P9-ELP-008

Christina Foyle's

Party
Book

Christina Foyle's

Party Book

Peebles Press

New York : London

© 1968 Christina Foyle
First published in this edition 1973
by Peebles Press International
New York : London
ISBN 0 85690 004 4

Printed and bound in Great Britain

CONTENTS

Publisher's Note:

This book is charming as well as practical. In trying to maintain its distinctive British manner, we have minimized the textual changes necessary to accommodate American cooking methods, but some British measurements do need translation. For your guidance, we list below some of the more frequently encountered items.

Liquid Measure

1 pint = 2 cups
1 gill = $\frac{1}{4}$ pint

Solid Measure

English		American
1 lb.	Butter or other fat	2 cups
1 lb.	Flour	4 cups
1 lb.	Granulated Sugar	2 cups
1 lb.	Brown Sugar	$2\frac{3}{4}$ cups
1 lb.	Confectioner's Sugar	3 cups
1 lb.	Syrup or Treacle	1 cup
1 lb.	Dried Fruit	2 cups
1 lb.	Chopped Meat	2 cups
1 lb.	Lentils or Split Peas	2 cups
1 lb.	Coffee (unground)	$2\frac{3}{4}$ cups
1 lb.	Breadcrumbs	4 cups
$\frac{1}{2}$ oz.	Flour	1 level tablespoon
1 oz.	Flour	1 heaped tablespoon
1 oz.	Syrup or Treacle	1 tablespoon
1 oz.	Sugar	1 level tablespoon
1 oz.	Jam or Jelly	1 level tablespoon
$\frac{1}{2}$ oz.	Butter	1 level tablespoon

Dessertspoonfuls are equal to heaping tablespoonfuls.

Also, some ingredient translations:

Golden Syrup	Maple Syrup
caster or castor sugar	granulated sugar
demerara sugar	light brown sugar
chipolata sausages	cocktail frankfurters
single cream	light cream
double cream	heavy cream
top of milk	medium cream
Russian salad	Russian salad dressing
Italian salad	Italian salad dressing
salad cream	creamy salad dressing
baking beans (as weights in pie crusts)	use any heavy dried beans
puff of lazy garlic	finely chopped garlic to taste
potted shrimps	extra small shrimps
ratafias	small cakes or biscuits flavored with apricot cordial or liquors
fruit squash	use concentrated, sweetened, frozen fruit juices, thawed but undiluted

Mark Numbers refer to British oven temperatures only.

ENTERTAINING

Every woman loves to entertain—to show off her husband, children, and the home they have built together. But let's face it not everybody wants to spend hours slaving over a hot stove or hours in preparing lavish meals. Some of us who are busy business women or have small children to care for, have no time for extensive preparations and therefore tend to give up the idea of inviting friends in for dinner or even for a few drinks. But giving a party does not necessarily require a great deal of work. As my book will show you, a successful party can be both an inexpensive and impromptu affair. Nowadays one does not need an excuse for a party, and they are an excellent means of making new friends—so why not have a party. . . tomorrow?

Happy entertaining

Christina Foyle.

7

INTRODUCTION

Whatever type of party you are having it is essential to plan in advance so that the minimum of work and preparation is necessary on the 'big day'. Food for buffet type parties and sandwiches can be kept fresh by covering with napkins and damp towels. Party rooms can be brightened with flowers, and attention should be paid to soft lighting and quiet background music to create a pleasant atmosphere for conversation.

Your invitations, whether written or verbal, should give the details of the party, the time it commences and the approximate time that it will end. You should also let your guests know what food to expect so that they can have a meal beforehand if necessary!

Give each arrival a really warm welcome, and use their christian names if you know them well enough. People who you do not know well, should be welcomed just as warmly—make them feel that you are glad that they could come. You should shake hands with ladies first and then the men. If the party is a small one, newcomers can be introduced to each person present, otherwise it is best to introduce them into one group and make certain that conversation has started before rushing off to get them a drink.

Sometimes a party goes over the time set and some guests look as though they are never going to leave. The important thing is to stay happy and smiling no matter how tired you feel. Never suggest coffee until it is obvious that the guests intend to leave.

When your guests finally depart, see them to the door or to their car and thank them warmly for coming. At this stage you should not prolong their departure by making conversation but do wait while they drive off. You should see that no lady has to travel home alone, even if she insists that she will be alright. Either offer to take her home yourself when the last guests are leaving or ring for a taxi. If she travels by taxi, it is a good idea to telephone later, to see that she arrived home safely.

When your last guests have left you can relax a little and survey the scene of your successful party. Empty glasses, dirty cups, and plates full ashtrays and leftover food litter every available table. It is best to empty ashtrays and glasses and move all crockery to the kitchen before going to bed and if you open the window it will ensure that there is no lingering smell in the morning.

COCKTAIL PARTIES

Cocktails

AMERICANO

⅔ Sweet Martini Vermouth
⅓ Campari
Ice

Pour over ice in large wine glass. Fill with soda, stir and add a twist of lemon peel and a dash of Angostina.

BAMBOO

¼ Dry Martini Vermouth
¼ Sweet Martini Vermouth
½ Dry Sherry

Stir well and strain into a glass.

COUNT ROSSI

½ Martini Dry Vermouth
½ Martini Sweet Vermouth
2 ice cubes

Put ice into a small tumbler. Squeeze peel of lemon over, serve with slice of orange.

PERFECT COCKTAIL

⅓ Martini Dry Vermouth
⅓ Martini Sweet Vermouth
⅓ Dry Gin

Shake: Strain into Cocktail Glass.

SWEET MARTINI

⅔ Martini Sweet Vermouth
⅓ Dry Gin

Pour into glass. Add a cherry or twist of lemon. (For those who prefer it Sweet but white use Martini Bianco).

DRY MARTINI

½ Martini Dry Vermouth
½ Dry Gin

Stir well with ice. Strain and serve with twist of lemon peel or an olive.

VODKATINI

⅔ Martini Dry Vermouth
⅓ Vodka

Stir and serve with a twist of lemon peel.

LONG MARTINI

Take a tall glass. Add plenty of ice, a good measure of Martini Sweet, Bianco or Dry. Top up with soda, bitter lemon or lemonade. Add a slice of lemon.

MARTINI 'ON THE ROCKS'

Take a tall glass. Add several cubes of ice and pour over Martini Sweet, Bianco or Dry. Serve.

MANHATTAN

½ Scotch Whisky
¼ Martini Dry Vermouth
¼ Martini Sweet Vermouth
Dash of Angostina

Stir, strain into glass. Serve with cherry.

EPEE

¾ Brandy
¼ Martini Sweet Vermouth

Stir and strain into a glass.

SILVERSTONE

½ White Rum
½ Martini Bianco Vermouth

Stir with ice and a little bitter lemon.

TORINO

⅓ Martini Dry Vermouth
⅓ Martini Bianco Vermouth
⅓ Martini Sweet Vermouth
Dash of Angostina

Stir and serve with an olive or cherry.

COCKTAIL PARTIES

ASTI COCKTAIL

Into a champagne glass put a lump of sugar soaked in Angostura Bitters. Then add a measure of brandy and a slice of orange. Fill the glass very slowly with Asti Martini.

ASTI CUP

1 glassful brandy
2 liqueur glassfuls Curacao
1 liqueur glassful Grand Marnier
Small slice of peeled cucumber
1 bottle Asti Spumante
Sliced orange
3-4 sprigs of fresh mint

Place in a large pitcher and serve with sprigs of fresh mint on top.

ANGELS KISS

A few drops of Grenadine
½ tablespoonful lemon juice
Top up with Asti Spumante

To be served in glasses frosted with lemon juice and castor sugar.

PASSION FRUIT COOLER

1 part Gin
1 part Tree Top Orange and
  Passion Fruit Drink
¼ part Cherry Brandy
Dash Angostura Bitters

Place all the ingredients in a large glass with crushed ice. Stir with a bar spoon and strain into cocktail glasses. Add a cherry and a squeeze of lemon peel on top.

BLACK TULIP

The white of 1 egg
½ glass blackcurrant flavoured
  cordial
½ glass dry gin

Shake well with ice. Strain into a cocktail glass.
Serves 1 person.

Cheese Treats

Need something light but sustaining, quick to serve and easy to eat, savoury rather than sweet? Try these Cheese Treats. They go splendidly with drinks when you have friends in. They make a handsome trayful for people who like to nibble while they're watching television. And the children will love them when they come home from school.

One of the nice things about such mouthfuls as these is that they can be eaten with fingers or forks, and don't demand the concentration of full-scale knife-and-fork food—so you won't miss some vital clue by diverting your eyes from the screen during a thriller! Similarly, guests and family can serve themselves—so the hostess doesn't have to spend her time hopping up and down to keep the party fed. Cheese Treats can be served hot or cold, so if your trayful starts the evening hot and finishes up cold, it's no great tragedy.

Quantities? As a general rule, make two or three different Treats from among the following recipes, and assume that each guest will eat three or four of these tempting snacks.

Cheese Sausage Bumbers

¼ lb. beef sausages
4 long rolls
¼" slices Cheddar cheese

Method

Grill sausages for 15 minutes. Split rolls and toast on both sides. Put two sausages on the bottom half of each roll. Cover with sliced cheese and return to grill to brown.

10

How to present a selection of biscuits and cheeses

COCKTAIL PARTIES

Chicken Sticks

3 oz. cream cheese
2 level tablespoonfuls mayonnaise
3 level tablespoonfuls Crunchy
  Peanut Butter
6 oz. diced cooked chicken
1 level tablespoonful brown pickle
½ level teaspoonful salt
Little pepper
1 level tablespoonful curry
  powder
12-14 Pretzel sticks

Method
Beat cream cheese, mayonnaise and peanut butter together. Stir in the chicken, peanuts, pickle, seasonings and curry powder, and mix well. Shape mixture into 12-14 small balls. Place a pretzel stick in each ball and chill until ready to serve.
12-14 chicken sticks.

Cheese Scotch Eggs

4 hard-boiled eggs
6 oz. grated Cheddar cheese
1½ oz. flour
1 level teaspoonful salt
½ teaspoonful Worcester sauce
Pinch cayenne pepper
1 egg
1-2 tablespoonfuls milk or cream
Dried breadcrumbs

Method
Mix the cheese, flour and seasonings, add the beaten egg and milk or cream, and beat well. Using wet hands, coat the eggs completely with the cheese mixture. Roll them in breadcrumbs. Fry in hot, deep fat to a golden brown, taking about 2 minutes to allow the cheese mixture to cook through. Drain and cool.

Cheese and Bacon Whiz

8 long rolls
2 oz. grated Cheddar cheese
2 tablespoonfuls tomato ketchup
3 rashers cooked streaky bacon,
  chopped
12 black olives, chopped
Pinch garlic salt

Method
Split and toast rolls. Mix all other ingredients. Fill rolls, sandwiching the two halves together. Wrap each roll in aluminium foil and leave in a cool place until needed. Leave foil on and heat through in a moderate oven at 350°F. (Mark 4), for 10-15 minutes.

Bangers with Zing

Whether it's the children's Guy Fawkes party or the grown-up's informal get-together, bangers on sticks and delicious concoctions in which to dip them are a great success.
Make little sausages from chipolatas by twisting the skin at the point where it is to be broken. Twist off and re-mould sausages into shape and fry until golden brown. Pierce with cocktail sticks and arrange on a sandwich loaf like the probes on Venus! Before serving, put the loaf and the sausages into a moderate oven to heat through. Sausages need mustard—straight or in a sauce. Try these and other ideas here for sauces and dips to serve with celery sticks, cheese cubes, pineapple cubes and potato crisps.

Eggs in Aspic

Try these at a teen-age party. They look very sophisticated indeed but are surprisingly, easy to make.
Prepare aspic jelly following the

Midnight feast

COCKTAIL PARTIES

directions on the packet; let it cool, but not set. Wet a jelly mould and pour a thin layer of the jelly over the bottom. Allow this to set in the coolest place you have. Arrange diced tomatoes on this and cover again with jelly. Repeat the process with a layer of sliced, cold hard-boiled eggs, and a layer of cooked ham cut into shapes. Let the jelly set between each layer. Finally cover completely with aspic jelly and leave to set firmly. Turn out when you want it—as you would any ordinary jelly; serve garnished with tomato and watercress.

Teenburgers

5½ fluid oz. (1 small can)
  Carnation milk
1 lb. fresh minced beef
2 oz. fresh breadcrumbs
1 small onion, grated
2 tablespoonfuls chopped green
  pepper
1 tablespoonful prepared mustard
½ teaspoonful salt, pepper

Method
Lightly mix all ingredients together. Divide into 8 portions and shape into hamburgers. Fry in hot fat for about 15 minutes, turning occasionally. Serve with fried onions and tomatoes or in hot rolls.

Party Dips

Hot Tomato Sauce

1 can condensed tomato soup
  (10½ oz. size)
2 teaspoonfuls made mustard
1 tablespoonful vinegar
2 tablespoonfuls chopped chives
  or finely chopped onion

Method
Put contents of can of tomato soup in saucepan with mustard and vinegar. Heat until piping hot, add chives or onion. Use as a dip for sausages.

Tomato Mustard Dunking Sauce

¾ pint thick mayonnaise
2 teaspoonfuls made mustard
2 tablespoonfuls tomato purée
1 teaspoonful sugar
Salt and pepper

Method
Blend ingredients together and season to taste. So right as a dip for sausages.

Garlic Cheese

8 oz. cream or curd cheese
2 teaspoonfuls made mustard
2 cloves garlic pressed or finely
  chopped
2 tablespoonfuls top of milk

Method
Beat cream cheese. Stir in mustard and garlic. Mix to a soft dipping consistency with top of the milk. Serve with potato crisps or celery sticks.

Piquant Ham Dip

¼ pint thick white sauce
2 teaspoonfuls made mustard
1 teaspoonful soft brown sugar
2 tablespoonfuls wine vinegar
4 oz. minced ham

Method
Blend together white sauce, mustard, sugar and vinegar. Heat gently to dissolve sugar. Add ham and bring to boil. Adjust seasoning to taste. Serve with celery sticks, cheese cubes or pineapple cubes.

Top picture Eggs in Aspic   *Teenburgers*

COCKTAIL PARTIES

Philly Cucumber Dip

2 x 3 oz. packets Kraft "Philly"
1 good tablespoonful well drained
finely chopped unpeeled
cucumber
Few drops of Worcester sauce
Garlic salt
2-3 tablespoonfuls milk

Method
Beat "Philly" until smooth. Work cucumber into "Philly" and mix well together. Add milk according to the consistency required. Serve with a selection of cocktail biscuits and crisps.

Liver Dip

4 oz. liver sausage
¼ pint thick white sauce
1 tablespoonful made mustard

Method
Mash liver sausage with a fork. Gradually beat white sauce and mustard into it. Use as a dip for potato crisps, pineapple cubes, celery sticks.

Basic recipes for open sandwiches

Shellfish Smorbrod

Cover buttered bread with crisp lettuce. Heap 2 oz. de-frosted Norwegian prawns or other cooked shellfish on the lettuce and decorate with a twist of thinly cut lemon—pipe with mayonnaise at the last minute.

Fish Smorbrod

Place lettuce on buttered fine wholemeal bread and on this arrange Norwegian brisling or sild and garnish with tomato and lemon.

Smoked Fish Smorbrod

Spread wholemeal bread or toast with lemon-flavoured butter. Top with sliced smoked salmon, smoked mackerel, smoked eel, raw kipper fillet or buckling. Garnish with scrambled egg, lemon and parsley.

Egg Smorbrod

Take a slice of white buttered bread and arrange on it slices of hard-boiled egg covered with a lattice of anchovy fillets. Garnish with tomato slices or stuffed olives or strips of red pimento and parsley.

Meat Smorbrod

Use white or wholemeal bread covered with a medium-thick slice of liver pâté. Decorate with a little Cranberry sauce and a fanned gherkin or fresh cucumber twists and cocktail onions.
On buttered brown or white bread arrange thinly cut slices of ham, salami, cold roast beef, pork or veal in eye-catching designs. Decorate with Russian salad or onion rings or asparagus tips and mayonnaise according to taste. Garnish with chopped chives or parsley.

Cheese Smorbrod

Take dark rye bread thickly spread with butter. Cover with slices of Jarlsberg cheese. Pipe with garnish made from whipped cream, horseradish sauce and lemon juice mixed together. Top with radish rings or radish rose.
Butter rye bread containing caraway seeds and place on it slices of Norbo. Add eye—and taste—appeal with crisp sweet pepper rings.

PATIO PARTIES

Oliver Twist

3 slices pork luncheon meat
  (or 4 slices cut lengthwise)
2 cooked prunes (stoned)
1 slice of fresh orange
Lettuce
Parsley
1 tablespoonful horseradish cream
Buttered bread

Method

Cut meat across in thin slices. Fold three slices, one in front of the other on to the buttered bread. Spoon on the horseradish cream centrally. Slice orange half-way through centre leaving top half still joined. Bend halves in opposite directions and fix lightly in a twist on the cream. Place prunes either side of twist. Tuck small piece of lettuce and parsley into the cream. For alternative method, arrange the four flat slices of meat, slightly overlapping each other on the bread. Garnish as before.

Danwich International

2 slices canned ham
1 dessertspoonful Italian Salad
1 tomato slice
2 cucumber slices
Lettuce
Parsley
Buttered bread

Method

Fold the meat slices and arrange on the buttered bread to give a little height. Place a small piece of lettuce on top. Spoon on the Italian Salad centrally. Place the tomato slice between the two pieces of cucumber. Cut through all three and twist, then place in position on top of the Italian Salad. Tuck sprig of parsley into one side of the twist.

Hans Andersen's Favourite

1 slice liverpâté
Few slices butter-fried mushrooms
1 gherkin
1 rasher crisply fried bacon
1 tomato slice
Lettuce
Buttered rye bread

Method

For a neatly cut slice, chill the pâté before opening. Place liverpâté on the buttered bread. Heap cooked, sliced mushrooms in the centre. Slice end of gherkin and fan out. Place it to one side of mushrooms. Arrange bacon strip across. Garnish with twisted slice of tomato. Tuck lettuce to one side of tomato.

The Epicure

Portion of chicken
1 bacon roll
2 slices cucumber
1 slice tomato
Watercress
Lettuce
Buttered white bread

Method

Arrange lettuce leaf to cover the bread. Place chicken portion on top. Put the tomato slice between the two pieces of cucumber. Cut through all three to make a twist, and place in position on the Danwich. Tuck in the bacon roll and a sprig of water cress.

Lamb Cutlet Pastries

8 lamb cutlets
1 tablespoonful salad oil
1 tablespoonful lemon juice
1 teaspoonful dried leaf marjoram
Salt and pepper

17

A typical patio layout

PATIO PARTIES

Pastry
1 lb. plain flour
1 level teaspoonful salt
4 oz. butter
4 oz. lard
4 tablespoonfuls water

Method
Mix salad oil, lemon juice, marjoram, salt and pepper together in a shallow dish. Brush lamb cutlets with oil and lemon mixture and marinate in remaining mixture, turning occasionally, for at least 2 hours. Grill for 3-4 minutes on each side. Put aside to become quite cold.

To make pastry: Sift together flour and salt. Rub in fat until mixture resembles fine breadcrumbs. Add water and mix together to form a stiff dough. Roll out pastry thinly. Using a cutlet as a pattern, cut round 1 inch away from cutlet, allowing end of bone to stick out 2 inches. Make 16 of these patterns. Place cutlet on one pattern, wet edges and put another on top. Press edges together and crimp all the way round. Garnish with a pastry leaf and brush with milk. Bake in a hot oven, 425°F. (Mark 7) for 15 minutes. Serve hot or cold.

Serves 8 persons.

Chicken with Pineapple

4-6 oz. diced chicken
2 rashers of lean bacon—finely chopped
4 oz. mushrooms—peeled and finely chopped
1 small can evaporated milk ⎫
¼ pint water ⎬ *For the sauce*
1½ oz. flour ⎪
1 oz. butter ⎭

1 small onion—skinned and finely chopped
1 cup Patna rice — 1 pint hot chicken stock or water
Small knob butter
1 small can whole kernel corn
1 small can pineapple tidbits

Method
Melt the small knob of butter in a pan then add the chopped onion and fry until golden brown. Add 1 teacupful of rice and continue to fry a further few moments—stirring well. Add 1 pint of hot salted stock or water. cover with a lid and allow to simmer gently until all moisture has been absorbed—about 20 minutes.

To make the Sauce
Melt the 1 oz. butter and gently fry the bacon and mushrooms. When cooked strain from the pan and use remaining fat to make the white sauce with the flour, evaporated milk and water. Season well. Return the mushrooms/bacon mix to the pan together with the diced chicken. Continue to heat through gently. Meanwhile heat the corn and pineapple in their canned liquor. When hot drain.

To serve
Make a ring of rice round the edge of the serving dish. Place the chicken sauce in the middle. Garnish with the corn and pineapple.

Serves 4-5 persons.

Cheese Charlotte

Few slices thinly cut brown and white bread and butter
3 eggs, separated
2 level teaspoonfuls gelatine dissolved in 2 tablespoonfuls water

2 oz. double-cream cheese
2 oz. grated Cheddar cheese
½ teaspoonful French mustard
Pinch salt and cayenne pepper
¼ pint single cream
Watercress

Method

Line a buttered Charlotte mould or 5″ cake tin with the bread, using alternate fingers of white and brown. Whisk the egg yolks until thick, and add the dissolved gelatine. Stir in the cheese, seasonings and cream, then fold in the stiffly whipped whites. Turn the mixture into the Charlotte mould and chill. Turn out and serve garnished with watercress.

The Beefeater

2 slices underdone roast beef
1 dessertspoonful remoulade
    sauce
Fried onions
Tomato
Gherkin
Lettuce
Fresh horseradish
Buttered bread

Method

Arrange the beef on the buttered bread. Lay a piece of lettuce at one end. Spoon on the remoulade sauce in the centre. Add a scattering of fried onion. Sprinkle a little freshly grated horseradish on to the remoulade. Place a gherkin fan to one side and finish off with a good twist of tomato.

Copenhagen Chicken Cocktail

1 chicken
1 cupful mayonnaise
2 tablespoonfuls tomato ketchup
2 tablespoonfuls lemon juice
1 teaspoonful Worcester sauce
1 teaspoonful curry powder
Salt and pepper
Salt and pepper to season
1 lettuce
1 cupful freshly diced cucumber
1 tomato

Method

Boil or steam the chicken with a sliced onion, 2 carrots and salt until the meat is tender and comes easily from the bone, about 45 minutes. Cut the chicken meat into strips. Mix the mayonnaise with the seasonings. Add the chicken meat and mix carefully. Shred the lettuce very finely. Divide the lettuce and the diced cucumber between 4 dessert glasses or plates and pile the chicken salad on top. Garnish with a slice of tomato.

Picnic Rice and Ham

12 oz. cooked rice (4 oz. rice and
    ½ pint liquid)
1 x 13½ oz. can crushed pineapple,
    drained
1½ oz. brown sugar
2 oz. butter or margarine
2 oz. diced green pepper
2 teaspoonfuls soy sauce
1 teaspoonful prepared mustard
8 slices boiled or baked ham cut
    about ⅛″ thick

Method

Combine cooked rice with pineapple, brown sugar, butter, green pepper, soy sauce and mustard. Place slices of ham on 12″ squares of aluminium foil. Top meat with rice mixture. Fold foil over ham and rice and turn edges over two or more times to seal. Bake at 350°F. for about 30 minutes.
Serves 8 persons.

PATIO PARTIES

Devilled Crab

2 x 7 oz. cans crab meat
2 packets onion sauce mix (see note)
1 pint milk
1 level tablespoonful Dijon mustard
2 tablespoonfuls Worcester sauce
2 tablespoonfuls chopped parsley
1 canned red pimento, chopped
Salt and pepper
Grated Parmesan cheese

Method

Discard any sinewy pieces from crab meat and flake. Make up the 2 packets of sauce mix with ¾ pint milk, not 1 pint as directed. Stir in the mustard, Worcester sauce, parsley and red pimento. Check seasoning. Fold in the flaked crab meat, divide mixture between 4 individual heatproof dishes or serve in one large dish. Dust with Parmesan or other grated cheese. Place under a moderately heated grill until bubbling. Serve Melba toast or crispbreads and butter separately.

Serves 4 persons.

N.B. When fresh parsley is not available use a packet of onion sauce mix and one of parsley sauce mix. To extend devilled crab, serve with a plain omelette cooked in butter with a puff of lazy garlic added.

Esrom Danwich

3 slices Esrom cheese
1 stuffed olive, sliced
Lettuce leaf
Danish Buttered Bread

Method

Tuck a piece of lettuce on one corner of bread. Put on the slices of cheese evenly. Garnish each slice with a piece of the stuffed olive.

Tuna Fish Mousse

2 x 7 oz. cans solid pack tuna fish
½ x 10 oz. bottle Salad cream
1 tablespoonful double cream
Salt and pepper
1 level teaspoonful gelatine
4 tablespoonfuls water
2 dill cucumbers
Lettuce leaves, shredded for garnish
Prawns for garnish

Method

Mix the tuna fish, salad cream, tomato ketchup, cream, salt and pepper together. Dissolve the gelatine in the water, meanwhile dice the cucumbers, keeping a few slices back for garnish. Stir the cucumbers and gelatine into the tuna mixture, pour into a suitable mould, place in a refrigerator or cold place to set. When firm turn out onto a serving dish and garnish with shredded lettuce, prawns and slices of dill cucumber.

Beefburgers and Sausageburgers

Allow 1 beefburger and sausageburger per person. Remember to take a large frying pan.

8 frozen beefburgers
8 sausages
Lard or oil for cooking
8 rolls
8 long soft rolls

Method

Fry beefburgers and sausages in lard. Split baps and rolls in half. Serve hot beefburgers between baps and sausage between long rolls.

Make 2 sauces, one spread and a salad to serve with the burgers.

21

Picnic rice and ham

Top picture Tuna Fish Mousse   *Beefburgers and sausageburgers*

Bacon Roll ups

PATIO PARTIES

Bacon Roll-Ups

4 oz. sardines
6 hard-boiled egg yolks
6 oz. cooked rice (2 oz. rice and
    ¼ pt. liquid)
2 tablespoonfuls grated onion
Salt and pepper to taste
2 teaspoonfuls prepared mustard
Dash of hot sauce
2 tablespoonfuls mayonnaise
12 slices bacon, cut into halves

Method
Mash sardines and egg yolk. Mix with rice and onion. Season with salt and pepper. Add mustard, hot sauce and mayonnaise. Blend well. Spread mixture on bacon slices. Roll and fasten with wooden cocktail sticks. Place on a rack on a shallow baking tray and bake at 450°F for 15 to 18 minutes, or until bacon is crisp. Serve hot.
Makes 2 dozen rolls.

Danish Summer Salad

1 chicken
2 hard-boiled eggs
½ cupful olives
½ cupful sliced green pepper
½ cupful sliced fresh tomatoes
½ cupful raw cauliflower in small
    pieces
½ cupful finely shredded lettuce
Dressing
½ cup olive oil
4 tablespoonfuls lemon juice or
    vinegar
Little chopped fresh mint or dried
    mint
Salt and pepper

Method
Boil or steam the chicken with 1 sliced onion, 2 carrots and salt until tender, about 45 minutes. Remove meat from bone and cut into fine strips. Slice the eggs. Mix the dressing and leave for 1 hour. Mix all ingredients in a big bowl and carefully add the dressing.

Mediterranean Flan

Pastry
8 oz. plain flour
½ level teaspoonful salt
4 oz. butter
2 tablespoonfuls cold water
Filling
1 large onion
½ oz. butter
2 eggs
Salt and pepper
½ pint milk
6 oz. peeled prawns
2 tomatoes

Method
To make pastry: Sift together flour and salt. Rub in butter until mixture resembles fine breadcrumbs. Add water and mix to a stiff dough. Turn on to a floured board and quickly knead until smooth. Roll out and use to line two 7″ flan rings. Chill. Fill with crumpled kitchen foil or greaseproof paper and baking beans. Bake in a hot oven, 425°F. (Mark 6) for 15 minutes.
To make filling: Chop onion finely and fry without colouring in butter until soft. Beat eggs, salt and pepper. Warm milk, then blend into eggs. Place cooked onion and prawns in the bottom of flan cases. Strain in egg and milk mixture. Arrange sliced tomatoes on top. Bake in a moderate oven, 350°F. (Mark 4) for about 35 minutes until custard is set.
Serves 8 persons.

PATIO PARTIES

Dane's Delight

> 2 slices cold roast pork
> 1 tablespoonful pickled red
>   cabbage
> 1 prune
> Orange slice
> Lettuce
> Buttered bread

Method
Lay the meat on the bread in a slightly circular shape, if possible. Mound the pickled red cabbage into the centre. Crown it with an orange twist. Tuck a small piece of lettuce and a stoned prune on opposite sides of the twist. Add a small piece of crispy crackling if available.

Picnic Fancy

> 1 hard-boiled egg
> 1 rasher of streaky bacon
> 1 slice tomato
> Lettuce
> Cress
> Buttered rye-bread

Method
Slice a hard-boiled egg lengthwise using an egg slicer for neatness. Arrange lettuce at one end of bread. Place egg slices in two rows to cover the bread completely. Place a piece of cold, crisply fried streaky bacon on top. Slice the tomato and twist it into position across the bacon. Tuck a little cress in by the tomato.

The Continental

> 4 thin slices salami
> 4 thin slices onion rings
> Lettuce
> Parsley
> Buttered bread

Method
Press lettuce into butter on one corner. Fold salami slices loosely in half. Arrange on buttered bread in a fan shape. Snip discreetly through two of the onion rings. Link them all together in a chain over the salami slices. Decorate with the parsley sprig.

Weekly Meeting

> $\frac{1}{2}$ fillet of plaice
> 1 dessertspoonful remoulade
>   sauce
> 1 lemon slice
> Lettuce
> Parsley
> Tomato
> Buttered bread

Method
Prepare the bread and cover it generously with fresh lettuce. Coat the fillets in egg and breadcrumbs and fry quickly on both sides until golden brown. Drain on absorbent paper and allow to cool slightly. Place the fillet while still warm on the lettuce and garnish with remoulade sauce, a generous twist of lemon and a sprig of parsley. Add a gay touch of red with a snippet of tomato.

The Miller's Choice

> 2 sticks Samsoe cheese
> 3 slices tomato
> Leaf of lettuce
> Buttered bread

Method
Place lettuce leaf on buttered bread. Place tomato slices slightly overlapping each other to form a triangle on the lettuce. Arrange sticks of Samsoe on top.

PATIO PARTIES

Savoury Flan

Pastry
> 5 oz. flour
> $\frac{1}{2}$ teaspoonful salt
> Pepper   Cayenne
>   Season to taste
> 3 oz. margarine
> 2 oz. grated parmesan cheese
> 2$\frac{1}{2}$ tablespoonfuls egg yolk and
>   milk to mix

Method
Sift together the flour and seasonings, rub in the fat very lightly and mix in the grated cheese. Mix with egg yolk and milk, pressing lightly together to give a firm paste. Roll out and line flan case reserving some for the lattice strips. Bake blind in the oven at 350°F (Mark 4) for 15 minutes.

Filling
> 1 lb. Haddock or Cod Fillet
> $\frac{1}{4}$ pint mayonnaise
> Pepper, salt and nutmeg
> $\frac{1}{4}$ pint double cream
> $\frac{1}{2}$ oz. gelatine dissolved in
>   1 tablespoonful water
> 2 oz. shrimps, cucumber and
>   parsley to garnish

Method
Poach fish with bay leaf and peppercorns for about 15 minutes. Drain fish bone, flake and mash very lightly. Stir in the mayonnaise and seasoning. Half whip the cream, fold in lightly and stir in the carefully dissolved warm gelatine. When it is just beginning to set, pour into the flan case. Roll out strips of pastry, place on flan in lattice pattern. Sprinkle with parmesan cheese. Put under hot grill for 5 minutes. Garnish with shrimps, cucumber and parsley.
Serves 6 persons.

Corn Cheese Omelette

> 4 eggs
> Salt and pepper
> Butter
> 7-oz. can sweet corn kernels
> A few puffs lazy garlic
> 2 oz. cheese, grated

Method
Lightly beat the eggs with a fork, just sufficient to mix whites and yolks, season with salt and pepper. For those who prefer a drier omelette separate whites and yolks from half the eggs. Whisk the whites and fold into the yolks and whites with a little top of the milk. Pour egg mixture into an 8" omelette or frying-pan, in which a good knob of butter has been heated until foaming. As soon as eggs coat pan, start to stir slowly with the back of a fork to form large creamy flakes. Tilt pan occasionally to take in liquid egg. When sufficiently set, add filling, cook a minute or two longer, fold omelette into half-moon shape. Turn out onto hot plate and serve at once.
Serves 2 persons.
Filling: drain corn kernels, heat in a knob of butter with a puff or two of lazy garlic. Quickly stir in cheese. Spoon at once onto omelette.

Danish Chicken Salad

> 1 chicken
> 7 oz. white processed cheese
> $\frac{1}{2}$ cup milk
> 4 teaspoonfuls lemon juice
> 1 cupful fresh cooked asparagus
> 1 cupful blanched almonds

Method
Boil or steam the chicken with 1 sliced onion, 2 carrots and salt until

the meat is tender and comes easily from the bone, about 45 minutes. Cut the chicken meat into fine strips. Mix the cheese with the milk until smooth. Add the lemon juice, sliced asparagus and almonds to the cheese dressing. Serve on lettuce with the chicken.

Cheese and Asparagus Boats

6 oz. shortcrust pastry
1 x 10 oz. can asparagus tips
2 oz. butter
6 oz. grated Cheddar cheese
Salt and pepper
Pinch mustard
2 tablespoonfuls cream or
*   top of milk*

Method
Roll pastry out thinly and use to line 12-15 small boat-shaped cases. Line cases with greaseproof paper and fill with baking beans. Bake in a fairly hot oven at 400°F. (Mark 6) for 10 minutes. Remove baking beans and greaseproof paper and return to oven for further five minutes. Drain liquid from asparagus tips and chop coarsely. Fill into boat-shaped cases. Cream butter, gradually add cheese, seasoning and cream, beating well to smooth, creamy consistency. Spread cheese paste on top of each boat and when required place in moderate oven at 350°F. (Mark 4) for 15 minutes. Serve at once.

Cottage Cheese Jack O'Lantern

Small ripe melon
2-3 x 8 oz. cartons Cottage cheese
2-3 dessert apples

Other flavours to taste, such as
*   1 oz. chopped ginger or nuts*
or
*   1 teaspoonful ground cinnamon*
Sugar to taste

Method
Cut a slice off the top of the melon. Hollow out flesh to serve separately. Cut out eyes, nose and a mouth. Blend Cottage cheese with unpeeled chopped apples and other flavourings as liked. Sweeten to taste. Pile Cottage cheese mixture into the melon. Serve with ginger nuts.
Melon Cream: mix melon with soured cream, 1 carton or to taste. Sweeten as liked. A sprinkle of chopped crystallised ginger and walnuts is delicious over this.

Champignons a la Grecque

$\frac{1}{2}$ lb. small button mushrooms
$\frac{1}{2}$ gill white wine
$\frac{1}{2}$ gill water
$\frac{1}{4}$ gill olive oil
Juice of $\frac{1}{2}$ lemon
1 small bay leaf
Pinch of thyme, coriander and
*   fennel*
1 tablespoonful chopped onion
Salt and pepper

Method
Put all the ingredients except the mushrooms into a pan. Allow to simmer for 5 minutes. Wash the mushrooms and cut into halves or quarters; depending on size. Add to the saucepan and simmer for a further 6 minutes. Leave in the liquor to cool. This quantity could be suitable for 2-4 portions depending on the other dishes with which it is served.

Top picture Cottage cheese Jack O' Lantern   *Champignons a la Grecque*

PATIO PARTIES

Dressed Crab

1 crab (approximately 4 lb.)
2 carrots
1 onion
Peppercorns
2 bay leaves
Pinch of dill seeds

Method

Plunge live crab into boiling water with the above ingredients, cook for approximately 12 minutes per lb. Remove from pan and plunge into cold water.

Ingredients for dressing crab

Salt pepper and mustard
1 oz. breadcrumbs
Chopped parsley
1 hard-boiled egg (white and yolk sieved separately)
Paprika
Lemon butterflies
$\frac{1}{4}$ pint double cream
$\frac{1}{4}$ pint mayonnaise
2 teaspoonfuls chopped gherkins
$\frac{1}{2}$ teaspoonful crushed dill seeds
1 teaspoonful lemon juice

Method

Carefully remove pincers and legs. Lift apron and discard, together with the gills, any green flesh and the small sac near the head. Remove all the brown meat from the shell, put into a bowl. Crack the pincers and legs. Remove all white meat and place in a separate bowl including white meat from around the shell. Reserve smaller legs for decoration. Gently tap the inside edge of the shell to break along the natural marking, then scrub clean and dry. Cream the brown meat, add the breadcrumbs to stiffen and season with pepper and a little vinegar. Shred the white meat and mix with the mayonnaise and double cream. Season with lemon juice, gherkins, dill seeds and salt and pepper. Arrange the white meat each side of the shell leaving a space down the centre for the brown meat. Roll the brown meat into sausage shapes, place down the centre of the shell and flatten slightly with a fork. Mark the dividing lines with the sieved egg white and yolk, and parsley. Sprinkle white meat with paprika. Decorate with lemon butterflies. Place the shell in the centre of a serving dish, supported on one or two of the small legs. Use the remaining legs for decoration.

Serves 4 persons.

Cheese and Asparagus Pie

Pastry

8 oz. plain flour
Salt and pepper
2 oz. butter
2 oz. lard
Cold water

Filling

6 oz. grated cheese
13 oz. can asparagus, drained and chopped
$\frac{1}{2}$ pint milk
2 eggs, beaten
Salt and pepper

Method

Sift the flour with the salt and pepper. Rub in the butter and lard. Add enough cold water to bind together into a stiff pastry. Roll out and use to line a 9 in. ovenproof flan dish with straight sides. Trim the edges. Arrange the cheese in the base of the flan and cover with the asparagus. Mix the milk with eggs and season with salt

and pepper. Pour into the flan. Roll out the pastry trimmings and cut into strips, using a pastry wheel. Arrange as shown, moistening the ends well. Decorate the edge of the flan. Bake at 425°F. (Mark 7) for 15 mins., then lower the temperature to 350°F. (Mark 4) and continue to cook for 35-45 mins.
Serves 4-6, hot or cold.

Salmon and Cheese Soufflé

1 oz. butter
1 oz. plain flour
¼ pint milk
9 oz. fresh salmon, skinned, boned
  and finely flaked
Pinch cayenne pepper
½ tablespoonful salt
3 oz. grated Cheddar cheese
½ teaspoonful lemon juice
3 eggs, separated

Method
Melt butter, add flour and cook gently for one minute. Remove from heat, add milk and bring to the boil, stirring well. Add salmon, seasoning, cheese and lemon juice. Stir until cheese has melted. Allow to cool and then beat in egg yolks. Whisk egg whites until stiff and fold into cheese.

Pineapple Drops

4 oz. flour
1 level teaspoonful dry mustard
¼ teaspoonful salt
4½ oz. grated Cheddar cheese
1 egg
¼ pint milk
Pineapple chunks

Method
Sieve the flour, mustard and salt into a bowl and add 4 oz. cheese. Mix the egg and milk and add to the dry ingredients, stirring all together. Drain the pineapple and coat each chunk with the batter. Fry in deep fat until golden brown. Sprinkle with remaining cheese. Makes about 20 drops.

Kebabs Alfresco

4 lamb's kidneys
1 lb. rump steak—thick
8 small tomatoes
¼ lb. mushrooms
8 oz. can pineapple slices
1 clove garlic
Salt and pepper
Olive oil
12 pickled onions
2 x 16 oz. cans baked beans with
  tomato sauce
8 metal skewers—about 8" long

Method
Wash and halve the kidneys, cut out core. Cut steak into 1½" cubes. Wash tomatoes and mushrooms, drain pineapple and cut into sections. Crush the garlic in salt in a large dish, pour in sufficient oil to cover the base and sprinkle with pepper. Place all ingredients except pineapple on the skewers and marinate in the oil for about 15 minutes, turning the skewers frequently. Preheat the grill on the highest setting then place kebabs under for about 4 minutes, turn them so that the food is evenly cooked (unless a rotary spit is used). Reduce the grill heat, put the pineapple on the skewers and continue cooking for 4-5 minutes. Meanwhile, halve the pickled onions and put in a saucepan with the baked beans and allow to heat through. Arrange the kebabs on the beans and serve immediately.

Kebabs Alfresco

PATIO PARTIES

Barbecue Cream Sauce

1 onion
2 tablespoonfuls oil
1 clove garlic (optional)
¼ pint tomato ketchup
2 teaspoonfuls ready mixed
mustard
2 tablespoonfuls wine vinegar
1 teaspoonful Worcester sauce
2 teaspoonfuls soft brown sugar
1 x 5 oz. carton soured cream

Method
Chop onion roughly and cook gently in oil for about 2-3 minutes. Stir in other ingredients, except soured cream and cook for 5 minutes. Add soured cream, heat through but do not allow to boil.
Note: This sauce is best made the day before for the flavours to be able to mature. Do not add the soured cream until the sauce has heated through again.

Mustard Sauce

2 level tablespoonfuls prepared
mustard
2 level tablespoonfuls thin honey
2 level tablespoonfuls soft brown
sugar

Method
Measure mustard, honey and sugar into a saucepan. Stir over gentle heat until boiling, then simmer for 5 minutes.

Spiced Cheese

Mix together half a teacupful creamed butter and the same quantity of grated cheese, and season with a pinch of cayenne pepper, a pinch of mixed spice and a few drops of Worcester sauce.

Australian Kebabs

1½ lb. lean lamb from leg or
shoulder
8 dried apricots, plumped
1 tomato, quartered
8 small onions, par-boiled
1 green pepper, deseeded
4 button mushrooms
Oil

Tomato Sauce

1 small onion, chopped
1 x 1 lb. tin tomatoes
1 tablespoonful oil
1 bay leaf
Salt and pepper

Method
Trim the meat and cut into even sized cubes. On 4 skewers thread the kebab ingredients in this order. Season well and brush with oil. Grill under medium heat, turning, for 15 minutes. Serve with 8 oz. patna rice plainly boiled and tomato sauce. '
To make the sauce: simmer all ingredients in a small saucepan for 20 minutes, remove bay leaf and serve.
Serves 4 persons.

Cottage Cheese and Horseradish Spread

8 oz. Cottage cheese
1 teaspoonful grated horseradish
or
2 teaspoonfuls creamed
horseradish sauce
Salt and pepper

Method
Blend together Cottage cheese and horseradish, or horseradish sauce. Season with salt and pepper.

34

Australian Kebabs

PATIO PARTIES

Chilled Cheese and Cucumber Soup

> 1 oz. butter
> 1 oz. plain flour
> 1½ pints milk
> 1½ level teaspoonfuls made
>   mustard
> 1½ level teaspoonfuls salt
> ¼ level teaspoonful pepper
> 8 oz. grated Cheddar cheese
> 2 level tablespoonfuls mayonnaise
> ¼ pint single cream
> 1 small cucumber, peeled and
>   finely diced

Method

Melt butter in a medium-sized saucepan, add flour and cook for 1 minute. Remove from heat and add milk gradually, stirring constantly. Bring to the boil, add seasonings and cheese. Pour soup into a bowl, cover with damp greaseproof paper and leave until cold. Remove paper carefully, stir in mayonnaise, cream and cucumber. Cover and chill for several hours.

Tivoli

> 4 slices hard-boiled egg
> ½ oz. Danish-style caviar
> ½ oz. mayonnaise
> 4 slices tomato
> Lettuce
> Buttered bread

Method

Place a lettuce leaf slightly larger rhan the bread on the butter. Arrange the slices of egg and tomato in two lines side by side on the lettuce. Pipe mayonnaise down the middle. Spoon the Danish-style caviar on to the mayonnaise.

Quick Summer Soup

> 2 cans tomato juice (14 oz. size)
> 1 pint chicken stock or
>   1 pint water and a chicken
>   stock cube
> 8 heaped tablespoonfuls fresh
>   white breadcrumbs
> 8 spring onions or
>   2 tablespoonfuls chopped chives
> Cucumber rings
> 2½ oz. carton double cream,
>   lightly whipped

Method

Warm together tomato juice and stock. Pour over breadcrumbs and season. Cut onions into thin rings. Stir chopped onions or chives into soup. Leave until cold. Pour into serving dish, garnish top with cucumber rings and teaspoonfuls of whipped cream. This soup is best served chilled. Hand finger croutons separately.

FINGER CROUTONS

Cut thin slices of bread into fingers. Fry until evenly golden. Drain and cool on paper.
Serves 8 persons.

Chef's Special

> 3 slices cooked gammon
> 2 slices tomato
> 1 slice cucumber
> Strip of scrambled egg
> 1 level teaspoonful chopped chives
> Buttered white bread

Method

Arrange gammon slices on the buttered bread in a nicely rounded shape. Place egg strip diagonally across the meat. Put the cucumber slice between two firm slices of tomato, all of equal size.

36

A selection of open sandwiches

Slice through all three leaving a piece at the top holding them together. Twist halves in opposite directions and place across the egg strip. Sprinkle chopped chives on the egg. An alternative garnish can be made using a dessertspoonful of Russian salad, with a triple twist of tomato and cucumber slices. A sprig of parsley and a small piece of lettuce tucked into the salad give a final touch of colour.

Orange Layer Cake

Cake
> *3 eggs*
> *3 oz. castor sugar*
> *3 oz. plain flour*
> *1 level teaspoonful baking powder*
> *1½ oz. butter*

Filling
> *1 (11 oz.) can mandarin oranges*
> *1 level teaspoonful cornflour*
> *1 teaspoonful lemon juice*

Butter cream
> *4 oz. butter*
> *6 oz. icing sugar*
> *2 tablespoonfuls lemon juice*

Method
Prepare a moderate oven 350°F. (Mark 4). Grease and line two 7 in. sponge tins. Whisk eggs and castor sugar together in a bowl over a pan of hot water until mixture leaves a trail. Remove bowl from pan and whisk until cool. Sift together flour and baking powder and carefully fold into whisked mixture, cutting through with a metal spoon. Melt butter and fold into mixture carefully. Pour into prepared tins and shake tins gently to level mixture. Bake for 30 to 35 minutes, until firm and golden brown. Allow to cool in tins for 5 minutes, then turn out carefully; cool thoroughly on wire racks. Drain oranges and blend syrup in a saucepan with cornflour. Mix well and bring to boil, stirring continuously. Add lemon juice. Reserve 5 orange segments and add the remainder to pan. Mix well and cook for 3 minutes, stirring continuously and breaking down orange segments. Allow to cool. Cream butter and icing sugar together until light and creamy. Beat lemon juice in gradually. Split each cake through the middle to form 4 layers. Sandwich 2 layers together with butter cream. Spread top with orange mixture, cover with third layer and spread with butter cream. Place final layer on top and spread remaining butter cream in swirls on top of cake. Arrange reserved orange segments on top of butter cream.

Rissotto for 50

> *3 lb. uncooked long grain rice*
> *1 lb. 8 oz. chopped onion*
> *2 lb. diced green pepper*
> *1 lb. 4 oz. mushrooms sliced*
> *14 oz. butter, margarine or oil*
> *6 pint rich chicken stock*
> *2½ tablespoonfuls salt*
> *1 lb. 8 oz. grated cheddar cheese*

Method
Saute rice in butter until it glistens (is golden in colour). Add onions and green pepper. Continue cooking for 5 minutes, stirring constantly to prevent over-browning the rice. Add chicken stock, salt and mushrooms. Heat to boiling, stir once. Cover, reduce heat to simmer, 20 minutes or until rice is tender. Remove from heat. Toss lightly with grated cheese.
Serves 50 persons.

Rissoto for 50

PATIO PARTIES

Entertaining on a summer's evening is so easy with these amusing individual quiches, or home-made chicken liver pâté served with toast and accompanied by a refreshing old fashioned lemonade. As a special finale give your guests this exciting apricot dessert made with a hint of apricot brandy.

Individual Quiches

6 oz. shortcrust pastry
1 tablespoonful corn oil
1 small onion—finely chopped
2 rashers of streaky bacon—finely chopped
1 level tablespoonful chopped parsley
½ level teaspoonful salt
Pinch pepper
1 oz. cheese—grated
2 tomatoes—skinned and sliced

Method

Roll out the pastry and line six 3" patty tins. Bake blind with baking beans in a hot oven 400°F (Mark 6) for 5 minutes. Remove the baking beans and bake for a further 5 minutes. Heat the corn oil. Add the onion and bacon and fry without browning. Remove from the pan and drain. Whisk the egg yolk and milk. Stir in the onion, bacon, parsley, salt, pepper and cheese. Divide the mixture between the six pastry cases. Bake in a moderately hot oven 375°F. (Mark 5) for 15 minutes, or until the filling is set. Garnish each quiche with a slice of tomato.

Chicken Liver Pate

1 lb. chicken livers
1 tablespoonful corn oil
1 small onion—finely chopped
2 oz. breadcrumbs
1 egg—lightly beaten
1 level teaspoonful salt
Pinch pepper
½ level teaspoonful powdered mace
1 tablespoonful brandy
½ lb. streaky bacon
2 oz. melted butter

Method

Mince the chicken livers, and heat the corn oil. Add the onion and fry until soft without browning. Drain and stir into the minced chicken livers with the breadcrumbs, egg, salt, pepper, mace and brandy. Mix well. Remove the bacon with a knife. Use to line a 7½" x 4" x 2" loaf tin. Spoon in the pâté mixture. Cook in a slow oven 325°F. (Mark 3) for 1½ hours. When cooked, leave the pâté in the tin. Cover with a piece of greaseproof paper and place weights on top. Leave overnight in a cool place. Remove the weights and paper from the pâté and pour over the melted butter. Leave to set. Turn out and cut into slices. Serve with slices of toast and butter.
Serves 6 persons.

Apricot Dessert

1 lb. apricots
¼ pint water
3 oz. sugar
A little milk
1½ oz. cornflour
2 eggs—separated
¼ pint single cream
1 dessertspoonful apricot brandy—optional
Angelica for decoration

Method

Halve and stone the apricots. Place in

Top picture California Raisin Squares

Chicken liver pâté

a saucepan with the water and sugar. Cover and cook slowly for 15 minutes or until tender but not mashed. Rub the apricots through a sieve reserving a few for decoration. Make the purée up to 1 pint with milk. Blend the cornflour and egg yolks with a little of the apricot purée. Put the remainder on to heat. Stir in the blended cornflour and bring to the boil, stirring. Cook for a further 3 minutes, stirring all the time. Pour into a large mixing bowl and leave to cool. Stir in the cream and apricot brandy if used. Whisk the egg whites until stiff and fold lightly into the apricot mixture. Pour into a wetted 1 lb. loaf tin and chill. Turn out and decorate with the reserved apricots and pieces of angelica.
Serves 6 persons

Old Fashioned Lemonade

4 lemons
3-4 oz. powdered glucose
1 pint boiling water
1 pint cold water
1 sliced lemon for decoration

Method
Wash the lemons and remove the zest. (The yellow outer skin). Squeeze the lemons and strain the juice into a glass serving jug. Place the zest and powdered glucose in a measuring jug and pour over the pint of boiling water. Leave to infuse for 15 minutes. Strain into the serving jug. Stir in the pint of cold water and chill thoroughly before serving. Serve in tall glasses decorated with slices of lemon.
Serves 6 persons.

California Raisin Squares

1 egg (lightly beaten)
6 oz. soft brown sugar

1½ oz. butter or margarine
1 oz. lard (melted and cooled)
3 oz. plain flour
½ level teaspoonful salt
½ level teaspoonful baking powder
¼ level teaspoonful vanilla essence
6 oz. seedless raisins (coarsely chopped)
3 oz. plain chocolate (small pieces

Method
Beat egg, sugar, butter and lard together in a basin. Add sieved flour, salt and baking powder. Stir in vanilla essence, raisins and chocolate, and mix together thoroughly. Spread mixture into a greased 7½" shallow square tin, and bake in a moderate oven 350°F. (Mark 4) for 35 minutes. Turn out, and cut into squares while still warm.
Makes 16 squares.

Darwin Easter Charlotte

1 x 29 oz. can peach halves
2 packets sponge fingers (about 1-1¼" wide)
2 level tablespoonfuls custard powder
2 oz. castor sugar
1 tablespoonful lemon juice
1 tablespoonful powdered gelatine
¼ pint evaporated milk
2 egg whites
Cherries for decoration

Method
Drain syrup from peaches and make up to ½ pint with water, if necessary. Add the lemon juice and sugar, and tip into a saucepan. Begin to heat. Mix the custard powder with 2 tablespoonfuls

Darwen Easter charlotte

cold water. Stir into the peach syrup. Stir and cook until thick. Mix the gelatine with 2 tablespoonfuls cold water, then stir into the sauce. Remove from heat and allow gelatine to dissolve completely. Add the evaporated milk and mix well. Pour into a bowl and set aside until just beginning to thicken. Grease the inside of a 7" bottomless cake tin. Place on a flat serving dish. Stand sponge fingers in an upright position all around the pan. Chop half the peaches into small pieces and add to the half-set jelly. Beat the 2 egg whites until very stiff and fold in. Pour half this mixture into the lined pan. Cover with sponge fingers, then tip in the rest of the mixture. Put away until firm and set. Decorate with peach halves and cherries.
Serves 6 persons.

Danish Teatime Squares

1 oz. shelled almonds
6 oz. butter
6 oz. castor sugar
3 eggs
6 oz. plain flour,
1½ level teaspoonfuls baking powder
½ level teaspoonful mixed spice
1 oz. chopped mixed peel

Method
Prepare a moderate oven 375°F. (Mark 5). Grease and line a tin, about 7½ in. by 11 in. Place almonds in a small basin. Cover with boiling water and leave for 3 to 4 minutes. Drain off water and remove almond skins. Carefully split almonds in half lengthways. Cream butter and sugar until light and fluffy. Beat the eggs together lightly with a fork and add to creamed mixture gradually, beating well after each addition. Sift together flour, baking powder and mixed spice and fold into creamed mixture. Add peel and mix lightly. Turn into prepared tin and smooth surface. Arrange almond halves in rows on top. Bake for 30 to 35 minutes, or until firm and browned. Allow to cool in tin for 4 to 5 minutes, then turn out carefully and cool on a rack. Cut into 12 squares to serve.
Makes 12 squares.

Strawberry Gateau

Sponge mixture
4 oz. butter
4 oz. castor sugar
2 eggs
4 oz. self-raising flour
Filling
½ pint double cream
½ lb. strawberries
Little icing sugar for dusting top

Method
To make sponges: Beat butter and sugar together until light and creamy. Beat in eggs, one at a time, adding a little flour with the last egg. Fold in flour, then divide mixture between 2 greased and floured 7" sandwich tins. Bake in a moderately hot oven, 375°F. (Mark 5) for about 20 minutes. Turn out and leave to cool.
To make filling: Lightly whip cream and slice strawberries, leaving 8 whole for decoration. Split each sandwich in half. Fill one sandwich with cream and sliced strawberries, spread another layer of cream and strawberries on top and place bottom of other sandwich on this. Pile on remaining cream and

A selection of open sandwiches

strawberries. Sieve a little icing sugar over the sponge top, cut into 8 equal sections and lift on to gateau. Decorate with remaining strawberries.
Serves 8 persons.

Barbecued Bangers

2 lb. sausages
1 medium onion, finely diced
½ cupful tomato ketchup
⅓ cupful olive oil
1 cup water
⅓ cup Demerara sugar
¼ teaspoonful Worcester sauce
1 teaspoonful salt
Juice of ½ lemon
1 tablespoonful wine vinegar
1 teaspoonful Tabasco

Method
Grill sausages lightly on all sides. Put in uncovered baking dish. In frying pan, saute onion in 1 tablespoonful oil until transparent. Mix together remaining ingredients and add to onions. Cook over low flame for 20 minutes to reduce. Pour sauce over sausages. 20-30 minutes before serving, put sausages in medium oven 325°F. (Mark 3) and heat thoroughly.

Sour Cream Dip with Crisps

Take two containers of sour cream, put in bowl. Add a packet of dried salad dressing mix—any flavour, onion, cheese, French—and ½ teaspoonful Tabasco, mix well. Put on tray and surround with potato crisps.

Devilled Eggs

6 hard-boiled eggs
2 tablespoonfuls mayonnaise
1 teaspoonful vinegar
½ teaspoonful salt
¼ teaspoonful Tabasco
¼ teaspoonful paprika
1 teaspoonful prepared mustard

Method
Cool eggs, remove shells and cut into lengthwise halves. Slip out yolks and mash with mayonnaise and remaining ingredients. Refill egg whites with yolk mixture.
Makes 12 halves.

Stuffed Celery

2 oz. packet cream cheese
1 teaspoonful salad cream or
    mayonnaise
½ teaspoonful Tabasco
Celery stalks, washed and cut into
    4" lengths

Method
Allow cream cheese to reach room temperature, and add salad cream or mayonnaise and Tabasco. Mix well with fork, stuff into celery stalks.

Snack Style Prawns

2 lb. frozen cooked prawns
2 onions, sliced in rings
8 bay leaves
1 cup salad oil
⅔ cupful white vinegar
1 teaspoonful salt
2 teaspoonfuls celery seed
2½ teaspoonfuls capers and juice
½ teaspoonful Tabasco

Method
Thaw prawns, wash in cold water, drain. Alternate prawns and onion rings in shallow dish. Add bay leaves. Combine oil, vinegar, salt, celery seed, capers and Tabasco and mix well. Pour over prawns and onions. Cover and store in refrigerator at least 24 hours.

Barbecued bangers, sour cream dips with crisps, devilled eggs, stuffed celery, snack-style prawns

PATIO PARTIES

'Danwich' is the registered trademark of The Danish Centre Ltd. for Danish open sandwiches.

Giving a Danwich party is great fun. The food is gay and colourful —and the Danwiches can be made well in advance.

Danwiches stay fresh for several hours if left in a cool place, lightly covered with damp greaseproof paper or a damp cloth until needed. You will want to make as many varieties as you can manage, and do have a Danish cheese board with fresh fruit afterwards.

Serve from a central point and each guest should have a plate, with knife, fork and napkin. Let people help themselves informally to the cheese board.

Danish lager and 'snaps' (Akvavit) are the traditional accompaniments in Denmark, but wine or non-alcoholic fruit cups and tea or coffee all go well with Danwiches.

When preparing for a party requiring a large number of each variety, avoid making the Danwiches separately. It is quicker and neater to butter all the required slices of bread, next add the topping to each piece, and finally arrange all the garnishes.

Allow two or three Danwiches for each guest, with cheese and fruit to follow.

To make a Danwich

"Danwich" is the registered trademark of The Danish Centre for Danish Open Sandwiches.

Here are the step-by-step instructions to successful Danwich-making.

Cut the bread into $\frac{1}{4}$" thick slices, about 2" x 4"—approximately half a slice from an ordinary loaf. Do not use a full slice or the topping will look skimped. Spread each piece with a good layer of butter, making sure the bread is completely covered. Arrange the topping— fish, meat, cheese, poultry, etc., neatly on the bread. Use sufficient to ensure the finished Danwich will have a generous well-rounded look. Decorate the topping with a selection of salads, mayonnaise, vegetables or fruit. Use a cake slice to serve them from trays or large plates. Eat them with a knife and fork.

Garnish Gaily

Garnish for colour and flavour. A little practice soon gives deftness to cutting gherkins fans, onion rings, strips of meat jelly or scambled egg.

Tomato twists. Slit slices through centre leaving a top piece holding halves together. Twist halves in opposite directions. Place in position. Use cucumber, beetroot, lemon and orange slices similarly.

Radish roses. Leave a small leaf on each radish. Cut radish in sections from base towards the stalk. Leave in cold water to open.

Gherkin fan. Slice a gherkin several times for two-thirds of its length, leaving a joined portion at top. Press slices apart to form fan.

48

PATIO PARTIES

Fish

A generous layer of butter prevents moisture from the fish reaching the bread. As in every kind of Danwich you will find it also adds inestimably to the flavour. Three Danwiches each are usually sufficient for a satisfying meal.

Pickled Herring with onion rings, tomato, lettuce and parsley.

Tuna fish on lettuce, with mayonnaise, a twist of lemon and parsley.

Anchovy fillets on new potato salad with slices of tomato.

Meats

Succulent slices of home-cooked bacon or canned hams and other meats provide a delicious variety of toppings. Salami, cocktail and Frankfurter sausages make excellent Danwiches, too. Notice how these meats are cut and arranged to cover the bread neatly and completely. Many of the suggested garnishes are interchangeable. Experiment to find your own favourite flavour combinations.

Middle Gammon slices, scrambled egg, tomato and cucumber twists, chopped chives.

Corner Gammon slices with pineapple, lettuce heart, half a glacé cherry.

Collar Bacon, sliced, with potato salad, pickles, tomato twist, chopped parsley.

Back Rashers (2), crisp-fried, with sliced mushrooms, tomato, cucumber twist.

Streaky Bacon rashers, crisp-fried, with apple sauce on lettuce.

Streaky Bacon, crisp-fried, with hard-boiled egg, tomato and cucumber twist, cress.

Pork Luncheon Meat, horseradish cream, lettuce, prune, orange twist.

Canned Ham with lettuce, vegetable salad, mushrooms and cucumber twist.

Chopped Pork and Tongue, vegetable salad, watercress, radish rose.

Lunch Tongue slices, lettuce, green pepper ring filled potato salad, tomato twist.

Chopped Pork and Ham, Russian salad, tomato twist and lettuce.

Liverpate, butter-fried mushrooms, bacon, gherkin fan tomato twist.

Liverpate with savoury meat jelly, crisp cucumber slices.

Cocktail Sausages sliced in potato salad, crisp-fried bacon and tomato garnish.

Frankfurter Sausage (split lengthwise) lettuce, tomato and spring onion salad.

Salami, horseradish cream, onion rings, cress.

Salami with onion rings and parsley.

Poultry

Fresh-frozen Danish chickens are reared on a natural diet. They are meaty, tender and flavoursome. Make party Danwiches with quarters of freshly roasted or grilled Danish spring chickens. Alternatively, add the chicken meat to potato salad or combine it with ham and tongue in mayonnaise.

Cold roast chicken, lettuce, cucumber, tomato and bacon rolls.

Chopped roast chicken in mayonnaise on lettuce, with gherkin and tomato.

Roast chicken and lunch tongue with Russian salad, cress, tomato, radish.

49

West Coast Cookies

Top picture Various Hors d'oeuvres   *General patio layout*

BUFFET PARTIES

"Come for Dinner" invitations are always accepted with pleasure if your guests know that they can expect good food, good company and a welcoming and relaxed hostess. But how hard it is to prepare the dining table, the food and the house single handed and yet have time to dress and titivate oneself properly before the first visitors arrive! The good hostess wants to have everything perfect with the minimum of fuss and effort and without having to run in and out of the kitchen constantly during the meal. A Buffet Dinner Party is an excellent way of entertaining without too much formality—guests enjoy helping themselves and coming back for "seconds".
Home entertaining *can* be fun and a good hostess makes it so.

Mushroom and Sweet Pepper Salad

> 4 oz. button mushrooms
> 1 small (2-3 oz.) sweet pepper
> ½ small clove garlic (optional)
> Good shake pepper
> 1 dessertspoonful vinegar
> 2 dessertspoonfuls vegetable oil
> ¼ teaspoonful salt

Method
Wash and dry the mushrooms and trim the stalks to within ¼" of the caps. Place them on a board, stalk side downwards, and slice thinly. Wash the pepper, cut off the stalk, remove all the seeds and slice the flesh across finely. Cut some of the circle into rough quarters. Chop the garlic very finely and squash with the blade of a knife, or the cut surface may be rubbed over the serving dish. Make a French dressing by whipping together the vinegar, oil and seasonings, until it is emulsified (this is easy with a small pear-shaped wire whisk, or shaken in a screw top bottle). Stir in the garlic and onion and pour over the mushrooms and peppers. Leave to marinate for several hours.
Serves 3 persons.

Grapefruit Meringues

> 2 grapefruits
> 8 teaspoonfuls ginger wine
> 2 egg whites
> 4 oz. castor sugar
> Cherries and angelica

Method
Cut the grapefruits in half. Remove core and separate the flesh from the individual sections. Pour two teaspoonfuls of ginger wine over each half. Whisk egg whites until stiff and then whisk in the sugar a little at a time. Pile meringue on each half grapefruit, decorate with a cherry and angelica and brown in a moderate oven 375°F (Mark 5) for 10-15 minutes. Serve hot.

Clear Beetroot Soup

> 2 pints rich white stock
> 1 small raw beetroot
> 1 celery stick
> 1 small onion
> ½ teaspoonful peppercorns
> Salt to taste
> 2 egg whites and shells
> ½ gill sherry

Method
Place all the ingredients in a saucepan, after peeling and scalding the onion.

BUFFET PARTIES

Whisk constantly till almost boiling, then remove whisk. Bring stock rapidly to the boil, then draw pan to side of stove. Stand for about 15 minutes, then strain through a jelly bag. Reheat to boiling point, but do not allow to boil. Stir in sherry, then pour into heated cups. Garnish with a steamed egg white, cut into tiny stars. Serve with a bowl of whipped cream. Season with salt and pepper.

Salmon Mousse

1 lb. salmon off cuts or
1 x 1 lb. tin pink salmon
¼ pint white wine
Salt and pepper
2 level tablespoonfuls mayonnaise
1 x 5 oz. carton soured cream
1 level tablespoonful tomato
*   Ketchup*
Dash Worcester sauce
1 level tablespoonful chopped
*   parsley*
½ cucumber—peeled and diced
Water
1 level tablespoonful gelatine
Juice of ½ lemon
Slices of cucumber for garnish

Method
Place the salmon in a buttered baking dish. Pour over the wine. Sprinkle with salt and pepper. Cover and bake in a moderate oven 350°F. or Mark 4 for 20 minutes. Drain the fish liquor and reserve. Skin and remove any bones from the salmon and flake without mashing. (If using canned salmon, drain and flake). Stir in the mayonnaise, soured cream, Ketchup, Worcester sauce, parsley and diced cucumber. Make the fish liquor up to ¾ pint with water. Heat and sprinkle in the gelatine.

Stir until dissolved. Add the lemon juice and allow to cool. When on the point of setting, stir ½ pint of the gelatine into the salmon mixture. Pour into a wetted 1 lb. loaf tin. Chill until set. Turn the mousse onto a wire tray and garnish with slices of cucumber. Warm the remaining ¼ pint of gelatine. Allow to cool and when on the point of setting, spoon over the mould to glaze. Chill until set. *N.B.* If using canned salmon, dissolve the gelatine in ¾ pint water and correct seasoning.

Fish Mousse

A buffet-party special. Looks very delicious and is great fun to make.
4 eggs
3 8-oz. tins salmon
*   (or 1½ lb. cooked white fish)*
1 oz. powdered gelatine
*   (enough for 2 pints liquid)*
1 tablespoonful plain flour
½ pint milk
1 oz. butter
Salt and pepper
1 tablespoonful castor sugar
2 teaspoonfuls dry mustard
¼ pint double cream (optional)
5 tablespoonfuls cold water
Vinegar

Method
Drain liquid from fish, and add enough vinegar to make up to ¼ pint. Add butter, heat till it has melted, then leave to cool. Flake the fish. Mix flour sugar and mustard in top of double boiler. Add eggs singly, and beat in well. When smooth, gradually stir in fish liquid and milk. Cook stirring constantly, until mixture thickens. Remove from heat. Stir in gelatine until dissolved add fish. Turn into

53

Mushroom and sweet pepper salad

Top picture Salmon Mousse   *Fish mousse*

bowl and set in a cool place. When cold and thick, season, and fold in the lightly whipped cream. Turn into 2½-3 pint mould rinsed with cold water, and leave till set. Turn out and serve on a bed of peas, decorated with egg slices and radishes.
Serves 8 persons.

Chicken and Mushroom Pate

1 lb. chicken livers
½ lb. lean pork
½ lb. fat bacon rashers
½ lb. mushrooms
1 medium sized onion
1 oz. butter
¼ pint double cream
2 eggs
1-2 cloves garlic
2 bay leaves
¾ teaspoonful thyme

Method
Clean the livers thoroughly and put into a pan with the diced pork. Chop the bacon into large pieces, slice the onion and add both to the pan. Add the thyme, 1 bay leaf and salt and pepper, together with the stock. Cook over a gentle heat until all is tender, but not soft. Drain off the stock and allow the meats to cool. The meat must then be ground down to a fine paste; this can be done with an electric blender, a mouli, or with fine blades on a mincer. The mushrooms and crushed garlic are added to the mixture during the blending stage. Now beat in the butter and cream, also the beaten eggs and lemon juice. Heat the vermouth, set alight, then add to the mixture.
Check seasonings, then turn into a prepared ovenproof pate mould. Stand in a tin of water and bake in oven

325°F., mark 3 for about 2 hours. Place a piece of kitchen foil on the surface and a weight on the top and allow to cool.
Garnish and serve with fresh crisp toast.

Pork and Cucumber Salad

10 oz. cooked leg of pork (cold)
½ cucumber
¼ pint plain yoghurt
1 tablespoonful chopped chives
¼ teaspoonful dry mustard
¼ teaspoonful garlic salt
1 teaspoonful lemon juice
Salt and pepper
4 lettuce leaves
1 tomato

Method
Cut the pork and cucumber into small strips and mix together in a bowl. Prepare the dressing by mixing all the ingredients together just before using. Toss lightly with the pork and cucumber and serve in cupped lettuce leaves. Garnish with sliced tomato.
Serves 4 persons.

Prawn Cocktail with Soured Cream Sauce

½ lettuce, shredded
6 ozs. shelled prawns
1 tablespoonful tomato ketchup
Dash Worcester sauce
Salt and pepper
1 carton Soured Cream
Paprika (optional)
4 whole prawns
4 lemon wedges

Method
Divide lettuce and shelled prawns between 4 glasses. Blend together

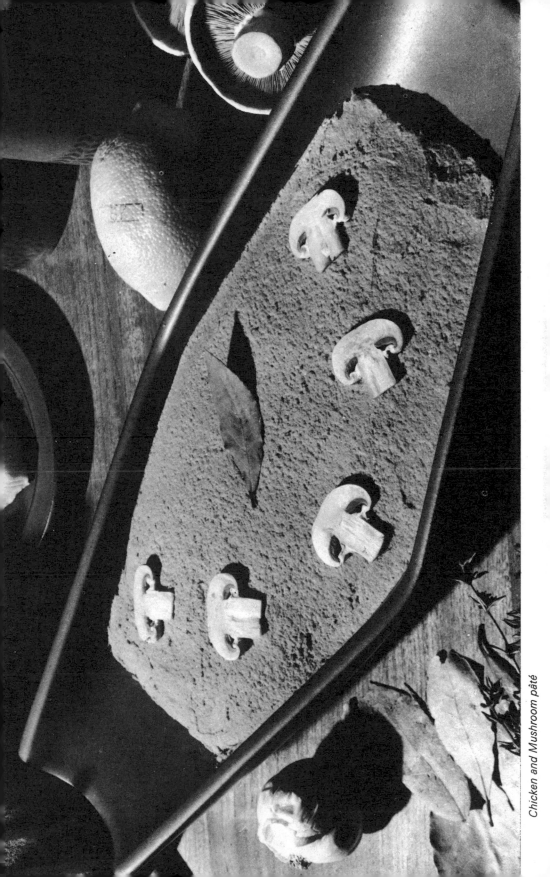

Chicken and Mushroom pâté

ketchup, Worcester sauce, seasoning and soured cream. Pour over sauce just before serving. Sprinkle with paprika. Garnish with whole prawns and lemon wedges, slit halfway up between the skin and the flesh so that they sit on the edge of the glass. Here is another colourful and piquant meal starter or luncheon salad.

Elizabethan-Style Chicken

4 large or 8 small chicken
   drumsticks
1 onion—sliced
$\frac{1}{2}$ level teaspoonful salt
Milk
2 oz. flour
2 oz. butter
6 tablespoonfuls Salad Cream
2 level teaspoonfuls gelatine
5 tablespoonfuls water
Cucumber and red pepper skins—
   cut in fancy shapes
Salt and pepper
$\frac{1}{2}$ pint aspic jelly

Method

Lay the drumsticks in a large saucepan, add the onion and salt, just cover with water. Cook until tender. Drain off the stock, remove the skin from the chicken and allow the drumsticks to cool. Dissolve the gelatine in the water. Make the stock up to $\frac{1}{2}$ pint with milk and make a thick white sauce with the butter, flour and stock. Fold the salad cream into the sauce and adjust the seasoning. Stir in the dissolved gelatine. Coat the drumsticks with the sauce. If it becomes too thick, warm over a low heat.
Decorate the chicken with the cucumber and red pepper. Coat the drumsticks with aspic jelly. The coating of aspic is optional if they are eaten the same day.
Serves 4 persons.

Antipasto

Italian Hors d'oeuvre.
   Fillets of anchovies
   Rolled anchovies
   Small mushrooms, cooked in a
      very little vinegar
   Pickled beetroot, cut into tiny
      shapes
   Pickled onions
   Hard-boiled eggs
   Pimentos
   Sliced tomatoes
   Sardines
   Olives, green and black

Method

Using as many of the above ingredients as you can, arrange them either on individual plates or on one large serving dish so that the colours form as attractive a picture as possible.

Braband Pan Fry

2 eggs
2 lb. potatoes
3 oz. lard
1 (12 oz.) can pork luncheon meat
Parsley to garnish

Method

Hard boil eggs for 10 minutes. Place under running cold water, shell and cut in halves. Peel potatoes and cut into $\frac{1}{2}$" cubes. Melt lard in a large frying pan, and fry potatoes slowly for 15-20 minutes. Add the meat, cut into cubes, and fry quickly to brown. Turn into a heated serving dish and garnish with hard-boiled eggs and parsley.
Serves 4 persons.

Top picture   *Elizabethan-style Chicken*   *Antipasto*

BUFFET PARTIES

Roast Poussins with Mushrooms

4 poussins weighing 1¼ lbs.
or 2 chickens weighing 2½ lbs.
1 bunch parsley
1 red or green pepper
1 oz. butter
3 bay leaves
1¾ lbs. mushrooms
½ lb. streaky bacon
¾ pint chicken stock

Method

Place one large mushroom and a good sprig of parsley inside each baby chicken. Put the chickens into a large baking dish, pour in the stock, add the bay leaves, salt and pepper. Cover the chicken breasts with two rashers of bacon each. Put into the oven 425°F., mark 7, for 10 minutes. Reduce the oven temperature to 375°F., mark 5, and cook for a further 45 minutes or until the meat is tender. Do not cover the dish during roasting, and remove the bacon for the last 15 minutes of cooking time. Prepare the kebab garnishes, allowing one or two skewers for each chicken. Thread rolled bacon rashers, mushrooms and chunks of pepper onto the skewers; brush with melted butter, season with salt and pepper and cook in the oven for 15-20 minutes. Put the remaining mushrooms onto a sheet of kitchen foil, sprinkle with salt and pepper, seal the edges of the kitchen foil together and cook in the oven for 15 minutes.

To assemble the dish: place the chickens on a large meat platter, stand the kebabs upright in the tail end of each chicken. Pile the baked mushrooms onto the front of the dish and garnish with parsley.

To serve the dish: using a sharp knife divide the chickens through the centre; or quarter them if using the larger birds. *Serves 8 persons*

Chicken a la King

1 pint diced cooked chicken
3 tablespoonfuls butter or chicken fat
½ cup shredded green pepper (optional)
12 oz. sliced mushrooms
3½ tablespoonfuls flour
½ pint hot chicken stock
¼ cup scalded milk
¼ cupful scalded cream
4 tablespoonfuls sliced pimento
Salt and pepper to taste
2 egg yolks
4-6 tablespoonfuls sherry
1 tablespoonful minced parsley

Method

Remove gristle and skin from chicken before measuring. Melt fat. Add pepper and mushrooms. Simmer till soft, in about 5 minutes. Add flour. Stir till blended. Add stock to the milk, and stir into mixture. Cook over low heat till smooth, thick and boiling. Draw pan to side of stove. Stir in cream, pimento, salt and pepper and chicken. Beat egg yolks slightly. Stir in a little of the hot sauce. When blended, stir slowly into remainder of sauce and chicken. Stir in sherry and parsley. Serve on a heated flat dish. Garnish with more minced parsley and hot triangles of puff pastry, separated by little groups of asparagus tips or green peas. This makes a good filling for hot patty cases for a party. *Serves 6-8 persons.*

Roast Poussins with Mushrooms

BUFFET PARTIES

Mincemeat Hornes

*Puff pastry using 8 oz. plain flour
or
1 packet prepared puff pastry
10 oz. can Mincemeat
¼ pint double cream—whipped
Beaten egg white to glaze
9-10 cornet tins*

Method
Heat oven to 450°F. (Mark 8). Roll out the pastry into an oblong, approximately 12" x 6". Cut the pastry into strips ½" wide. Moisten one side of the strip of pastry with water and wind round the cornet mould from the point upwards, keeping moist surface on the outside. Finish overlap on underside of tin and trim neatly. Place on baking sheet. Glaze the pastry with beaten egg white and bake in the pre-heated oven for about 10-12 minutes, or until golden brown. Place on a cooling tray, remove the tins, cool and store until required. Place one teaspoonful of whipped cream into the bottom of each horn case, and top with Mincemeat.
Makes 9-10 horns

Copenhagen Kebabs

*1 (8 oz.) can cocktail sausages
6 rashers streaky bacon
12 button mushrooms
3 tomatoes
1 small green pepper
1 oz. butter*

Method
Prepare a medium grill. Drain can of sausages and discard liquid. Remove rind and bone from bacon and cut each rasher in half. Flatten pieces with back of a knife and roll up each one. Wash mushrooms and cut each tomato into quarters. Remove seeds and pith from green pepper and cut into 12 small pieces. Arrange, on each of 6 skewers, 3 sausages, 2 bacon rolls, 2 pieces of tomato, 2 pieces of green pepper and 2 pieces of mushroom. Brush with melted butter. Grill for 20-25 minutes and serve on a bed of boiled rice.
Serves 6 persons.

Baked Potatoes

*4 large even-sized potatoes
1 oz. butter
4 oz. cheese
Salt and pepper*
Garnish
See below

Method
Scrub the potatoes, prick and bake at 400°F. (Mark 6) for 1-1½ hours, depending on size, until they feel soft. Cut a cross or zig-zag in the top of each and remove the cooked potato. Place in a bowl and beat in the butter, cheese, salt and pepper. Refill the potato skins, smoothing the tops. Garnish as desired and replace in the oven to reheat for 10-15 mins.
Suggestions for garnishes:
Cheese: Top the filled potato with a slice of cheese. Replace in the oven until the cheese is just melted.
Eggs: Make a hollow in the top of the filled potato and break in an egg. Replace in the oven until the egg is just set, about 15 mins.
Bacon: Use streaky bacon to make bacon rolls. Thread on a cocktail stick and grill until crispy. Garnish the potato with the bacon roll on its stick, topped with a coloured cocktail onion or pickled onion.

Baked potatoes

Tomato: Top the filled potato with tomato slices before reheating.
Sausage: Arrange sliced cooked sausages on the filled potato, reheat. Garnish with parsley.

Spiced Stuffed Marrow Boats

1 medium-sized marrow
1 oz. dripping
1 large onion (chopped)
1 lb. minced beef
4 oz. mushrooms (chopped)
Pinch of mixed herbs
2 oz. white breadcrumbs
¾ teaspoonful Tabasco
Salt to taste
2 oz. melted butter

Method
Peel marrow thinly and cut a slice from the top. Remove seeded part with a spoon. Melt dripping in a saucepan, and fry onion until tender but not browned. Add beef and cook for 10 minutes, stirring occasionally. Add mushrooms and herbs, and cook for a further 5 minutes. Stir in breadcrumbs, Tabasco, and salt to taste. Pile meat mixture into hollow of marrow. Brush over with melted butter. Wrap in foil and bake in a fairly hot oven (Gas No. 6 400° F.) for about one hour. Remove from foil, and serve.
Serves 6 persons

Tomatoes Tabasco

7-8 firm tomatoes
8 oz. cottage cheese
1 level tablespoonful salad cream
½ level teaspoonful lemon juice
4 oz. cooked cold chicken, meat or
    corned beef (chopped)
½ cucumber

Salt
Just over ¼ teaspoonful Tabasco

Method
Cut a circle 1" in diameter out of the top of each tomato, remove pulp and turn upside down to drain on kitchen paper. Mix together cottage cheese, salad cream, lemon juice and meat. Chop cucumber and add to cottage cheese mixture, add salt to taste and Tabasco. Pile mixture into tomato shells, and garnish with parsley.
Serves 8 persons

Prune and Chicory

Soak plump prunes—3 per sandwich— in cold water for an hour or two. Remove stones, drain well, then fill each with a dessertspoonful of Cottage Cheese. Take buttered slices of brown bread, spread with mayonnaise then top with slices of cucumber. Season well. Arrange small chicory leaves on one side and place 3 cheese-stuffed prunes on top.

Salt Brisket and Horseradish Cottage Cheese

Cover slices of buttered white bread with two folded slices of brisket. Pile between the meat rolls a heaped tablespoonful of Cottage Cheese blended with a level teaspoonful horseradish sauce, a teaspoonful of bramble jelly and a little whipped cream. Top with a pickle to taste, and thinly sliced onion rings.

Cottage Baps

Butter a split white roll. Arrange slices of tomato on top, season and top with 1 heaped tablespoonful Cottage Cheese

Top picture
Spiced Stuffed Marrow Boats

Prune and chicory, Salt brisket and horseradish, cottage baps

blended with 2 chopped anchovies and a little mayonnaise. Season with pepper. Pile on tomato and place a cross of anchovy on top.

Steak Curry

6 oz. desiccated coconut
1½ pints milk
3 lb. chuck steak
Oil
6 oz. blended white vegetable fat
1½ lb. onions, peeled and cut in rings
Little green ginger, chopped
3 level teaspoonfuls strong curry powder
3 level teaspoonfuls flour
3 level teaspoonfuls salt
4 level tablespoonfuls ground almonds
6⅓ oz. tube Concentrated Tomato Paste
3 cartons plain yoghurt
2 bananas

Method

In a bowl soak the coconut with the milk for ½ hour. Cut the steak into 1" cubes. Heat just enough oil in a large saucepan to cover the base (an 8 pint flameproof casserole can be used for preparing the curry from start to finish). Fry the steak until each piece is sealed. Put meat on one side. To the pan add the vegetable fat. Sauté onions in the fat until soft but do not brown. Stir in the ginger, curry powder, flour, salt and ground almonds. Simmer together for 10 minutes. Add tomato paste and mix well. Strain liquid from the coconut into the pan and add yoghurt. Mix well. Add meat and turn the contents into an 8-pint heatproof casserole. Cover and cook in the oven at 325°F. (mark 3)

for 2 hours until the meat is tender. Serve garnished with bananas sliced lengthwise and sprinkled with lemon juice. Add parsley (optional).

ACCOMPANIMENTS: fluffy rice — allow 1¼-1½ lb. Cook in plenty of boiling salted water until tender, about 15 minutes.

Chutney—Indian Mango and the hotter Rajput Mango. Tomato and Onion Salad—thinly slice ½ lb. peeled onions lengthwise. Place in a bowl, sprinkle evenly with 2 level teaspoonfuls salt and leave for ½ hour. Halve ½ lb. skinned tomatoes, remove seeds and thinly slice. Squeeze the juice from the onions and discard the juice. Toss onions and tomatoes together and serve in small bowls garnished with freshly chopped parsley.

Open Sandwich of Anchovy Salad

1 small tin anchovies
4 slices rye bread
3-4 medium cold boiled potatoes
6 black olives
Cayenne pepper

Method

Carefully save the oil when taking the anchovies from the tin. Chop the anchovies, stone and chop the olives, and finely dice the potatoes. Mix all together with the oil from the anchovies and season with pepper. Spread on rye bread.

Open Sandwich of Pacific Prawns

4 slices brown bread
4 Pacific prawns, cooked and peeled
2 medium sized spring onions

Open sandwich of Anchovy Salad

BUFFET PARTIES

Mayonnaise
Cayenne pepper

Method

Spread the bread with some of the mayonnaise. Finely chop the prawns and the onions, using some of the green of the onions. Mix well together and cohere lightly with more mayonnaise. Spread the mixture on the bread and season carefully with the cayenne pepper. If raw, poach the prawns in a little salt water with a bay leaf for 10 minutes.

Pork and Potato Salad Bar

1 lb. potatoes
3 tablespoonfuls mayonnaise
1 tablespoonful finely chopped
*   chives, onion or leek top*
1 small lettuce
1 large (12 oz.) can Chopped pork
*   and ham*
Radishes

Method

Boil potatoes in their skins. Drain and peel; cut into $\frac{1}{4}$" cubes and place in a bowl. Add mayonnaise and chives. Wash lettuce and arrange on a serving dish. Cut the meat into 8 slices and arrange alternately on lettuce with potato salad, to form a bar. Garnish each end with radish 'roses'.
Serves 4 persons.

Shrimp Hors-d'oeuvre

1 (10$\frac{1}{2}$ oz.) can condensed
*   Cream of Mushroom Soup*
2 tablespoonfuls lemon juice
2 tablespoonfuls mayonnaise
8 oz. shelled shrimps
Green salad

Method

Mix soup, lemon juice and mayonnaise.

Add the shrimps. Arrange on a bed of fresh green salad and serve.
Serves 10 persons.

Party-style Chicken

1 deep-frozen chicken, 2$\frac{1}{2}$ lb.
3$\frac{1}{2}$ oz. butter
1-2 teaspoonfuls saffron yellow
*   colouring*
6 oz. long-grain rice
2 oz. plain flour
$\frac{1}{4}$ pint milk
1 (7$\frac{1}{2}$ oz.) can mushrooms
Seasoning
1 canned red pepper

Method

Thaw chicken, then remove giblets; simmer giblets in water to make stock. Wipe chicken and truss. Melt 2 oz. butter in a large saucepan, add chicken and turn in butter to coat. Cover and cook slowly for $\frac{3}{4}$-1 hour, until tender, turning occasionally during cooking. Boil a large saucepan-ful of water, add colouring, salt and rice and bring to boil, stirring. Boil for 12 minutes. Drain thoroughly and rinse in hot water. Melt 1$\frac{1}{2}$ oz. butter in a small saucepan, add flour and cook for 2 minutes. Stir in $\frac{1}{2}$ pint stock and the milk and bring to boil; simmer for 3 minutes. Drain mushrooms and add to sauce with seasoning to taste. Cut red pepper into thin strips. Place chicken on a warm serving dish and spoon mushroom sauce over. Press rice into castle tins and turn out around the chicken. Garnish top of each mound of rice with a small piece of red pepper and arrange remainder over breast of chicken.
Serves 4 persons.

Dishes illustrated are: Potted Shrimps, Shrimp and Parmesan Soufflé, Shrimp boats, Shrimps Ensalada de Arroz, Shrimp Sauce

BUFFET PARTIES

Seafood Specials

Shrimp dishes

Shrimp Ensalada de Arroz

6 oz. carton potted shrimps
4 oz. Patna rice
3 oz. red or green peppers
Chives or spring onions
Chopped parsley
Chopped lettuce
Salad oil

Method
Thaw the potted shrimps. Cook the Patna rice in boiling salted water. Leave to cool. Chop the red or green peppers finely, add a few chopped chives or spring onions, a little parsley and lettuce. Add the shrimps and mix all the ingredients together. Season well. Add a little salad oil and a pinch of nutmeg. Serve on a bed of chopped lettuce.
Serves 4 persons

Shrimp Boats

2 x 2 oz. cartons potted shrimps
2 doz. 3½-4ins. pastry boats
Red and green pimentos
Radishes, gherkins

Method
Make or buy the pastry boats. Make ½ pint of thick white wine sauce. Mix in the thawed potted shrimps. Fill the boats with the mixture. Garnish with slices of red and green pimento, radish, gherkins, etc. Fold over and seal the edges by crimping. Fry in hot fat for 4-5 minutes. Serve hot or cold.
Enough for a small party

Shrimp Sauce

2 oz. carton potted shrimps
1 oz. butter
1 oz. plain flour
½ pint milk

Method
Thaw the potted shrimps. Make a white sauce in the usual way using butter, plain flour and milk. Season well and add half the shrimps. Crush the rest of the shrimps and stir in. Stir until the butter has melted and the shrimps heated. Serve with grilled white fish or any type of poached fish.

Shrimp and Parmesan Souffle

6 oz. carton potted shrimps
½ pint white sauce (½ pint milk, 1 oz. flour, 1 oz. margarine, seasoning)
2 oz. grated Parmesan cheese
½ teaspoonful English mustard
4 eggs
1 teaspoonful tomato purée

Method
Separate eggs. Make white sauce, add the thawed potted shrimps, cheese, tomato purée and English mustard. When the sauce has cooled slightly, beat in egg yolks. Whisk egg whites until stiff. Fold in the shrimp and cheese sauce to the white of eggs. Pour the soufflé mixture into a greased soufflé dish. Place in a hot oven. Bake at 400°F. or Mark 6 for 30 minutes.
Note: Serve immediately the soufflé is taken from the oven. This is a wonderful light supper dish.
Serves 4 persons.

Open sandwich of Pacific Prawns

Dishes illustrated are: Scampi Meuniere, Seafood Sauce, Italian Scampi Salad, Butterfly Scampi, Scampi Provencal, Bacon and Scampi Delights

BUFFET PARTIES

Scampi dishes

Fried Scampi

2 x 4 oz. packets scampi
Flour
Cooking Oil
1 egg white

Method

Thaw the scampi. Drain, make up a light batter and allow to stand for $\frac{1}{2}$ hour. Whip egg white until stiff and fold into batter immediately prior to dipping scampi. Heat oil to 365°F., drop and cook for 1-2 minutes until golden brown. Be sure not to overcook. Serve piping hot with Tartare Sauce.

$\frac{1}{4}$ pint thick mayonnaise
Juice of $\frac{1}{2}$ lemon
1 tablespoonful chopped gherkins and capers
1 teaspoonful chopped onion

Mix all ingredients together and serve with the fried scampi.
Serves 4 persons.

Scampi Meuniere

2 x 8 oz. packets scampi
Lemon
Chopped parsley
Flour
Butter

Method

Thaw the scampi. Drain. Roll in seasoned flour. Fry briefly in butter. Remove from pan, squeeze on a little lemon juice. Put a piece of butter into the pan. When it has become noisette—brown and nutty—pour quickly over the scampi. Add a few pinches of parsley. Serve immediately, while butter is still foaming.
Serves 4 persons.

Butterfly Scampi

2 x 8 oz. packets scampi
1 egg
2 tablespoonfuls flour
$\frac{1}{4}$ teaspoonful ground ginger
Nut oil

Method

Thaw the scampi. Drain. Make batter; beat egg, add flour gradually, salt and pepper to taste, and ground ginger. Stick 2 scampi together on wooden cocktail sticks to form 'butterfly'. Dip in batter. Deep-fry in *hot* nut oil for 30 seconds. Drain. Serve with *seafood sauce*.
Serves approx. 25 persons.

Seafood Sauce

1 tablespoonful soya sauce
1 tablespoonful nut oil
1 teaspoonful brown sugar
1 small onion
$\frac{1}{2}$ teaspoonful chilli powder
$\frac{1}{2}$ tablespoonful wine vinegar

Method

Blend soya sauce and nut oil, (sesame oil if you can get it makes this sauce extra-delicious), with brown sugar, finely chopped onion (if possible use a spring onion and include the green stem), chilli powder, and wine vinegar. Serve in shallow bowl. Delicious with prawns or scampi, either fried as above, or just as they come from the packet!

Bacon and Scampi Delights

2 x 8 oz. packets scampi
1 lb. streaky bacon
Deep fat for frying
Lemon juice

BUFFET PARTIES

Seasoning
Bread crumbs
Stuffed olives

Method

Thaw the scampi. Drain. Stretch the streaky bacon, place a couple of scampi onto the bacon and roll up. Dip in beaten egg and roll in breadcrumbs. Fry in deep fat for 3-4 minutes. Serve on a cocktail stick and garnish with a stuffed olive. Serve hot or cold.
Serves approx. 30 persons.

Scampi a la Ajillo

8 oz. packet scampi
4 tablespoonfuls olive oil
4 cloves garlic
2 tablespoonfuls chopped parsley
1 teaspoonful chopped chilli pepper

Method

Thaw the scampi. Drain. Pour olive oil into frying pan. Add scampi, garlic, parsley and chilli pepper. Fry together for 2 minutes. Serve hot.
Serves 2 persons.

Scampi Provencale

8 oz. packet scampi
8 oz. rice
3 oz. butter or margarine
1 onion
2 oz. green or red peppers
1 clove garlic
1 tin peeled tomatoes
¼ pint dry white wine

Method

Cook the rice in salted water. Thaw the scampi. Drain on absorbent paper. Melt the butter or margarine in frying pan. Add chopped onion and chopped green or red peppers and chopped garlic. Fry for 2-3 minutes. Season well. Add pulped strained tomatoes and dry white wine. Add scampi and continue to cook slowly for a further 5 minutes. Mix the scampi with the cooked rice and serve piping hot.
Serves 3 persons.

Italian Scampi Salad

8 oz. packet scampi
4 oz. shell macaroni
4 oz. frozen peas and carrots (mixed)
1 tablespoonful chopped parsley
1 tablespoonful chopped chives or spring onion tops
2 oz. butter
4 oz. cucumber
Freshly ground black pepper
4 tablespoonfuls mayonnaise
1 lettuce
4 oz. tomatoes

Method

Cook the macaroni in boiling, salted water for 12-15 minutes. Drain and wash under running water to remove starch from the shells. Cook vegetables in salted water. Drain and cool. Thaw and drain scampi. Melt butter in frying pan and add the scampi. Fry in butter for 1-2 minutes. Allow to cool. Dice the cucumber and place into a mixing bowl, then add the cooked scampi, macaroni, vegetables, chives, black pepper and mayonnaise. Mix together. Serve the scampi salad on a bed of chopped lettuce and garnish with chopped tomatoes and parsley.
Serves 4 persons.

BUFFET PARTIES

Crabmeat and Scallop dishes

Crab Cocktail

2 x 4 oz. packets crabmeat
2 oz. chopped lettuce
2 tablespoonfuls dairy cream
2 tablespoonfuls thick mayonnaise
1 tablespoonful tomato ketchup
1 teaspoonful chopped spring
*   onion tops*
$\frac{1}{2}$ teaspoonful chopped gherkins
$\frac{1}{2}$ teaspoonful chopped capers
1 chopped hard-boiled egg
Parsley and lemon

Method
Thaw the crabmeat. Divide the lettuce into 4 glasses. Put 2 oz. of crabmeat in each glass. Make the sauce by mixing the mayonnaise, tomato ketchup, cream, spring onion tops, gherkins and capers. Pour a little of the sauce over each cocktail. Garnish the tops of the cocktails with parsley, egg and a twist of lemon.
Serves 4 persons.

Crab and Bacon Rolls

2 x 4 oz. packets crabmeat
2 eggs
8 oz. bacon
1 teaspoonful soya sauce

Method
Thaw the crabmeat. Drain. Mix crabmeat with egg yolks. Cut the bacon into 2″ lengths. Make batter by beating egg whites with soya sauce. Wrap bacon round a portion of crabmeat. Dip into batter. Heat oil and deep fry rolls for 30 seconds. Drain on absorbent paper.

Crabmeat Sauce

4 oz. packet crabmeat
$\frac{1}{2}$ pint white sauce ($\frac{1}{2}$ pint milk,
* $\frac{1}{2}$ oz. flour, $\frac{1}{2}$ oz. margarine,*
*   seasoning)*
1 tablespoonful Anchovy essence
Tomato purée

Method
Thaw the crabmeat. Make up white sauce, add anchovy essence and continue to cook. Add a little tomato purée to improve the colour. Add the crabmeat. Serve this sauce with poached turbot or halibut.

Crabmeat Mayonnaise

2 x 4 oz. crabmeat
4 tablespoonfuls mayonnaise
1 egg
1 chopped green pepper
2 tablespoonfuls chopped chives or
*   spring onion tops*
Chopped Parsley
Cucumber

Method
Thaw the crabmeat, and mix with the mayonnaise, green pepper, chives and parsley. Season well. Pile the crab mayonnaise in the centre of a dish and garnish with slices of egg and cucumber. Serve with slices of buttered brown bread.
Serves 4 persons.

Fried Scallops with Bacon

8 oz. packet Scallops
1 egg
Breadcrumbs
8 rashers of crisp-fried streaky
*   bacon*

Method
Thaw the scallops. Dip into beaten egg

Dishes illustrated are: Crabmeat Sauce, Coquilles St. Jacques a la Creme, Crab and Bacon Rolls, Crabmeat Mayonnaise, Crab Cocktail, Fried Scallops

and roll in breadcrumbs. Fry in deep oil until golden brown. Wrap the bacon round the scallops and secure with cocktail stick.

Coquilles St. Jacques a la Creme

8 oz. packet Frozen Scallops
$\frac{1}{4}$ pint white wine
$\frac{1}{4}$ pint water
Squeeze of lemon juice
$\frac{1}{2}$ oz. butter
$\frac{1}{2}$ oz. flour
$\frac{1}{4}$ pint double cream
Seasoning
Cayenne pepper
1 oz. grated Gruyere cheese

Method

Thaw the scallops, place in a shallow pan and poach them in the wine, water and lemon juice for 10 minutes. Allow to cool. Strain off the liquor and slice the scallops. Melt the butter, flour and seasoning together with the fish liquor. Stir until boiling and continue to cook for 3-4 minutes. Add the cream and boil again until syrupy, add the scallops to the sauce and place into either shells or dish. Scatter cheese over the scallops and brown under grill.
Serves 4 persons.

Dressed Crab

1 medium sized crab
1 dessertspoonful white wine vinegar
1 oz. fresh white breadcrumbs
Salt and pepper
1 level dessertspoonful mayonnaise
1 hard-boiled egg
Watercress and lettuce

Method

Remove the legs and large claws by twisting sharply. Prize the body from under the tail out of the shell. Remove the stomach sack from the shell and deadman's fingers (grey feathery pieces) from underneath the body and discard. Scoop the dark meat out of the shell and place in a basin. Stir in the vinegar, breadcrumbs and salt and pepper to taste.

Wash and scrub the shell. Dry and oil. Remove the white meat from the body, legs and claws using a skewer. Place the white meat in a separate basin and stir in the mayonnaise. Spoon an equal amount of the dark meat either side of the shell. Fill the centre with white meat.

Garnish with lines of finely chopped egg white, sieved egg yolk and chopped parsley.

Serve the dressed crab on lettuce and watercress.

The legs may be used as a garnish if liked.
Serves 4 persons.

Anchovy Cream Sauce

4 tablespoonfuls mayonnaise
$\frac{1}{4}$ pint double cream
Dash Worcester sauce
Anchovy essence
1 teaspoonful finely grated onion

Method

Mix mayonnaise and cream with grated onion. Season with Worcester sauce and add anchovy essence to taste. Chill before serving.

BUFFET PARTIES

Prawn dishes

Prawn Cocktail

2 x 4 oz. packets peeled prawns
Shredded lettuce
3 teaspoonfuls tomato ketchup
Worcester sauce
Cayenne pepper
Chopped parsley
Lemon
½ pint salad cream
    (or home-made mayonnaise)

Method
Half fill six stem glasses with shredded lettuce. Divide thawed prawns between the 6 glasses. Take the salad cream or mayonnaise (beat yolks of 2 eggs with pepper, salt, squeeze of lemon juice, add ⅓ pint olive oil, drop by drop, stir in 1 tablespoonful fresh-frozen cream) ; add tomato ketchup, dash of Worcester sauce. Spoon over prawns. Dust with Cayenne pepper, garnish with parsley and lemon twist.
Serves 6 persons.

Prawns in Aspic

8 oz. packet peeled prawns
1 pint aspic jelly
2 oz. quartered tomatoes
2 oz. sliced pimentos
2 oz. cooked button mushrooms
2 oz. sliced cucumber
2 oz. gherkins (sliced lengthways)
2 oz. stuffed olives

Method
Line a 6″ ring mould with some of the jelly. Decorate the bottom with thawed prawns and other ingredients. Cover with a thin layer of aspic. Allow to set. Repeat until the mould is filled. Leave to set. Turn out and decorate with parsley.
Serves 4 persons.

Sweet and Sour Prawns

2 x 4 oz. packets peeled prawns
1 tablespoonful sherry
2 onions
2 green peppers
¼ cupful of chicken stock
4 sliced pineapple wedges
    (tinned)
1 tablespoonful cornflour
2 teaspoonfuls soya sauce
½ cupful vinegar
½ cupful sugar

Method
Marinate the prawns in sherry. Add salt and pepper to taste. Gently fry onions (sliced into rings) and sliced green peppers, until tender. Add the chicken stock and pineapple wedges. Cover and cook for 3-5 minutes. Blend cornflour, soya sauce, vinegar, sugar, and add to the mixture. Stir until it thickens. Stir in prawns. Cook for 30 seconds. Cover. Turn heat off. Leave covered for 2 minutes before serving. (Can be kept warm). Serve with boiled rice.
Serves 6-8 persons.

Prawn Puffs

4 oz. packet peeled prawns
1 lb. raw Cod or Haddock
Juice of one lemon
Seasoning
1 tablespoonful Anchovy essence
    or tomato purée
5 oz. self-raising flour
Deep fat for frying

BUFFET PARTIES

Method

Flake raw fish, add roughly chopped thawed prawns, seasoning, lemon juice and tomato purée or anchovy essence. Mix the flour into this mixture thoroughly. Divide the mixture into 32 portions and roll into small balls. *Note:* These do not have to be egged and crumbed. Drop into hot fat for 3-4 minutes or until evenly brown. Serve on cocktail sticks with a mayonnaise and tomato dip. i.e. $\frac{1}{2}$ pint thick mayonnaise, juice of $\frac{1}{2}$ lemon, dash of Lea and Perrins sauce and 1 tablespoonful tomato ketchup.
Serves 4-6 persons.

Savoury Prawn Slices

8 oz. packet peeled prawns
8 oz. cheese crust pastry
1 chopped medium size onion
1 chopped green pepper
4 medium size tomatoes
4 oz. packet frozen peas
3 large eggs
$\frac{1}{4}$ pint milk
2 oz. grated cheese
Seasoning to taste

8 oz. plain flour
3 oz. mixed fat
2 oz. grated cheese
$\frac{1}{2}$ teaspoonful dry mustard
Water or egg to mix

Method

Thaw the prawns. Make pastry and roll out into an oblong. Line an oblong tin, crimp edges at the side (this prevents any mixture from overflowing). To the peas, chopped onion, green pepper and sliced tomatoes, add the prawns. Beat the 3 large eggs well. Add seasoning to taste, and milk. Pour the beaten egg and milk onto the prawns and vegetable mixture. Pour this over the pastry. Sprinkle cheese over the top and bake in a hot oven, 400°F. or Mark 6 for 25-30 minutes. Allow to cool, cut down the centre and cut into slices.

Prawn and Cheese Tortilla

Allow for each person:
2 oz. packet peeled prawns
2 eggs
1 oz. butter
1 oz. Parmesan cheese
A little chopped parsley

Method

Thaw and chop the prawns. Beat eggs, season well and add prawns and cheese. Melt butter in a small omelette pan, add the mixture. Allow to set and turn over, continuing to cook. When cooked divide into two portions and serve quickly, garnishing with parsley.

Spanish Sea Food Salad

4 oz. packet peeled prawns
6 oz. carton potted shrimps
4 oz. packet crabmeat
1 Cos lettuce
4 tomatoes
7 black olives
$\frac{1}{4}$ pint mayonnaise
4 oz. cooked white fish
   (Cod or Haddock)
4 tablespoonfuls lemon juice
2 tablespoonfuls chopped onion
1 teaspoonful prepared mustard
Seasoning (black pepper)
Pinch of saffron

Method

Thaw out the seafood. Prepare the Cos lettuce and arrange in a salad bowl. Mix the prawns, shrimps and crabmeat, together with the cooked white fish. Arrange the fish in the bowl on the bed of lettuce. Garnish with wedges of tomato and black olives. Make the dressing by mixing the mayonnaise with lemon juice and onion, mustard and seasoning to taste. Infuse the saffron in a teaspoonful of boiling water and add this to the dressing. Pour the dressing over the salad. Serve chilled.

Serves 4 persons.

Cottage Cheese and Prawn Open Sandwich

3 x 2 oz. packets peeled prawns
6 slices Danish Rye bread or
    Wholemeal bread
1 bunch watercress
Seasoning
6 oz. Cottage cheese
Chopped chives or spring onion tops

Method
Spread each slice of bread with 1 oz. Cottage cheese which has been well seasoned. Place a pile of thawed prawns down the centre of the bread. Garnish each side of the prawns with sprigs of watercress. Sprinkle the chives or spring onion tops over the prawns.

Serves 6 persons.

Prawn Curry

1 quart fresh prawns or
1 × 6 oz. packet frozen prawns
1 tablespoonful corn oil
1 large onion—chopped
2 level tablespoonfuls cornflour
1 chicken stock cube
2 level teaspoonfuls curry paste
½ level teaspoonful salt
1 level tablespoonful demerara
    sugar

1 × 7 oz. can tomatoes
1 bay leaf
¾ pint water
8 oz. plain boiled rice

Method
Peel the prawns and remove the veins. (If using frozen prawns, defrost). Heat the corn oil. Add the onion and fry until soft without browning. Add the cornflour, stock cube, curry paste, salt, sugar, tomatoes and bay leaf. Stir in the water and bring to the boil, stirring. Cover and simmer for 30 minutes. Add the prawns and simmer for a further 20 minutes. Serve with plain boiled rice.

Halibut Steaks in White Wine Sauce

4 halibut steaks (4 × 6 oz. each)
1 bay leaf
6 peppercorns
¼ pint white wine
White sauce
Milk
2 egg yolks
Lemon slices for garnish

Method
Trim the fish and place in a buttered baking dish, with bay leaf and peppercorns. Pour over the white wine. Cover and bake in a moderate oven, 350°F. or Gas Mark 4, for 20-30 minutes. Remove the fish and place on a serving dish. Keep warm. Strain the fish liquor and make up to ½ pint with milk.

Make up the white sauce as directed (see index), using the fish liquor. Allow to cool slightly and stir in the egg yolks. Reheat without boiling and pour into a sauceboat. Garnish the fish with lemon slices and serve the sauce separately.

Dishes illustrated are: Prawn Cocktail, Prawns in Aspic, Spanish Sea Food Salad, Savoury Prawn Slices, Prawn Puffs, Prawn and Cheese Tortilla

BUFFET PARTIES

Hans Andersen's Lattice Flan

Pastry
 4 oz. plain flour
 Pinch of salt
 2 oz. butter
 2 oz. lard
 Water
Filling
 4 oz. Samsoe cheese
 3 oz. white breadcrumbs
 1 (7 oz.) can chopped pork and ham
 1 (5 oz.) can garden peas
 ½ pint milk
 1 egg
 Salt and pepper

Method

Prepare a moderate oven 375°F.(Mark 5). Sift together flour and salt into a mixing bowl. Cut fats into small pieces and add to flour. Rub in with fingertips until mixture resembles fine breadcrumbs. Add about one tablespoonful water and mix together with fork. Press together lightly to form a firm dough. Roll out to a circle, about 9½″ in diameter. Line pie plate and turn under excess pastry at rim. Cut up and flute edge; prick base lightly with fork. Cut some strips from cheese, about ¼″ thick, ½″ wide, and as long as possible. Reserve to form a lattice. Grate remaining cheese and add to breadcrumbs. Mix well together. Use half breadcrumb mixture to form a layer on base of flan. Cut the meat into cubes; reserve 12 cubes for garnish. Place remaining meat cubes in a layer on breadcrumbs. Drain peas and spread over meat layer. Cover with most of remaining breadcrumb mixture. Whisk milk, egg and seasonings together with fork. Pour over ingredients in pie plate. Sprinkle remaining breadcrumb mixture over, place pie plate on baking sheet and cook for 1-1¼ hours until filling is set and golden brown. Arrange cheese strips in a lattice on top of flan and cook for a further 10 minutes, until cheese has slightly melted. Just before serving, place a cube of meat in each hole of the lattice. Serve hot or cold.
Serves 4-6 persons.

Savoury Snacks

Chickenburgers

Mix one jar of Chicken Spread with a beaten egg and some bread crumbs. Make into flat cakes and bake in a moderate oven (350°F., Mark 4) for 15 minutes. Serve in hot rolls.

Salmon Potato Cakes

Mix 1 teacupful of well-flavoured mashed potatoes with a jar of Salmon Spread. Add a squeeze of lemon juice and a little tomato ketchup, shape into 4 flat cakes and fry in a little hot fat. Garnish with lemon and parsley.

Crab and Cheese Snack

Spread slices of hot buttered toast with Crab Spread. Top with a slice of processed cheese and grill until just melting and golden.

Savoury Chicken Potatoes

Bake large potatoes in their jackets, cut open, spread with butter and Chicken Spread.

Top picture   Prawn Cocktail with soured cream sauce   Dressed crab

BUFFET PARTIES

Cottage Cheese Crusts

2 small round bread rolls
4 oz. cream cheese
1 teaspoonful chopped chives (or
green of spring onions)
Pepper

Method
Cut the rolls in two and carefully remove the crumb. They can be deep fried a golden brown or, if new, use them as they are. Mix the cheese, chives and sage together and season with pepper. Fill the crusts with the mixture.

Cheese Tartlets

Make up 4 oz. cheese pastry. Roll out very thinly. Stamp into 20 rounds with a 3″ cutter and line patty pans. Prick with a fork. Lightly beat a large egg, add, $\frac{1}{4}$ pint milk, 2 oz. grated cheese. Season with Worcester Sauce and pepper. Fill patty pans just short of pastry rims. Bake at 400°F. (mark 6) for about 20 minutes. Serve warm garnished with parsley sprigs. Makes 20.

Kedgeree

Serve kedgeree half-way through any kind of celebration party. Make it before the party starts, and keep it hot in a low oven until you need it. It's easy to make in quantity—the limit being the size of your largest saucepan.

3 hard-boiled eggs
Salt and pepper
$\frac{1}{2}$ lb. rice
1 lb. smoked haddock (cooked and
flaked)
2 oz. butter

Method
Put 4 pints of salted water in a large saucepan and bring to the boil. Sprinkle in the washed rice and boil quickly until cooked (about 12-18 minutes, according to type of grain). Strain, then put rice in colander under running cold water. Put butter in the hot pan, melt, then add the drained rice. Stir over very low flame until reheated. Add fish and chopped eggs. Season lightly with pepper. Mix well and turn into a warm serving dish, dot with butter and keep hot in a low oven.

Prawn and Orange Salad

Prawns
Lettuce leaves
Beetroot cubes
Orange segments
Radish slices
Hard-boiled egg slices

Iced Pear Salad

3 level tablespoonfuls mayonnaise
4 oz. crumbled Cheshire cheese
1 red pepper, tinned
$\frac{1}{8}$ pint double cream
2 large pears
4 lettuce leaves
Watercress

Method
Turn refrigerator up to maximum. Mix mayonnaise with Cheshire cheese, chopped red pepper and the cream, and spread in ice tray. Place in freezing compartment, and stir every half hour until mixture is frozen, about 1 - 1$\frac{1}{2}$ hours. Wipe pears (peel if skins are tough), cut in half and remove core. Place each half pear on a lettuce leaf, pile iced cheese mixture on pear and garnish with watercress sprigs. Serve immediately, or pear halves may discolour.

Top picture Kedgeree

Prawn and Orange Salad

BUFFET PARTIES

Scallop of Herring Roes and Mushrooms

1 lb. soft herring roes
½ lb. button mushrooms
4 oz. butter
1 oz. flour
½ pint milk
4 oz. grated cheddar cheese
Triangular croutes of fried bread
1 tablespoonful fine breadcrumbs
Parsley

Method
Dice the mushrooms and cook in hot butter for 4 minutes, seasoning well with salt and freshly ground black pepper. Divide between four scallop shells or individual dishes. Cook the roes in hot butter with seasoning and add these to the shells. Prepare a sauce with the remaining butter, the flour and milk. Add a little more than half of the cheese to the sauce and check the seasoning. Pour over the roes and mushrooms. Top with cheese and breadcrumbs and put into a hot oven, 450°F. or Mark 8 until golden. Place triangles of fried bread in the edges of the scallop, add a touch of parsley and serve at once.
Serves 4 persons.

Pate Whirls

From a small white loaf cut 4 slices. Remove crusts. Cut each slice into 4—giving 16 pieces. Melt 1½ oz. butter. Brush a baking tray lightly with a little butter. Arrange bread squares over the tray. Brush squares with the remaining butter and bake in the oven at 425°F. (mark 7) for 15 minutes. Cool. Beat 2 oz. butter until smooth, beat in the contents from any one of the varieties of Pâtés until the mixture is creamy. If too soft, chill. Pipe a whirl onto each bread square. Garnish. Makes 16.

Garlic Cheese Dip

Mix together 5 fl.oz. soured cream and 3 oz. cream cheese. Stir in a puff Lazy Garlic and a little snipped chive. Serve in a bowl with pretzels, cauliflower florets, carrot sticks and crisps for dunking.

Cumberland Boats

Make up 4 oz. cheese pastry (4 oz. flour etc.). Roll out and line 20 small boat tins. Prick well and bake at 400°F. (mark 6) for about 10 minutes. Cool. Beat 6 oz. cream cheese with 2 teaspoonfuls Cumberland Sauce. Pipe into the boats. Garnish with radish slices. Makes 20.

Pumpernickle Nibblets

Either cut small rounds from slices of pumpernickle or use the ready-cut circles of pumpernickle. For 16 circles, cream together 1 oz. butter with 1 teaspoonful Anchovy Essence. Spread over the bread. On each, place a slice of tomato and a twist of cucumber. Garnish with a slice of stuffed olive and a piece of pickled walnut tucked into the cucumber. Makes 16.

Walnuts on Horseback

Drain the walnuts from a 10 oz. jar Sweet Walnuts. Rind 10 rashers of streaky bacon, cut No. 4 or 5. Roll a rasher of bacon round each walnut, place on grill rack, join side down. Grill until bacon is crisp. Pierce each with a cocktail stick. Serve hot. Makes 10.

BUFFET PARTIES

Party Dips

Recipes to help you add glamour to your meals.

There's no mystery about making sauces. Not much bother, either, once you have mastered the basic recipe.

Making a Basic White Sauce

1 oz. butter
1 oz. flour
½ pint milk
Seasoning (omitted in sweet sauces)

To make a pouring sauce you'll need:
½ oz. butter
½ oz. flour
Seasoning (omitted in sweet sauces)

Method

Put the butter, flour and seasoning in a saucepan and cook for a few minutes. Don't let the mixture brown. Add the milk slowly, stirring well all the time. Bring to the boil slowly, still stirring. Cook for a few minutes.

9 Savoury Variations

using ½ pint basic sauce.

Anchovy Sauce

Add a few drops of anchovy essence to the sauce and use rather less salt.

Caper Sauce

After the sauce has boiled add 1 teaspoonful chopped capers and a squeeze of lemon juice to it.

Cheese Sauce

Add 1½ oz. grated cheese to the cooked sauce.

Mustard Sauce

Add 1 teaspoonful made mustard and 1 teaspoonful vinegar to cooked sauce.

Onion Sauce

Cook a small onion in half a pint of milk. Chop or sieve the onion and use the milk to make the sauce. Add the onion.

Parsley Sauce

Add 1 teaspoonful chopped parsley (dried in muslin) to the sauce.

Shrimp Sauce

Add a few picked shrimps to the plain sauce, or the anchovy recipe. Reheat and serve.

Mayonnaise

1 level teaspoonful sugar
1 level teaspoonful dry mustard
½ level teaspoonful salt
Pinch of cayenne pepper
1 egg
¾ pint corn oil
3 tablespoonfuls French vinegar

Method

Put the sugar, mustard, salt, pepper and egg into a mixing bowl. Mix well. Add the corn oil gradually beating all the time. Stir in the vinegar. This mayonnaise will keep in a screwtop jar in a refrigerator for several weeks.

Hot Sausage Dip

Make 1 lb. chipolata sausages into cocktail sausages by twisting each in half and cutting into two. Grill or oven-cook and keep hot in the oven at 300°F (mark 1). Pierce each with a cocktail stick. Offer a selection of well-labelled mustards (Dijon, German and French) as dips with the hot sausages.

Hot Sausage Dip

BUFFET PARTIES

Three "Pots"

Succulent devilled kidney, chicken with a hint of orange and spicy ham with sweet pepper garnish, all from one basic sauce.

Basic Sauce
6 oz. butter
6 oz. flour
3 pints stock made with beef stock cubes

Method

Melt butter in a saucepan, stir in flour and cook slowly over a low heat, stirring continually until well browned but not burnt. Gradually add the stock. Bring to the boil and simmer for 5 minutes. Cool and divide between three smaller pans or better still flameproof serving dishes.
FIRST PAN: Skin, halve and core 1½-2 lb. lamb's kidney, sauté in 1 oz. melted butter for 10-15 minutes. Add to the basic sauce 2 level teaspoonfuls German Mustard, 4 tablespoonfuls Sauce Diable, a few drops Worcester Sauce. Add sauté kidneys. Bring to the boil and simmer for 5 minutes. Check seasoning. Garnish with chopped parsley.
SECOND PAN: To the basic sauce add 2 level teaspoonfuls French Mustard, 4 tablespoonfuls Cumberland Sauce, 1 teaspoonful lemon juice and 1½ lb. cooked, diced chicken. Bring to the boil and simmer for 5 minutes. Check seasoning. Garnish with grated orange rind and orange slices.
THIRD PAN: Add to basic sauce 1 teaspoonful Hot Tomato Ketchup, 4 tablespoonfuls Derby Sauce, ¼ level teaspoonful Lazy Garlic, 1 canned red pimento (chopped) and 1½ lb. cooked

diced lean ham. Bring to the boil and simmer for 5 minutes. Garnish with strips of canned red pimento.
ACCOMPANIMENTS: serve the 'pots' with a green salad and French dressing, fluffy rice, bread sticks or long French bread.

Stuffed Mushrooms

Pâté with chopped gherkin, garnished with hard-boiled egg and raw carrot. On a bed of cress, filled with chopped hard-boiled egg and diced celery coated in mayonnaise. Prawns in cream cheese whipped with raw egg yolk and a little white wine vinegar.

Ham and Chicken Brochette

½" thick slice uncooked gammon (1 lb.)
2 tablespoonfuls cranberry sauce
6 oz. cooked chicken

Method

Remove rind from gammon and snip the fat at 1" intervals. Spread 1 tablespoonful cranberry sauce over one side and grill for about 10 minutes under a moderate heat. Turn the gammon, spread with remaining sauce and grill a further 10 minutes till tender. Cool. Cut into 24 cubes. Cut chicken into 18 pieces. Alternate ham and chicken on 6 skewers. Arrange round a pyramid of potato salad. Serve more cranberry sauce and herb-dressed lettuce separately.
N.B. For the potato salad boil 2 lb. potatoes in salted water. Drain. Cut in cubes. Gently turn in home-made mayonnaise. Garnish with snipped chives.

Stuffed Mushrooms

BUFFET PARTIES

Cheese and Celery Dip

1 oz. margarine
1 level tablespoonful flour
1 (10½ oz.) can condensed Cream
of Celery Soup
4 oz. grated cheese
Pinch of paprika

Method
Melt margarine in saucepan. Add the flour, mix together and cook one minute. Add the soup and grated cheese and stir well until boiling. Pour into a very hot decorative fire-proof dish, sprinkle with paprika and keep hot while serving.
Serve as a "dip" with potato crisps, fingers of dry toast, wholemeal bread, small plain biscuits, short sticks of washed celery, or cubes of ham and pineapple.
Serves 10 persons.

Dips

Mix together half a tablespoonful of any Spread or Minced Food with a little creamed cheese, mayonnaise or thin cream seasoned with Paprika. Spread on fresh potato crisps or let the guests dip their crisps into different bowls.

Spicey Tomato Dip

3 cloves of garlic
2 level dessertspoonfuls cornflour
15½ oz. can Tomato Soup
3 tablespoonfuls Olive Oil
5 tablespoonfuls White Vinegar
1 tablespoonful Malt Vinegar
Salt and pepper
1 teaspoonful dried horseradish
1 tablespoonful tomato ketchup

Method
Very finely chop or crush the cloves or garlic. Blend the cornflour with a little of the Tomato soup, and gradually stir in the rest of the soup. Turn into a saucepan with the rest of the ingredients. Bring to the boil, stirring all the time, and boil for 2 minutes. Turn into a Fondue dish. Heat up when required. Serve with fish or meat balls.

Tuna Fish Dip

1 tin (7 oz.) tuna fish
¼ pint double dairy cream
1 tablespoonful lemon juice
1 tablespoonful mayonnaise
2 tablespoonfuls green pepper or
parsley, finely chopped
Salt and pepper

Method
Drain and flake the tuna fish. Whip cream lightly, so it is thick, but not stiff. Stir in the lemon juice, mayonnaise and green pepper or parsley. Season to taste with salt and pepper. Serve dip in a half green pepper or small bowl with crisps.
Excellent for a party or T.V. snack. Delicious with ice-cold milk.

Bechamel Sauce

1½ oz. butter
1½ oz. flour
1 pint milk
Seasoning
Small pieces of carrot, turnips and
onion
1 stick of celery
1 small bunch of herbs
1 tablespoonful cream

Method
Make in the same way as the basic sauce. Add the herbs and vegetables after you have mixed in the milk.

92

Anchovy cream sauce dippers

BUFFET PARTIES

Simmer gently (a double boiler is best) for about threequarters of an hour. Strain and season to taste. Add the cream and reheat.

Bread Sauce

1 medium-sized onion
1 clove
½ pint milk
2 oz. fresh white breadcrumbs
Seasoning
1 tablespoonful cream and ½ oz. butter or
1 oz. butter

Method
Put the onion and clove in a saucepan with the milk and bring to the boil. Add the breadcrumbs and seasoning. Simmer for about 15 minutes, stirring occasionally. Remove the onion and clove and stir in the cream and butter.

Sweet Sauces

The basic sauce for these is usually made with cornflour or custard powder. Add about an ounce of sugar to half a pint.

Chocolate Sauce

Melt 2 oz. plain chocolate in the milk before making the sauce.

Fruit Sauce

Add a teaspoonful of lemon juice and ¼ pint of fruit puree to cooked sauce. Reheat and stir until smooth.

Dips

4 oz. tinned sweetcorn with chopped peppers
4 oz. chopped ham and 1 tablespoonful brown sugar
2 heaped tablespoonfuls fresh chopped chives or spring onion
3 tablespoonfuls chutney
4 oz. chopped tinned pineapple, well drained

Method
Very popular and easy to prepare. Make a basic dip of: 8 oz. Cottage Cheese and a carton of soured cream (or single cream with a little lemon juice), and add your favourite flavours. Serve dips in bowls and surround with biscuits, chopped raw carrot sticks and chicory leaves for dunking.

Smoked Salmon Fingers

4 large slices fresh toast
4 oz. smoked salmon
8 oz. button mushrooms
3 oz. butter
1 egg yolk
2 tablespoonfuls sherry
¼ pint cream
1 dessertspoonful flour
Freshly ground black pepper
Parsley

Method
Remove the crusts from the toast and butter lightly; cut each slice into 3 fingers and place on hot serving platter. Cut the mushrooms into good sized dice and toss in hot butter for 2 minutes. Prepare a sauce with the remaining butter, blending in the flour and cream. Add salt and freshly ground black pepper, together with the sherry and mushrooms. Allow to simmer for a few minutes, then stir in the egg yolk removing the pan from the heat. Check the seasoning, then spoon the creamed mushrooms onto the toast fingers. Top each finger with a roll of smoked salmon and parsley.

Little eats with cottage cheese

BUFFET PARTIES

Seafood Special

2 oz. Patna rice
1 oz. frozen peas
1 oz. red pepper, diced
3 tablespoonfuls Salad Cream
1½ tablespoonfuls Tomato Ketchup
4 oz. prawns, frozen
1 teaspoonful lemon juice
(4 small individual ring moulds to set the rice mixture)

Method
Cook the rice in boiling salted water for 12-15 minutes, drain, and cook the peas, as directed on the packet, blanch the pepper. While the rice, peas and pepper are still hot, mix them together, and press into the greased ring moulds, allow to cool, and place in the refrigerator until firm. Mix the salad cream and tomato ketchup together, and fold in the prawns and lemon juice. Remove the ring moulds from the refrigerator. Dip each mould into boiling water for a few seconds, and turn the rice borders out onto individual plates. Fill each one with the prawn mixture, and serve. Garnish with asparagus. *Serves 4 persons.*

Sweet Sour Scampi

1 lb. luxury scampi—defrosted
4 oz. flour
Pinch salt
1 tablespoonful Olive Oil
¼ pint water
1 egg white
2 level teaspoonfuls arrowroot
7 oz. bottle Tomato Ketchup
4 oz. Pineapple Juice
3 oz. Malt Vinegar

Method
Make a coating batter with the flour, salt, olive oil and water, beat until smooth. Fold whisked egg white into batter just before required. Heat fat until smoking. Toss scampi in seasoned flour (in a paper bag) dip in batter and drop into the hot fat. Cook until golden brown. Drain and keep hot. Blend the arrowroot with a little water and place in a saucepan with the ketchup, pineapple juice and vinegar, bring to the boil and boil until clear.
Pile the scampi in a suitable serving dish, pour some sauce over it. Serve the remaining sauce separately. Plain boiled rice may be served with this dish.

Salad Macedoine

12 oz. frozen mixed vegetables, or 1 can Macedoine of Vegetables
2 tablespoonfuls Olive Oil
¼ teaspoonful salt
2-3 dashes pepper
½ teaspoonful caster sugar
Pinch dry mustard
1 tablespoonful vinegar
Lettuce for garnish

Method
Cook the vegetables as directed, strain and cool. Put the olive oil, salt, pepper, caster sugar, and dry mustard in a small basin and whisk in the vinegar. Toss the vegetables through the dressing and serve in individual bowls garnished with lettuce leaves.

More little eats with Cottage Cheese

Chicory fingers filled with cottage cheese and sprinkled with garlic salt. Celery stalks filled with cottage cheese seasoned with onion salt and sprinkled with poppy seeds.

Top picture   *Sweet Sour Scampi*   *Seafood special*

BUFFET PARTIES

Butter Snaps

Cream 2 oz. butter and beat in 2 teaspoonfuls Sauce Robert. Pipe onto 10 Hotel biscuits, using a star pipe. Garnish with thin strips of green pepper and minute pieces of parsley. Makes 10.

Melon

A pair of medium-sized melons will be ample. Cut into wedges almost through to the base (remove the seeds or leave in position) and stand in small dishes for support. Serve with lemon to squeeze or sugar for dredging.

Coffee Special

Warm the glasses; pour 1-2 oz. Brandy and ½ oz. Tia Maria into each glass, fill the glasses with piping hot strong black coffee, add sugar if required, then stir it all together. Top with a spoonful of stiffly whipped cream.

Apple Soured Cream Bake

6 oz. flour
3 oz. caster sugar
2 teaspoonfuls baking powder
½ teaspoonful salt
½ teaspoonful cinnamon
¼ pint milk
4 oz. softened butter
1 egg
1 lb. apples
   peeled cored and diced
1 carton soured cream
1 egg, blended
1½ oz. soft brown sugar
1 oz. chopped walnuts

Method
Sift together dry ingredients. Add milk, butter and beaten egg. Beat until smooth. Stir in apples. Turn into greased ovenproof dish, about 6″ x 10″ x 2½″ deep.
For Topping: blend together soured cream and egg, and spread over mixture. Mix together sugar and walnuts and sprinkle over top. Bake in moderate oven, 350°F. or Gas Mark 4, about 1 hour. Serve hot.
Serves 6 persons.

Party Dessert

4 oz. fat (fork mix type)
4 oz. caster sugar
4 oz. self-raising flour
1 tablespoonful Cocoa
Pinch salt
2 eggs
1 tablespoonful milk
For decoration
   Fresh whipped cream
   Flaked almonds
   Tinned or fresh fruit
   Angelica

Method
Put all ingredients into a bowl. Beat together until a smooth mixture is formed. Turn into an oval 7″ x 5″ cake tin. Bake in oven 350°F. or Mark 4 for about 45 minutes. Cool on a wire tray. Spread cream around the edge and dip into flaked almonds. Decorate the top as illustrated with fresh cream and fruit.

How to make the party swing? Serve Peanut Butter Drumsticks. Made with cheese, chicken and energy giving Peanut Butter, young and old will be dancing the night away.

BUFFET PARTIES

Philly and Almond Roll

   2 x 3 oz. packets Kraft "Philly"
   1½ oz. Danish Blue Cheese
   2 oz. ham (chopped)
   8-10 stuffed olives (chopped)
   4 oz. chopped almonds

Method

Combine ingredients, mix thoroughly and beat until smooth. Place under grill or in hot oven until pale brown. Form "Philly" mixture into a roll and coat in toasted nuts. Roll up in kitchen foil or greaseproof paper. Chill thoroughly in refrigerator or leave overnight. Cut in slices ⅛" thick. Serve with salad or as an appetizer.

Pineapple Cheesecake

   2 x 8 oz. cartons of cottage cheese
   1 lemon
   8 oz. tin of pineapple rings
   ½ oz. powdered gelatine
   2 eggs, separated
   4 oz. castor sugar
   ¼ pint double cream, whipped

Crust

   6 digestive biscuits, crushed
   1 level tablespoonful castor sugar
   1½ oz. butter, melted

Method

Well oil a 7" cake tin. Sieve cottage cheese. Drain pineapple juice into a basin, sprinkle in gelatine. Keep one pineapple slice for decoration. Chop the remainder finely and add the cottage cheese with juice and grated lemon rind. Place basin with juice and gelatine over pan of hot water and allow gelatine to dissolve. Add sugar and blended egg yolks. Stir over heat until the consistency of pouring cream. Cool. When thick but not set blend into cheese mixture, lastly fold in stiffly beaten egg whites and whipped cream. Turn into prepared tin, and chill until set. Combine the crust ingredients together and sprinkle and press down lightly on top of cheesecake in tin, leave to become firm. Turn out on to a 10" flat plate. Decorated with wedges of pineapple and sprigs of mint.
Serves 8 persons.

Lime and Lemon Creams

   6 egg yolks
   8 oz. caster sugar
   1 lime
   ½ pint double cream
   Kirsch
   Nut (Almonds or pistachio)
   2 egg whites
   3 lemons
   1 slightly rounded dessertspoonful
     gelatine
   3 oz. ratafias
   Wafers

Method

Work the sugar and egg yolks together, gradually adding the juice from the lemons and lime. Whisk over a pan of hot water until the mixture is thick and creamy. Mix the gelatine with a little water, dissolve over a moderate heat. Add to the egg mixture whilst gelatine is still steaming. Stir vigorously. Whisk the cream to a thick pouring consistency, stir into the mixture. Put a few ratafias into the bottom of eight individual glass dishes, pour over a little kirsch, then fill the dishes with the lime and lemon cream. Chill in a refrigerator for at least 1 hour. Serve with wafers and decorate with chopped nuts.
Serves 8 persons.

Party dessert

Top picture   Pineapple cheesecake

Philly and Almond Roll

BUFFET PARTIES

Avocado Pear with Mushroom Cocktail

2 avocado pears
3 dessertspoonfuls tomato ketchup
3 dessertspoonfuls double cream
Dash Worcester sauce
¼ lb. button mushrooms
1 dessertspoonful mayonnaise
½ clove garlic

Method
Finely slice the mushrooms. Mix the ketchup and mayonnaise and add the finely crushed garlic and whipped cream. Season with salt, pepper and Worcester sauce. Half an hour before serving time, add the mushrooms to the sauce. Leave to stand in a cool place. Scoop out the centre of the halved pears, then fill with the mushroom cocktail.

Glazed Pear Shorties

Make a shortbread dough with 10 oz. plain flour 2 oz. cornflour, 8 oz. butter or margarine and 2 oz. caster sugar. This softer dough needs more careful handling than short pastry. Roll out and line ten 4¼″ shallow patty pans. Prick the bases and bake blind at 375°F. (mark 5) for 15-20 minutes. Remove from pans and cool. (These shells can be stored for a day or two in an airtight tin.) Whisk ½ pint double cream with 2 tablespoonfuls sherry and 2 tablespoonfuls thinned Apricot Syrup. Divide between shortbread cases. Place a drained, canned pear half in each. Glaze with more Apricot Syrup.
Decorate with angelica leaves, toasted, flaked or nibbled almonds, chocolate vermicelli or whirls of whipped double cream.

Raisin Avocado Pears

3 Avocado pears
2 oz. Seedless Raisins
Juice 1 small lemon
1 level tablespoonful grated onion
2 level tablespoonfuls mayonnaise
*   or salad cream*
Salt and pepper
Pinch cayenne pepper
Prawns

Method
Cut Avocado pears in half, and remove stone. Scoop out the flesh. To make filling, cover raisins with cold water, bring to boil, and leave to stand for five minutes, drain and dry. Mash Avocado flesh with a fork, add lemon juice, onion, mayonnaise, raisins, and season with salt, pepper and cayenne pepper. Mix thoroughly, place on serving dish and decorate with prawns.

Coeur a la Creme

2×8-oz. cartons cottage cheese
5 oz. carton soured cream (or
*   ¼ pint double cream soured with*
*   a little lemon juice)*
1 tablespoonful icing sugar
¼ teaspoonful salt
1 lb. strawberries
Sugar to taste
¼ pint cream

Method
Rub cottage cheese through a sieve. Beat with the cream, icing sugar and salt until smooth. Turn into the mould, lined with double-thick muslin. Pack tightly and chill for at least an hour or leave overnight in a cool place. Unmould and serve with strawberries, whole or sliced, sugar to taste and cream.

LUNCHEON PARTIES

A salad lunch for 4

Tomato Juice Cocktail

To a 1 lb. 3 oz. can of tomato juice add 2 teaspoonfuls Worcester Sauce. Chill thoroughly. Pour into 4 tall glasses and garnish with mint sprigs. For garlic lovers add a puff of Lazy Garlic before chilling.

Luncheon Platter

> 2 hard-boiled eggs
> 2 rounded teaspoonfuls Tartare
>   Sauce
> Cos lettuce, washed and drained
> Small bunch spring onions,
>   trimmed
> 4 firm tomatoes
> $\frac{1}{2}$ small cucumber
> 1 small red pepper
> 1 grapefruit
> 12 slices garlic sausage
> 4 slices cooked ham
> 4 tablespoonfuls Piccalilli
> 4 slices tongue
> 4 square slices Emmenthal cheese

Method

Halve eggs, remove yolks and mash thoroughly with tartare sauce. Pipe or spoon back into egg whites. Arrange lettuce on a large plate. Place stuffed eggs in the centre. Lay onions round the edge. Slice tomatoes and cucumber thinly, slice the de-seeded pepper in julienne strips. Cut grapefruit into segments removing membrane. Tuck three slices garlic sausage behind each egg. Roll ham into cornets and place between eggs, fill in situ with piccalilli. Roll tongue into cigar shapes with a grapefruit segment protruding from each end. Put in a wheel round the edge.

Arrange groups of tomato slices and alternate triangles of Emmenthal cheese with cucumber.

ACCOMPANIMENTS: garlic bread— blend 2 oz. butter with a few puffs Lazy Garlic. Make slashes through a long French loaf almost through to the base. Open up and spread with garlic butter. Form together and wrap in foil. Pop in a hot oven for about 10 minutes. Home-made mayonnaise and made-at-the-table oil and vinegar dressing.

Monday Bolognaise

> 2 onions
> 1 carrot
> 1 stick of celery
> 1 clove garlic (optional)
> 2 tablespoonfuls olive oil
> $\frac{1}{2}$ oz. dripping
> 4-8 oz. minced or finely cut up
>   cooked beef (or fresh minced
>   beef)
> 1 10$\frac{1}{2}$ oz. can condensed
>   Cream of Tomato or Tomato
>   Soup
> 1 bay leaf
> Seasoning
> 8 oz. spaghetti, boiled
> Grated cheese, preferably Parmesan

Method

Chop the onion, carrot, celery and garlic very finely. Fry in the oil and dripping in a saucepan until the onion softens (about 5 minutes). Add the meat and mix well with a fork to break it up. Add the other ingredients and taste for seasoning. Cover and cook 15 minutes. (30 minutes if using raw meat.) Drain the spaghetti, put onto hot plates and pour the meat mixture over. Sprinkle each plateful with grated cheese and serve.

103

LUNCHEON PARTIES

Neptune Soup

1 cod or hake's head
2 oz. butter
1 large onion
3 sticks celery
2 pints fish stock
1 pinch or small packet saffron
Salt and pepper
$\frac{1}{4}$ pint milk
1 heaped tablespoonful chopped
   parsley
$\frac{3}{4}$ lb. cod

Method
Cover the fish head with water and simmer for 25 minutes. Reserve stock, add butter and fry with finely chopped onion and celery quickly until transparent but not brown. Add 2 pints of the fish stock, saffron and salt and pepper. Simmer for 10 minutes. Stir in the milk and parsley. Skin the cod and cut into small pieces. Add to the soup and simmer for 5 minutes. Adjust seasoning and serve.
Serves 5-6 persons.

Danish Bacon Risotto

1 (8 oz.) middle cut bacon
   small green pepper
1 chicken stock cube
8 oz. long-grain rice
1 medium onion
1 oz. lard
1 small (7$\frac{1}{2}$ oz.) can button
   mushrooms
1 level dessertspoonful chopped
   parsley
3 oz. Samsoe cheese

Method
Remove rind from bacon and cut streaky end into $\frac{1}{2}$ in. pieces. Remove seeds and pith and cut green pepper into strips. Place in a saucepan, cover with water and bring to boil. Simmer for 5 minutes, then drain. Fill a large saucepan with water and add chicken stock cube. Bring to boil and add rice. Cook for 12 to 15 minutes and drain. Peel and roughly chop onion. Melt lard in a large frying pan and fry onion until soft. Add streaky bacon; continue to cook. Drain liquid from can and rinse mushrooms in cold water. Add to pan. Stir rice, parsley and green pepper into frying pan. Mix well, then pile into a heated serving dish. Grill back rashers of bacon and arrange on rice mixture. Serve with grated Samsoe cheese.
Serves 4 persons.

Sugar-baked Danish Ham Louisiane

1 medium-sized ham
Bay leaf
Cloves
Onion
Brown sugar
Ginger and nutmeg
1-2 pints flat cider

Method
Prepare and boil ham, using bay leaf, cloves and onion. When cooked, drain, trim and place in a high-sided baking tray. Dredge ham with brown sugar and sprinkle with ginger and nutmeg. Pour cider into tray and bake until brown and done. Slice as required for service. For service, place slices on platter and pour over sparingly Sauce Louisiane. Garnish with watercress.

Neptune Soup

LUNCHEON PARTIES

Holiday Surprise Pie

6 oz. hot cooked rice
   (2 oz. rice and $\frac{1}{4}$ pint liquid)
3 tablespoonfuls maraschino
   cherry juice
$\frac{1}{2}$ oz. gelatine
Coconut Crust
Scant $\frac{1}{2}$ pint hot water
8 oz. cream cheese
3 oz. sugar
$\frac{1}{4}$ pint double cream, whipped
Fruit topping

Method
Combine hot cooked rice and cherry juice. Cool. Dissolve gelatine in hot water and chill until a thick syrup consistency. Combine cheese and sugar until a smooth paste is formed and beat in the gelatine. Stir in the rice and fold in the whipped cream. Turn into Coconut crust. Chill. When pie has set for about one hour, spread with Fruit Topping.

Baked Gammon Platter

$2\frac{1}{2}$-3 lb. corner gammon
1 onion
1 bay leaf
2 peppercorns
1 level teaspoonful dry mustard
1 level tablespoonful demerara
   sugar
1 tablespoonful water
4 oz. mushrooms
6 tomatoes
Salt and pepper
1 oz. butter
Watercress

Method
Soak gammon for 2 to 3 hours or overnight in cold water. Drain well. Place in large saucepan and cover with cold water. Peel and slice onion and add to saucepan. Add bay leaf and peppercorns and bring to boil. Cover and simmer for 45 minutes. Prepare a moderate oven 350°F. (Mark 4). Remove gammon from saucepan, drain well and place in a roasting tin. Carefully peel off rind and score fat in strips with a sharp knife. Mix together mustard, sugar and water. Spoon over gammon. Roast for 30 minutes, basting occasionally with juices in pan. Wash mushrooms and dry with kitchen paper. Cut tomatoes in halves, sprinkle with salt and pepper and dot with butter. Place at one end of tin with gammon, place mushrooms at other end, and add remaining butter to them in small pieces. Return to oven and cook for a further 30 minutes. Serve on a large flat dish. Place gammon joint in centre and arrange tomato halves and mushrooms around. Garnish with watercress.

Tuna Fish Pie

1 ($10\frac{1}{2}$ oz.) can condensed
   Cream of Mushroom, Celery or
   Chicken Soup
3-6 tablespoonfuls water
1 (7 oz.) can tuna fish
3 packets potato crisps
1 small (4 oz.) can peas
2 teaspoonfuls lemon juice
Pinch pepper

Method
Heat soup with water. Add flaked tuna fish. Crush 2 packets of potato crisps and add to soup with drained peas, lemon juice and pepper. Pour into a casserole. Edge with remaining crisps and bake in a moderate oven 350°F., Mark 4, for 25 minutes.

Prawn Cocktail

1 packet of frozen prawns
Lettuce leaves
Dressing
2 tablespoonfuls double cream
2 tablespoonfuls salad cream
1 tablespoonful tomato ketchup
Few drops Tabasco

Method
Thaw prawns and pile into glasses on bed of chopped lettuce. Prepare dressing by mixing all ingredients together. Pour over prawns. Sprinkle with red pepper, and serve with lemon wedges and thinly sliced buttered brown bread.

Chicken Casserole

2 chicken joints
1 level tablespoonful flour
Pinch of salt and pepper
1 oz. butter
1 tablespoonful oil
3 oz. streaky bacon
2 medium onions
4 oz. mushrooms
1 teaspoonful mixed dried herbs
1 Golden Oxo cube
½ pint hot water
½ pint white wine
Parsley

Method
Mix flour with seasoning. Dip the chicken joints in it and coat well. Remove the rind and dice the bacon. Peel and slice the onions. Wash and slice the mushrooms. Heat the butter and oil in a frying pan and fry the chicken until golden brown. Put it in a casserole. Lightly fry the bacon and onions and add to the chicken. Add mushrooms and herbs. Sprinkle in the rest of the flour. Pour off any fat left in the frying pan. Add the hot water, stir to dissolve sediment. Add the Golden Oxo cube and stir until dissolved. Pour into the casserole. Cover and cook $1\frac{1}{4}$-$1\frac{1}{2}$ hours. 350°F (Mark 4) until the chicken is tender. Sprinkle with chopped parsley and serve.

Cottage Cheese and Ham Casserole

2 oz. button mushrooms
1 oz. butter
1 small green pepper
3 standard eggs
¼ pint milk
1½ oz. soft white breadcrumbs
½ lb. chopped ham
12 oz. cottage cheese
1 level teaspoonful made mustard
Seasoning to taste

Method
Slice and lightly fry mushrooms in the butter, put a few slices to one side for garnish. Remove stalk and pips from green pepper. Cut into slices and simmer in salted water for 5 minutes. Save 3 slices for decorating and dice the remainder. Beat the eggs with the milk and pour on to the breadcrumbs. Leave for 10 minutes and then add all other ingredients. Mix well, season to taste and put in a buttered casserole dish. Top with green pepper and mushrooms. Bake in a moderate oven, 350°F (Mark 4) for 30 minutes, until golden brown and set.
Serves 4 persons.

Holiday Surprise Pie

Top picture Prawn Cocktail, Chicken Casserole   Cottage Cheese & Ham Casserole

LUNCHEON PARTIES

Pork Paprika

1½ lb. boned shoulder pork
1 oz. lard
1 onion, peeled and chopped
1 tablespoonful paprika pepper
1 oz. flour
½ pint stock
1 can tomato purée (2½ oz. size)
Salt and pepper
6 oz. small button mushrooms
1 x 5 oz. carton Soured Cream

Method

Cut pork into 1½" pieces. Melt ½ oz. lard in a pan. Fry pork quickly on both sides until just beginning to turn brown. Remove from pan and drain on absorbent kitchen paper. Fry onion in pan for 2 minutes. Blend flour in remaining ½ oz. lard, add paprika and cook a further minute. Remove from heat and blend in stock. Add tomato purée. Return to heat and bring to boil stirring until thickened. Add pork. Season with salt and pepper. Cover pan and let goulash simmer for 1½ hours or until meat is tender. Two minutes before end of cooking time, add mushrooms. Just before serving, adjust seasoning if necessary. Pour over soured cream.
Serves 4 persons.

Herring Pizza

For a delicious and sustaining brunch, lunch or for an evening pizza party, here is a pizza with a difference. Herrings fresh from the sea with black olives, tomatoes and cheese make a mouth-watering topping. Herbs enhance the Mediterranean touch. And its unbelievably easy to make too.

Scone Dough

8 oz. self-raising flour
½ teaspoonful salt
1½ oz. butter
About ¼ pint milk

Topping

4 oz. grated Cheddar cheese
1 teaspoonful dry mustard
½ teaspoonful dried mixed herbs
½ lb. tomatoes thinly sliced
7 black olives
3 filleted herrings
Salt and pepper

For Scone Dough Sift together flour and salt and rub in butter until mixture resembles fine breadcrumbs. Bind together with milk to form a soft dough. Roll out lightly to a 12 in. circle on a greased baking sheet.

For Topping Mix grated cheese, mustard and herbs in a basin. Sprinkle over the dough. Arrange thinly sliced tomatoes on top and then the herring fillets in a radial pattern. Place the olives between the fillets. Sprinkle with salt and pepper. Bake in a moderately hot oven, 400°F. (mark 6) for about 30 minutes. Serve with a green and pepper salad.
Serves 3-6 persons.

Top picture Herring Pizza

Pork Paprika

LUNCHEON PARTIES

Rice Medley

2 dessertspoonfuls butter or
  margarine
4 oz. diced celery
12 oz. cooked rice
4 oz. prawns
2 oz. chopped cooked bacon
1 beaten egg
Pinch salt
2 oz. grated cheddar cheese
Dash pepper

Method
Melt butter in fry pan. Sauté celery until tender but not brown. Add rice, prawns, egg, salt and pepper. Heat thoroughly stirring constantly. Pour into a buttered casserole. Top with cheese and bacon. Place under grill until cheese is melted.
Serves 4 persons.

Bacon and Pineapple Grill

1 (8½ oz.) can pineapple slices
2 level tablespoonfuls demerara
  sugar
2 level teaspoonfuls dry mustard
½ teaspoonful Worcester sauce
4 pork chops, ¾ in. thick
Parsley or watercress to garnish

Method
Prepare a moderate grill. Drain pineapple. Place demerara sugar, mustard and Worcester sauce in a small basin and add 2 tablespoonfuls pineapple syrup ; stir thoroughly to blend. Remove rack from grill pan. Trim rind and dark skin from pork chops, snip fat around edge and place in grill pan. Spoon the sugar mixture over, and grill in a low position for 9 to 12 minutes, turning once. Add pineapple rings to grill pan for last 2 minutes'

cooking time. Arrange pork chops on a warm dish with a pineapple ring on each, and garnish with parsley or watercress.
Serves 4 persons.
Note: Gammon steaks are tasty served in this way. Grill for 15 to 20 minutes.

Scotch Orange

13 oranges, halved
2 tins Fruit Cocktail, drained
½ lb. smoked salmon, finely
  chopped
2 gills or ½ pint Cinzano Bianco

Method
Scoop out orange flesh, chop coarsely, and add to fruit cocktail. Mix in smoked salmon. Fill orange shells. Sprinkle with Cinzano Bianco. Garnish with curled slice of cucumber.
26 portions

Sole California

25 × 4 oz. fillets of sole, skinned

Method
Fold fillets in half and place in liquid to poach. When cooked, arrange on serving platter and garnish with California Sauce.
25 portions.

Catalina Shrimp and Rice

8 oz. rice, uncooked
1 pint pulped, tinned tomatoes
1 tablespoonful salt

Method
Put rice, tinned tomatoes and salt into a saucepan. Bring to the boil and stir once, cover the saucepan, lower the heat and allow to simmer for 15 minutes if using ordinary rice, and 25 minutes if using par-boiled. Fluff with a fork. Serve with shrimps, prawns or fish.

LUNCHEON PARTIES

Cod Creme Gratin

1 lb. peeled potatoes
1 oz. butter
1 tablespoonful cream
1 egg
1¼ lb. fresh cod
water
Glass white wine
1 oz. flour
1 oz. butter
1½ oz. Gruyere cheese, grated
1 tablespoonful cream
2 oz. peeled shrimps
2 teaspoonfuls Tabasco

Method

Make up duchesse potato. Poach fish for 10-12 minutes in water and wine. Melt butter, add flour and cook roux. Gradually add ½ pint cooking liquor, simmer to thicken sauce. Add cheese and melt in sauce. Add cream and the shrimps and Tabasco sauce. Divide fish into pieces, place in an ovenproof dish. Mask over with the sauce. Pipe with duchesse potato. Bake in hot oven, 425°F. (mark 7), to colour surface. Thin remaining sauce and serve separately.
Serves 4-5 persons.
A dash of Tabasco can also be used with any kind of fish used for frying. Fish fried in batter has a crisp golden coating. If you are just frying fish by coating it in bread crumbs, use the trick of rubbing a little Tabasco on both sides of the fish before dipping it in bread crumbs.

St. Valentine's Day Salad

The 14th February is famous in British folk-lore as the day on which young men were popularly supposed to choose their sweethearts, sending them posies or love tokens accompanied by verses.

Here is a delicious and pretty St. Valentine's Salad for you to prepare for your favourite man, husband now or husband to be. Serve it as a first course for a dinner for two or as part of a light lunch

Mould 8 oz. Cottage Cheese into a heart shape on a flat dish. Outline with cooked peas, then working outwards surround heart with a layer of finely grated carrot, mustard and cress, seeded black and white grapes and a circle of tomato slices, topped if liked with onion rings blanched for a minute in boiling salted water.

Creamed Casserole of Veal

1 lb. stewing veal
1 medium sized onion
4 oz. mushrooms
2 oz. butter
4 tablespoonfuls stock or water
1 level teaspoonful paprika pepper
1 tablespoonful lemon juice
1 level teaspoonful dried sage
Salt and pepper
¼ pint double dairy cream

Method

Cut veal into small cubes. Finely chop onion. Slice mushrooms. Melt butter. Gently fry veal, onion and mushrooms until lightly brown. Place in a casserole and add stock or water, paprika, lemon juice and sage. Season with salt and pepper. Cook in a warm oven 300°F. (Mark 3) until veal is tender—45-50 minutes. Just before serving stir in cream and adjust seasoning to taste. Reheat without boiling.
Serves 4 persons.

Top picture Cod Creme Gratin

St. Valentine's Day Salad

LUNCHEON PARTIES

Shashlik Kebabs

1 large onion, very finely chopped
1 clove garlic, crushed
1 level teaspoonful curry powder
$\frac{1}{8}$ teaspoonful ground ginger
1 oz. butter or margarine
1 (10$\frac{1}{2}$ oz.) can condensed
   Cream of Tomato, Mushroom or
   Chicken Soup
3-6 tablespoonfuls water
12 small white onions or shallots
2 medium green peppers, cut into
   1$\frac{1}{2}$" pieces
1$\frac{1}{2}$ lb. lean lamb or pork, cut into
   1$\frac{1}{2}$" cubes
2 tomatoes, cut in pieces
2 apples, each cut into 6 or 8
   pieces
12 oz. rice, freshly boiled

Method
For sauce, fry chopped onion, garlic, curry powder and ginger in butter until onion is tender. Add soup and water. Cook 5 minutes. Stir often. Simmer the onions and green peppers for 5 minutes in very little water. Drain. Thread the lamb or pork, pieces of pepper, onions, tomato and apple alternately onto skewers. Brush with the sauce. Grill gently, turning and brushing with sauce, approximately 30 minutes. Serve on rice with remaining sauce.
Serves 6 persons.

Porcupine Meat Balls

1 lb. minced beef
2 oz. uncooked long grain rice
1 medium onion, finely chopped
2 level tablespoonfuls finely
   chopped parsley
1 level teaspoonful salt
1 small egg, slightly beaten
1 (10$\frac{1}{2}$ oz.) can condensed

Cream of Tomato or Tomato
   Soup
1$\frac{1}{2}$ oz. dripping or cooking fat
1 clove garlic (optional)
1 soup canful water
4 oz. rice, boiled

Method
Mix together the beef with the rice, onion, parsley, salt, egg and 4 tablespoonfuls of soup. Shape into 16 1$\frac{1}{2}$" balls, using wet hands to avoid sticking. Heat the dripping in a large frying pan and add the chopped garlic. Brown the meat balls on all sides. Add the remaining soup and the water to the pan and stir well while bringing to the boil. Cover with a lid or upturned plate and simmer 40 minutes, stirring and turning occasionally. Serve on a bed of boiled rice.
Serves 4 persons.

Poultry Giblets and Rice

2 lb. giblets
2$\frac{3}{4}$ pints of water
2 lb. onions
1 teaspoonful pepper
1 teaspoonful salt
12 oz. butter
1-2 cloves of garlic
1 bouquet garni (herbs)
3$\frac{1}{2}$ lb. rice

Method
Cut giblets into small pieces and fry them slightly adding slices of onion and garlic, fry for 5 minutes and then add water, salt, pepper, herbs and leave to simmer for an hour. Before the giblets are tender add the rice which has been fried in butter previously, and leave it for another 15 minutes. The rice will absorb the gravy, and the dish will be served dry.

Top picture   Shaslik Kebabs   *Porcupine Meat Balls*

LUNCHEON PARTIES

Peppery Chicken

3 tablespoonfuls cooking oil
4 chicken joints
8 very small onions (peeled)
1 small green pepper (seeded and
    sliced)
4 rashers streaky bacon (chopped)
1½ oz. flour
¾ pint stock or water
1 teaspoonful Tabasco sauce
Salt
4 oz. small mushrooms (wiped)
4-6 oz. long grained rice

Method
Heat the oil in a frying pan, and fry
chicken joints quickly to brown, add
the onions. Remove chicken to casserole dish. Add green pepper and
bacon to frying pan, and fry for a few
minutes. Transfer to casserole. Stir the
flour into remaining oil in pan, cook for
a few minutes, stirring constantly.
Gradually stir in the stock or water,
bring to the boil, stirring. Add Tabasco
Sauce and salt. Pour into the casserole,
stir in mushrooms. Cover and cook in
a moderate oven 350°F. (mark 4) for
about 1 hour until the chicken is
tender. Serve with boiled rice, adding
some to the dish just before serving.
Serves 4 persons.

California Sauce

5 oz. dry white wine
3 pints bechamel sauce, thick
2 tins Fruit Cocktail, drained
Salt and pepper

Method
Add the wine to the bechamel sauce.
Stir in the drained fruit cocktail and
season to taste. On service, garnish
with heads of mustard and cress (not

stalks.)
Note: For main course service, it is
considered advisable to increase the
sauce, etc., by half again and double
the fish allowance.

Tivoli Bacon Roast

2½-3 lb. forehock ham
1 bay leaf
1 carrot
1 small onion
Stuffing
1 small (8 oz.) can prunes
2 oz. fresh white breadcrumbs
1 cooking apple
1 egg
Salt and pepper
2 tablespoonfuls milk

Method
Soak ham joint overnight in cold
water. Discard water and place joint
in a large saucepan. Cover with cold
water and add bay leaf, peeled carrot
and onion. Bring to boil and simmer
for 1 hour. Remove from water and
take off rind. Mark fat in a diamond
pattern, and place joint in a roasting
tin. Prepare a moderately hot oven
400°F. (Mark 6). Drain syrup from
can of prunes and reserve; stone
prunes and chop roughly. Place in a
bowl with breadcrumbs. Peel, core
and chop apple and add to bowl.
Chop onion, used in boiling of joint,
and add to mixture. Add remainder of
stuffing ingredients and mix well.
Form into 8 balls and place in roasting
tin with joint. Pour prune syrup over
joint and bake for 30 minutes, basting
occasionally with syrup. Serve hot or
cold.
Serves 6 to 8 persons.

118

Peppery Chicken

LUNCHEON PARTIES

Mediterranean Pilaff

2 oz. butter or margarine
1 small onion, chopped or 1 level
    tablespoonful dried onion
    soaked 30 minutes
1 small can chopped green and red
    peppers
6 oz. long-grain rice
1 (10½ oz.) can condensed
    Consommé
½ soup canful water
¼ teaspoonful vegetable extract,
    optional
Dash pepper
4 oz. grated cheese

Method
Melt the butter. Add onion, peppers and rice. Cook until lightly browned 6-8 (minutes). Add rest of ingredients except grated cheese. Cover. Simmer until tender (approximately 30 minutes).
Serve hot with grated cheese.
Serves 4 persons.

Creole Casserole

2 tablespoonfuls cooking oil
1½ lb. stewing steak
2 onions (sliced)
3 sticks celery (cut into 1" pieces)
8 oz. can tomatoes
2 medium-sized potatoes
    (peeled and diced)
¾ pint stock or water
1 teaspoonful Tabasco Sauce
Salt

Method
Heat the oil in a large saucepan. Cut the meat into cubes removing any excess fat. Brown the meat in the pan. Add the onions and celery and fry for a few minutes. Add the tomatoes, potatoes, stock or water, Tabasco sauce and salt. Bring to the boil, reduce heat and cover. Simmer for about two hours until the meat is tender. Alternatively, the stew may be cooked in a casserole in a warm oven 325°F. (mark 3) for about two hours.
Serves 4 persons.

Kebabs with Piquant Rice

1 oz. butter
6 oz. Patna rice
¾ pint water
1 stock cube
1 level teaspoonful salt
Pepper
1 oz. dry mustard
1 tablespoonful vinegar
1 level teaspoonful sugar
8 tomatoes
1 pepper
4 lambs kidneys
4 oz. button mushrooms
10 oz. cubed rump steak

Method
Melt butter and gently fry rice for 5 minutes without colouring. Crush stock cube in a small bowl with salt, pepper, mustard, vinegar and sugar. Blend with a little of the water and add this with the rest of the water to the rice. Boil quickly with the lid off until all the water has been absorbed (approximately 15 minutes). Stir frequently. Spread in a buttered dish and keep hot.
Halve tomatoes. Remove stalk and seeds from pepper and cut into 1" pieces. Plunge in boiling salted water for 1 minute, drain. Skin, core and halve the kidneys. Thread all the ingredients on skewers, 2 per person, brush with melted butter, season well and grill slowly turning once.

Kebabs with Piquant Rice

LUNCHEON PARTIES

Rice Chicken with vegetables

1 chicken (2½-3 lb.)
1 medium green pepper, cut in thin strips
8 oz. uncooked rice
1 teaspoonful salt
2 oz. sliced pimento
6 oz. chopped onion
2 oz. butted or margarine
1 pt chicken stock
½ teaspoonful pepper
6 oz. cooked peas.

Method
Simmer chicken in ½ pint of seasoned water for 30-45 minutes, or until tender, cool, remove meat from bones, set aside. Cook onion and green pepper in butter until tender. Add rice and brown slightly. Stir in stock, salt and pepper. Bring to boil, stir once, cover and simmer 15 minutes or until tender. Add chicken, pimento and peas. Mix lightly, cook covered 10 minutes longer.
Serves 6 persons.

Chef's Special Herbed Rice

8 oz. rice, uncooked
1 teaspoonful salt
½ teaspoonful Marjoram
1 oz. butter
1 pint chicken stock
½ teaspoonful Rosemary
½ teaspoonful Thyme
1 teaspoonful chopped parsley for garnish

Method
Bring to boil and add rice, seasoning and butter. Return to the boil, stir, cover saucepan with tight fitting lid, lower the heat and allow to simmer for 15 minutes if using ordinary rice, 25 minutes if using par-boiled, sprinkle with chopped parsley before serving. Serve with steak, roast beef, ham steaks or roast lamb.
Serves 4 persons.

Mayonnaise

2 egg yolks
1 level teaspoonful Dijon Mustard
½ level teaspoonful salt
½ level teaspoonful sugar
Shake white pepper
½ pint olive oil
1 tablespoonful white wine vinegar or 2 tablespoonfuls tarragon vinegar
2 teaspoonfuls lemon juice

Method
Put egg yolks in a basin with the mustard, salt, sugar and pepper. (If using an electric blender place ingredients in the goblet.) Add oil drop by drop, beating hard all the time until the sauce is thick and creamy. Add the vinegar and lemon juice to taste. Stir. N.B. This sauce will keep covered for one to two weeks in a cool place.
Variations:
Remoulade Sauce: for baked or grilled fish. Basic recipe plus 1 level tablespoonful German Mustard, few drops of Anchovy Essence and 3 chopped gherkins, 1 tablespoonful capers; 2 tablespoonfuls each of parsley, chives, fennel.
For other variations use the basic recipe and add 6 teaspoonfuls Sauce Robert *or* 6 teaspoonfuls lemon juice and 2 teaspoonfuls sugar *or* 3 tablespoonfuls finely chopped parsley *or* 3 tablespoonfuls soured cream *or* 2 level teaspoonfuls Dijon Mustard *or* 2 tablespoonfuls double or single cream.

LUNCHEON PARTIES

Spaghetti Francesca

1 packet of long spaghetti
½ lb. of cooked ham
1 large onion
1 medium sized tin of tomatoes
3 oz. grated Parmesan cheese
White breadcrumbs
Salt and pepper

Method
Fry the onion and tomatoes in olive oil. Season well. Add the chopped ham. Cook the spaghetti for twenty minutes in boiling salted water, and when tender, drain well and add the mixture to it. Put in an ovenproof dish, sprinkle the cheese and breadcrumbs on top, add a knob of butter and grill until brown.
Serves 8 persons.

Cold Ham with Chutney Louisiane

Use remaining ham left over from hot meal. Serve sliced, garnished with watercress. Hand separately in a sauceboat Chutney Louisiane. Method as for the hot sauce ; add extra chillies, ground black pepper and Worcester Sauce.

Grilled Halibut with California Fruit Sauce

25 rounds of bread, trimmed
25 fillets of halibut (steaks)
2 tins Fruit Cocktail
5 oz. rough white wine
3 pints bechamel sauce, thick
English cheese, finely grated

Method
Fry the trimmed bread slices in butter (margarine) until brown, or deep fry. Grill the halibut until tender ; place on the prepared bread. Add the drained fruit cocktail and wine to the bechamel sauce. Garnish the halibut with the sauce ; sprinkle with the English cheese and flash under the grill.
25 portions

Portuguese Fried Cod

Portuguese Sauce
½ oz. butter
1 medium onion, finely chopped
4 medium tomatoes
¼ green pepper
½ pint cider or inexpensive white wine
About 12 stuffed olives
1-2 tablespoonfuls seasoned flour
1 lb. cod fillets, skinned
Oil and butter for frying

Method
Make sauce by melting butter in a small saucepan. Cook the finely chopped onion till tender but not brown. Remove pips from green pepper, slice, and add to onion ; cook lightly again for a few minutes. Skin tomatoes, quarter, and shake out the pips. Tip into onion mixture and keep warm. Cut the cod fillets into pieces across the fish, about 2" wide. Coat in seasoned flour. Heat a good-sized frying pan and cover the bottom to a depth of ½" with oil, and add about 2 oz. butter for flavour and browning quality. When fat is hot lay the fish in the pan and let it cook briskly but not violently. As soon as one side is browned lightly turn and cook the other side of each piece. Add the cider and olives to the tomato mixture and bring it to the boil. Pour a little over the fish and serve the rest in a sauce boat.
Serves 4 persons.

Top picture Chef's special herbed rice

Rice chicken with vegetables

Portuguese Fried Cod

LUNCHEON PARTIES

Fried Chicken Danish style

1 deep-frozen chicken, 2½ lb.
5 oz. butter
1¼ lb. potatoes
½ large cucumber
Salt
Freshly ground black pepper

Method
Thaw chicken, then remove giblets. Wipe chicken with kitchen paper and cut into 4 even-sized portions. Prepare a moderate grill, remove rack and melt 3 oz. butter in the pan. Add chicken, baste and grill for 20-25 minutes, turning occasionally. Peel and wash potatoes and cut in ½" cubes. Dry on kitchen paper. Melt remaining butter in a large frying pan, add potatoes and fry for 10 to 12 minutes over a moderate heat, until golden brown and tender. Peel cucumber and cut into ¼" dice. Stir into pan and heat through for 2 minutes. Season with salt and black pepper. Arrange chicken on a warm serving dish and spoon vegetables around.
Serves 4 persons.

Maroc Bacon Rolls

10 lean slices bacon
4 oz. fresh white breadcrumbs
2 tablespoonfuls Olive Oil
½ teaspoonful parsley flakes
½ teaspoonful mixed herbs
Grated rind and juice 1 Maroc orange
2 small mushrooms (finely chopped)
1 small onion (finely chopped)
1 finely chopped garlic clove
    dash of garlic salt
Salt and pepper

Method
Make stuffing: mix breadcrumbs with remaining ingredients. If mixture appears to be dry moisten with a little boiling water. Taste for seasoning. Remove rind from bacon and place some of the stuffing on each slice and roll up. Secure with a skewer. Oil large oval ovenware dish and place rolls inside. Cook for 20 minutes at Mark 4-5 or 350°F. until bacon is cooked and crisp. Serve accompanied with tomato garnish.
Serves 10 persons.

Halibut with Provencal Sauce on Croutons

3 halibut steaks
Salt and pepper
½ oz. butter
2 tablespoonfuls cream
2 oz. grated cheese
3 large or 6 small slices of French
    bread fried in garlic butter
For the sauce
½ oz. butter
1 onion, sliced
½ oz. flour
½ pint water or stock
3 tablespoonfuls tomato purée
A few sliced black and green olives

Method
Season the fish, brush with the butter and cream and sprinkle with cheese, grill until the fish is well cooked. Sit the fish on the croûtons. Meanwhile melt the butter and sauté the onion until soft and transparent. Add the flour and cook the roux for a few minutes. Gradually stir in the water or stock and tomato purée. Finally add the olives and boil for a few minutes; season and serve poured over the hot fish steaks.
Serves 3 persons.

Boeuf Stroganoff

1½ lb. grilling steak
Dash pepper
2 level teaspoonfuls flour
2 oz. butter or margarine
4 oz. mushrooms, sliced
1 small onion
1 small clove garlic
1 (10½ oz.) can condensed
  Consommé
¼ pint sour cream or yoghourt
8 oz. noodles

Method

Cut meat into strips and dust in seasoned flour. Heat the butter and brown the meat. Add mushrooms, onion and garlic, and brown. Stir in soup. Cover Cook 20 minutes or until meat is tender. Stir often. Gradually add sour cream and cook over low heat 5 minutes. Serve over cooked noodles.

Serves 6 persons.

Rice Salad

5 lb. hot cooked rice, cooked in
  chicken stock
5 oz. onion, minced
1 tablespoonful pepper
8 oz. green pepper
5 oz. sweet pickle relish
4 oz. Pimiento, diced
8 fluid oz. french dressing
1 tablespoonful salt
2 lb. celery, diced
5 oz. sour pickle, diced
8 hard-boiled eggs, chopped
16 fluid oz. Mayonnaise

Method

Combine rice, french dressing, onion, salt and pepper. Let this mixture stand for about 30 minutes. Add the celery, green pepper, pickles, relish, pimiento, eggs and mayonnaise; toss lightly. Chill thoroughly then serve.

Yields 50 half-cup servings.

Chicken with Maroc Sauce

8 small chicken joints
Approximately 4 tablespoonfuls
  flour
1¼ pints chicken stock (cube)
5 oranges
Approximately 6 tablespoonfuls
  olive oil
1 clove garlic (optional)
2 tablespoonfuls fresh cream or top
  of milk
  Salt and pepper
To Garnish
1 orange
Small bunch parsley

Method

Wash and coat chicken joints in a little seasoned flour. Fry lightly in the olive oil with crushed garlic clove, if used. Drain. Add the flour to oil and cook to form roux. Add chicken stock gradually and cook over gentle heat to make sauce adding grated orange rind and juice. Place a little sauce in large Phoenix casserole then add drained chicken joints. Pour over remaining sauce and cook at 325°F. (Mark 3) in centre of oven for approximately 1½ hours or until chicken is tender. Just before serving add the cream or top of the milk and garnish with a few sprigs of parsley and orange rounds.

Serves 8 persons.

Accompaniments: Creamed, duchesse or sauté potatoes, green vegetable or salad.

Top picture Boeuf Strogonoff   Rice Salad

Halibut with Provencal Sauce on Croutons

LUNCHEON PARTIES

Salmon Scotch Eggs

1 x 7 oz. can middle cut salmon
2 teaspoonfuls grated lemon rind
Seasoning
2 tablespoonfuls breadcrumbs
2 egg yolks
1 tablespoonful chopped parsley
4 hard-boiled eggs
Flour
Beaten egg
Breadcrumbs

Method

Drain the salmon and combine with the lemon rind, seasoning, breadcrumbs, egg yolks and chopped parsley. Dust the eggs lightly with flour, and enclose each in a portion of the salmon mixture. Dust with a little extra flour, and coat with beaten egg and breadcrumbs. Chill for ¾ hour. Deep fry until golden brown. Serve either hot or cold with a salad.
Serves 4 persons.

Salmon Flan

6 oz. short crust
3 eggs
½ pint milk
Salt and pepper
8 oz. tin salmon
¼ cucumber

Method

Line an 8″ flan ring or shallow baking tin with pastry. Place a circle of greaseproof in the pastry case, put baking beans or crusts of bread in the paper to prevent the base of the case rising. Cook for 20 minutes at 400°F. or Mark 6. Remove paper and beans or bread crusts. Drain the salmon and flake. Beat the eggs, milk and season-ing together. Add salmon, mix well. Pour into pastry case. Bake for 30 minutes at 350°F. or Mark 4. Decorate the top with sliced cucumber.
Serves 6 persons.

Tossed Mutton with Rice

2 lb. rice
7 oz. butter

Method

Proceed as you would do for a stew but do not use flour, as the rice already contains flour. Before the meat has cooked, fry the rice in butter until golden, and then add to stew. The rice will absorb the gravy, so that the dish will be served dry.

Chicken Supreme Patties

Heat small can of Chicken à la King. Cut four slices of bread 1″ thick, cut into rounds with a cutter 3″ in diameter, in centre of each use a 2″ cutter to cut a circle ¼″ deep. Fry bread in hot deep fat, 370°F. till golden brown. Drain. Lift off centre circles with sharp knife. Fill each with Chicken à la King, replace centres. Serve hot or cold.
Serves 4 persons.

Chicken Supreme Salad Ring

Cook 6 oz. rice in boiling water salted to taste till tender (15 minutes). Drain. When cold, mix with 4–6 large lettuce leaves, finely shredded, 1 dessertspoon-ful oil, 1 teaspoonful salt, ¼ teaspoonful pepper; press mixture firmly into a ring mould, turn out gently onto a serving dish, fill centre with contents of 1 large can of Chicken à la King. Serve cold, with lettuce and tomato salad.
Serves 4 persons.

Top picture   Salmon Flan   *Tossed mutton with rice*

LUNCHEON PARTIES

Salmon Pancakes

4 oz. plain flour
Seasoning
2 eggs
⅓ pint of milk
2 tablespoonfuls single cream
Oil or butter for frying
1 oz. butter
1 x 7 oz. can middle cut salmon
2 tablespoonfuls grated lemon rind
2 teaspoonfuls lemon juice
Parsley

Method

Sieve the flour and seasoning. Separate the eggs, add the yolks to the flour and beat to a smooth paste with a little of the milk. Gradually beat in the remaining milk. Leave to stand for 1 hour. Stir in the cream and fold in the stiffly beaten egg whites. Make up batter into six pancakes, using either butter or oil. Turn pancakes on to a clean tea cloth. (If not being used immediately, place between sheets of buttered greaseproof paper and refrigerate. Reheat in a moderate oven, without removing greaseproof paper). Melt the butter, add the flaked salmon, salmon liquor, lemon rind and lemon juice, and heat through. Place some salmon filling on each pancake and roll up. Garnish with parsley, and serve accompanied by a suitable sauce, i.e. Hollandaise, Caper, Mousseline, etc.

Serves 3 persons.

Chicken Supreme Flan

Take one cooked short pastry flan case 7" in diameter. Mix contents of a small can of Chicken à la King with ½ pint white sauce. Heat, season to taste, pour into flan case, sprinkle top with 2 oz. grated cheese ; brown under grill, garnish with thin slices of raw tomato, cooked bacon rolls and parsley. Serve hot or cold.

Chicken Supreme Soufflé

Mix a large can of Chicken à la King with ½ pint thick white sauce, beat in two egg yolks, season to taste, add two egg whites whipped very stiff. Mix gently together, pour into a greased mould, and bake for approximately 45 minutes in a moderate oven, 350°F. (mark 4).

Also try: Chicken à la King with curry, or as a filling for Vol-au-Vents, Baked Potatoes, Omelettes, Baked Stuffed Marrow or Large Boiled Onions (scoop out the centre of each onion, chop finely, mix with heated Chicken à la King, refill onion, re-heat before serving). It's wonderful with winter and summer salads, in buttered rolls or for making super sandwiches.

Fruited Rice Dressing or Stuffing

1 lb. celery diced
1½ lb. butter or margarine
1 tablespoonful poultry seasoning
4¾ pints orange juice
4 tablespoonfuls salt
10 oz. onion, minced
6 oranges, orange peel, grated
4¾ pints water
5 lb. 4 oz rice, uncooked

Method

Saute celery and onions in butter until tender. Add orange peel, salt, poultry seasoning, orange juice, water, and rice. Bring to the boil. Stir well, reduce heat, cover with a tight-fitting lid or foil and simmer 25 minutes, or until tender.

Fruited rice dressing

LUNCHEON PARTIES

Hot Trifle

1 sponge cake
1 can apricots (medium size)
2 tablespoonfuls sherry
1 pint thick custard
½ oz. grated chocolate

Method
Slice the cake into four. Cut each slice in half. Arrange the cake around and in the bottom of an ovenproof dish. Drain the apricots. Pour the syrup and sherry over the cake. Place the apricots on the cake, reserving a few for decoration. Cover with foil and place in a moderately hot oven, 350°F. (mark 4) for 45 minutes. Make a thick custard and pour over the cake, when a skin forms arrange the apricots on the custard, sprinkle with the grated chocolate and pop back in the oven for a few seconds until the chocolate begins to melt.

Upside down pudding

3 tablespoonfuls ginger wine
4 oz. butter
6 oz. Demerara sugar
4 bananas
Glacé cherries
Sponge mixture made from
2 eggs
their weight in butter, sugar and plain flour
with 1½ teaspoonfuls baking powder

Method
Melt the sugar and butter in an oven dish. Stir in the ginger wine and arrange the sliced bananas and cherries in an attractive pattern.
To make the sponge: sift the flour and baking powder. Cream the butter, add

sugar and cream again. Then add eggs well beaten a little at a time and keep beating. Add the flour gradually, then enough milk to make a soft consistency. Pour this mixture over the fruit and bake for 1-1¼ hours at 350°F. When ready turn upside down and serve with whipped cream. As a variant you can use a small tin of pineapple instead of bananas.

Rice Imperial

3¼ pints milk (65 fluid oz.)
14 oz. Long Grain Rice
2 Vanilla pods
16 egg yolks
14 oz. sugar
1 teaspoonful vanilla essence
4 tablespoonfuls unflavoured gelatine
1½ pints double cream, whipped
1 lb. preserved fruit, diced finely, marinated in Kirsch
Red currant jelly, thinned with Kirsch

Method
Combine 2 pints milk, rice and vanilla pods in top of double boiler, cover and cook until tender. Set aside. Remove vanilla pods. Beat egg yolks with sugar, vanilla essence and 1¼ pints milk. Cook until mixture thickens, remove from heat; stir in the dissolved gelatine and strain through cone-shaped sieve. Add cooked rice. Cool until mixture begins to set. Fold in the whipped cream and preserved fruit. Pour into fancy moulds with hollow centres, or into individual moulds and chill. Unmould on very cold platter and surround with red currant jelly, thinned with Kirsch. Garnish with custard glaze. *Serves 25 persons.*

Rice Imperial

Lemon Chiffon Pie

LUNCHEON PARTIES

Hot Apricot Cream Charlotte

5 slices bread, without crusts
2 oz. butter, melted
2 tablespoonfuls Golden Syrup
  Jelly
16 oz. can apricots
1 carton Soured Cream

Method

Divide slices of bread in half making 10 fingers, cut 6 in half again, making small squares. Dip bread in butter and use smaller pieces to line 1½ pint oven-proof dish. Spread remaining fingers with Golden Syrup Jelly. Drain apricots and sieve, then blend in Soured Cream. Pour this mixture into lined dish and top with remaining fingers of bread. Bake in a moderately hot oven, 400°F. (Mark 6), for 20-25 minutes until bread is golden brown and crunchy on top.

Cranberry Tartlets

Roll out 6 oz. shortcrust pastry (6 oz. flour etc.) and line 4 individual Yorkshire pudding tins. Crimp edges, prick bases and bake blind at 425°F. (mark 7) for about 15 minutes. Cool. Divide a 5 oz. carton soured cream between the cases and top with a thick layer of Cranberry Sauce.

Coconut Crust

1 egg white
2 tablespoonfuls sugar
1 tablespoonful syrup
½ teaspoonful vanilla
6 oz. desiccated coconut

Method

Beat egg white until stiff but not dry. Gradually beat in the syrup, sugar and vanilla. Stir in the coconut. With back of spoon, press coconut mixture to bottom and sides of 10" pie dish, making the top edge of crust slightly higher than edge of dish. Bake at 350°F. mark 4, for about 20 minutes. Chill.

Lemon Chiffon Pie

5 oz. digestive biscuits
2 oz. melted butter
2 oz. castor sugar

Lemon Filling

3 oz. castor sugar
2 oz. pre-cooked rice
¼ oz. powdered gelatine
½ pint water
1 lemon, juice and thinly pared
  rind
1 egg white

Method

Crush biscuits (between two sheets of greaseproof paper or in a bag with rolling pin) and add sugar. Stir in melted butter with fork and mix until blended and crumbly. Spoon mixture over base and sides of shallow pie plate and press down to make firm crust. Chill while preparing filling. Dissolve half sugar in ¼ pint water and bring to boil. Add rice, cover with lid and set aside until required. Dissolve remaining sugar in ¼ pint water and bring to boil. Add lemon rind and simmer for 5 minutes. Meanwhile pour strained lemon juice over gelatine powder and leave to soak. Remove lemon-flavoured water from heat and strain liquid on to soaked gelatine, stirring well to dissolve it. Allow to cool. Allow reconstituted rice to cool thoroughly. When gelatine mixture is cool add egg white and whisk until thick, and frothy. Fold in rice and pour into chilled biscuit shell. Chill thoroughly and decorate with little extra grated lemon rind and a few lemon jelly slices. *Serves 4-6 persons.*

Fruit Fool

¼ *pint double cream*
¼ *pint cold custard (the same consistency as the cream)*
1 *lb. fruit (gooseberries, raspberries, etc.)*
About 4 oz. sugar
About ¼ pint water

Method

Cook the fruit with water and sugar. Sieve finely and leave to cool. Whip the cream until thick (don't overwhip). Fold into the custard. Fold in the cold fruit purée. Put into individual dishes and chill well. Top with whipped cream and serve with ratafia biscuits.

Coffee and Vanilla Milk Jelly

Here you are really making two separate milk jellos, of quite different flavours and colours, and combining them into one exciting two-tier jello.

¾ *pint milk*
¼ *pint strong coffee*
2 *oz. castor sugar*
1 *oz. gelatine*
4 *tablespoonfuls water*
Vanilla essence

Method

Dissolve 1 oz. sugar in hot coffee and ¼ pint of milk. Leave to cool. Dissolve ½ oz. gelatine in 2 tablespoonfuls water. Add the milk and coffee mixture. Add vanilla flavouring (see directions on bottle) to the remainder of the warmed milk and dissolve 1 oz. sugar in it. Leave to cool. Dissolve ½ oz. gelatine in 2 tablespoonfuls water. Add the vanilla-flavoured milk. Pour this jelly into a mould. Leave to set. Pour the cool coffee jello on top of the vanilla jello and leave to set. Turn out,

and decorate with cream and chocolate drops to match the colour and flavour. It's just as easy to make this two-tier jello in the bright colours children love.

Strawberries and Rice Louisiane

6 *oz. rice*
1½ *pints milk*
½ *teaspoonful salt*
4 *oz. sugar, sweeten according to taste*
2 *oz. butter*
1 *teaspoonful vanilla essence*
½ *oz. gelatine*
2 *tablespoonfuls water*
½ *pint double cream, whipped*
12 *peach slices*
12 *whole strawberries*
2 *tablespoonfuls Kirsch or Cointreau*
3 *oz. sugar*

Method

Combine rice, milk, 4 oz. sugar and salt in top of double boiler. Place over lower part of boiler and cook covered until rice is soft and creamy, about 1 hour. Stir occasionally. Blend in butter and vanilla.

Soften gelatine in water and stir into the hot rice to dissolve. Cool rice but do not let it become firm. Fold in whipped cream and turn into 3-pint fancy mould. Chill until well set.

Marinate peaches and strawberries in Kirsch or Cointreau and 3 oz. sugar, for 30 minutes. Turn out rice mould onto a cold serving dish. Decorate with peaches and strawberries.

Serves 6 persons.

Strawberries and Rice Louisiane

LUNCHEON PARTIES

Pink'n Pretty Parfait

*1 pint rice pudding, cooked and
    cold*
¼ pint double cream
¼ teaspoonful almond essence
*A few drops cochineal or pink
    colouring*
*1 large carton frozen strawberries,
    defrosted*

Method
Whip the cream and fold half into the
rice together with the almond essence
and colouring. Fill individual glasses
with alternate layers of rice and
strawberries. Top with the remaining
cream and a single strawberry. Four to
six portions.

Fruit Topping

12 dates, finely chopped
12 maraschino cherries, drained
*12 figs, drained and finely
    chopped*
¼ pint liquid from figs
2 tablespoonfuls brandy
2 oz. sugar
¼ pint water
1 tablespoonful gelatine
*3 tablespoonfuls liquid from
    cherries*

Method
Combine fruit, fig juice and brandy and
leave to stand. Combine sugar and
water, boil for 5 minutes. Soften
gelatine in liquid from cherries. Add to
boiling water; stir to dissolve. Add to
fruit mixture and then drain in a sieve
saving both liquid and fruit. Pour
liquid over pie and arrange fruit
mixture around the edge. Chill until
set, about two hours.
Serves 8 persons.

140

Lemon Syrup Cream

1 box lemon jello
11 oz. can mandarin oranges
1 lb. cottage cheese, sieved
1 lemon, grated rind and juice
*¼ pint double cream, lightly
    whipped*
*3 tablespoonfuls Golden Syrup
    Jelly*

Method
Make up jelly double strength with
½ pint heated juice of the mandarin
oranges and water. Allow to cool, then
stir into the sieved cottage cheese with
lemon juice and grated rind. When
nearly set, fold in cream and turn into
a 2 pint pudding basin or mould. Chill
until set. Dip the outside of basin into
very hot water for a few seconds then
turn out on plate. Arrange a star of
mandarin orange segments on top
and remaining mandarins around
outside of mould. Melt the Golden
Syrup Jelly and spoon over the
mandarins.
Serves 4-6 persons.

Truffles

3 oz. chocolate
1 egg yolk
½ oz. butter
6 oz. cake crumbs
2 tablespoonfuls ginger wine
*Chocolate vermicelli or cocoa
    powder*

Method
Melt the chocolate in a bowl over
boiling water. Cool slightly and then
add egg yolk, butter, cake crumbs and
ginger wine. Beat until smooth. Form
into balls and roll in chocolate vermicelli or cocoa powder.

Pink'n Pretty Parfait

DINNER PARTIES

INTRODUCTION

Giving a dinner party sounds all very grand, but if the menu is carefully planned it can be an easy as well as an enjoyable occasion. Have a simple first course—I suggest something like grapefruit, melon, potted shrimps, hors d'oeuvres (already arranged on individual dishes) or a good soup.

Simple Soup with Vegetables

$\frac{1}{2}$ lb. potatoes
$\frac{1}{2}$ lb. carrots
$\frac{1}{2}$ lb. onions
$\frac{1}{2}$ lb. turnips
1 parsnip
2 oz. butter
$1\frac{1}{2}$ pints water
1 oz. flour
1 pint milk
Seasoning
Chopped parsley

Method
Prepare the vegetables and cut them into small pieces. Melt the butter in a large saucepan, add the vegetables, cook and stir for a few minutes. Add the the nearly boiling water and a little seasoning. Bring to the boil and simmer until the vegetables are tender. Blend the flour with the remaining water and add to the vegetables. Cook for a few minutes. Put through a fine sieve and return to the saucepan. Stir in the milk and adjust the seasoning to taste. Bring to the boil. Serve hot, sprinkled with chopped parsley.

Lentil Cream Soup

4 oz. lentils
$\frac{1}{4}$ lb. carrots
$\frac{1}{4}$ lb. onions
A stalk of celery
Small piece of turnip
1 oz. butter
1 pint stock
1 pint milk
Seasoning
$\frac{1}{4}$ pint double dairy cream
Chopped parsley

Method
Wash the lentils, prepare and slice the vegetables. Melt the butter in a saucepan, add the vegetables and cook for approximately 10 minutes, stirring to prevent sticking. Add the stock and the milk, season and bring to the boil. Simmer gently until the vegetables are cooked. Sieve, return the soup to the saucepan and add double dairy cream. Reheat slowly. Chopped parsley should be sprinkled on the top when served. *Note:* If a thinner soup is preferred, add extra milk when adding cream.

Gaiety Soup

$15\frac{1}{2}$ oz. can Cream of Tomato soup
1 packet of demi-sel cheese
A little milk
1 teaspoonful onion juice
Salted almonds
Small biscuits or crackers

Method
Heat the soup according to the directions on the can. Blend the cheese with a little milk and onion juice until soft and creamy. Pipe or pile the cheese onto small biscuits and garnish with salted almonds or other large nuts. Pour the soup into a hot serving dish and float the biscuits on the top.

DINNER PARTIES

Almond Soup

Purée
1 pint milk
1 onion
1 head celery (white part only)
2 oz. blanched and chopped
*   almonds*
Sauce
1 oz. butter
1 tablespoonful flour
½ pint milk
Seasoning
½ pint double dairy cream

Method
Prepare the purée: pour pint milk into a saucepan and add the whole onion, sticks of celery and chopped almonds. Simmer gently for 1 hour, then remove the onion and celery. Sieve the almonds and milk. Prepare the sauce: melt the butter, add the flour and cook for a few minutes. Remove from heat and add ½ pint milk. Season well. Bring to the boil, stirring all the time. Remove from heat. Add the purée to the sauce and reheat, stirring continuously. Add the double dairy cream and continue cooking for a few minutes, but do not allow the soup to boil. Serve immediately.

Cheese Soup

1 small onion
1 stick celery
½ oz. butter
Seasoning
1 pint milk
¾ pint stock or water
½ oz. cornflour
2 tablespoonfuls water
2 oz. grated cheese
*   (Lancashire for choice)*

Method
Prepare the onion and celery and chop them finely. Melt the butter in a saucepan and toss the onion and celery in this until all the fat is absorbed. These should not be fried or browned. Add the seasoning, milk and stock, and simmer gently for about half an hour. Mix the cornflour to a smooth paste with 2 tablespoonfuls of water, strain and stir this into the mixture. Bring to the boil and continue to cook for five minutes. Add the grated cheese and simmer for a few minutes until it is melted. Add extra seasoning if necessary and serve.

Laced Tomato Soup

1½ lb. tomatoes
1½ pints stock (water and chicken
*   bouillon cube)*
1 oz. bacon scraps and rind or
*   bacon bone*
2 tablespoonfuls olive oil
Medium onion (roughly chopped)
Medium carrot (roughly chopped)
½ teaspoonful ground nutmeg
*   (optional)*
Sugar and lemon juice to taste
1 teaspoonful mixed herbs
Small can tomato purée
1 wineglassful Cinzano Red
Salt and pepper
Celery
Thickening
½ oz. cornflour mixed with
2 tablespoonfuls water to each
*   pint purée*
To Garnish
Chopped parsley

Method
Fry the bacon scraps with olive oil and fry off the carrot, onion and celery. Add

the washed and roughly chopped tomatoes. Add the stock and remaining ingredients including the wineglassful of Cinzano Red. Simmer the soup for $1\frac{1}{2}$ hours. Rub through a nylon sieve. Return soup to pan and thicken if necessary with cornflour blend. Taste for seasoning. Serve very hot sprinkled liberally with chopped parsley and accompany with crisp French bread. *N.B.* 2 tablespoonfuls of fresh cream can be stirred in at the end just before serving for a more creamy soup.
Serves 8 persons.

Iced Cucumber and Yogurt Soup

1 large unpeeled cucumber
2 cartons plain yogurt ($\frac{1}{2}$ pint)
$\frac{1}{2}$ small green pepper
1 clove of garlic (finely chopped)
Salt and pepper
2 tablespoonfuls wine vinegar
Chopped chives (optional)
$\frac{1}{2}$ pint chilled milk
Ice cubes
Chopped parsley

Method
Grate the cucumber on a medium grater into a bowl, stir in the yogurt. Chop the green pepper very finely, discarding pips and pith, add to the yogurt with the chopped garlic, salt and pepper, vinegar and chopped chives. Chill very thoroughly. Before serving add the milk and ice cubes. Sprinkle with parsley.
Serves 6 persons.

Cream of Almond Soup

3 oz. blanched almonds (finely chopped)
2 pints milk
$\frac{1}{2}$ onion
1 celery heart or 4 sticks (cut into 1" pieces)
1 oz. butter
1 oz. flour
Cayenne pepper
Small pinch ground mace
Salt
5 fluid oz. fresh cream
Garnish
1 oz. flaked almonds fried in butter

Method
Bring the almonds to the boil in one pint of the Milk with the onion and celery; simmer for half an hour, then remove the vegetables. Make a roux with the butter and flour, blend in the remaining pint of Milk and season with the pepper, mace and salt. Stir in the almond-milk. Simmer for ten minutes. Add the cream and bring the soup just to the boil. Serve garnished with the fried almonds. Instead of adding the cream to the soup it may be served separately.
Serves 6 persons.

Tomato Salad

Slice or quarter tomatoes and pour over a little oil and vinegar dressing.

Cottage Cheese Cocktail

1 tin of Fruit Cocktail
Creamed cheese

Method
Line a large glass or bowl with crisp lettuce, add the fruit cocktail and top with the creamed cheese, garnish with walnut halves.

Cottage Cheese Cocktail

Sole Rachel

4 large or 8 small fillets of sole,
*   skinned (reserve skin and bones)*
1½-2 oz. onion peeled
Bay leaf
Salt
Fleurons of puff pastry (optional)
6 mushrooms
3 tablespoonfuls cream
¾ oz. flour
Salt
1 oz. butter
1 gill dry white wine
1 egg yolk
Peppercorns

Method

Place fish skin and bones with onion, bay leaf, peppercorns, and 1 teaspoonful salt in a saucepan and just cover with water. Boil for 20-30 minutes. Wipe or wash mushrooms. Slice some for the garnish and chop the rest finely. Cook gently in ¼ oz. of butter, 1 tablespoonful of the cream, salt and pepper in a covered pan for 4-5 minutes. Strain. Place equal portions of the mushroom on half of each fillet, skinned side downward, fold over and lay in a heatproof dish. Pour over wine and 1 gill of the strained fish stock. Season. Cover with greaseproof paper and bake at 375°F. (Mark 5) for 20-25 minutes, or until the fish is cooked. Remove fish to a serving dish and keep hot. Melt rest of butter in a small saucepan, blend in flour, add strained liquor from the fish and bring to the boil stirring with a wire whisk. Boil for a minute or two, remove from heat, beat in rest of cream and the egg yolk, adjust seasoning, heat through then pour over the fish. Garnish with the slices of mushroom and fleurons of pastry if desired.

Baked Fish with Lemon Rice Stuffing

1 x 5 lb. fish (trout, haddock,
*   cod, bass, pike)*
Salt and pepper
12 oz. cooked rice
1½ oz. slivered almonds
2 tablespoonfuls minced parsley
1 tablespoonful grated lemon rind
½ teaspoonful basil
Butter or margarine

Method

Wash fish and season with salt and pepper. Combine rice, nuts, parsley, lemon rind, basil, ½ teaspoonful salt and a dash of pepper; mix well. Stuff prepared fish. Sew or close cavity with small skewers and lace with twine. To facilitate removal from pan to serving platter, place fish on greaseproof paper, or foil for baking. Brush fish with butter or margarine. Bake at 400°F for 45 minutes.
Serves 8-10 persons.

Plaice Mayonnaise

8 small fillets plaice
Salt and pepper
½ pint mayonnaise
½ pint aspic jelly
Gherkins
Lettuce, cucumber and tomatoes
*   for garnish*

Method

Skin the fillets and season with salt and pepper. Fold in half and steam between 2 buttered plates for 15 minutes. Allow to cool. Stir half the aspic jelly, when on the point of setting,

Top picture   *Baked Fish with Lemon Rice Stuffing*   *Sole Rachel*

into the mayonnaise. Coat the fillets, leave to set. Thinly slice gherkins and cut small diamond shape pieces of tomato and arrange on the fillets. Glaze with remaining $\frac{1}{4}$ pint of clear aspic and leave to set. Chop any remaining clear aspic on a wet board and decorate
Serves 4 persons.

Scallops Aix en Provence

4 oz. Patna rice
1 lb. haddock fillets—fresh or
frozen
Salt and pepper
$\frac{3}{4}$ oz. butter
$\frac{1}{2}$ oz. plain flour
$10\frac{1}{2}$ oz. can condensed chicken
soup
$\frac{1}{4}$ lb. prawns—fresh or frozen
4 tablespoonfuls white wine
6 scallop shells
Slices of cucumber—sliced and
halved for garnish

Method
Wash the fish and place in a small greased fireproof dish; season with salt and pepper; cover and cook in oven for 20-30 minutes, 350°F. (Mark 5). Cook the rice in boiling, salted water for 12-15 minutes; drain, cover and keep warm in the oven. Break the fish into flakes, discarding the skin and any bones. Melt the butter in a saucepan; add the flour and cook gently for 2 minutes. Add the soup and wine and cook for a further 3 minutes, stirring all the time. Gently fold in the flaked haddock and prawns and heat thoroughly. Arrange the cucumber slices and rice in an attractive border in the shells and fill the centres of each with the fish mixture.

'Pink Clouds'

1 lb. small mushrooms
1 lettuce
$\frac{1}{2}$ clove crushed garlic
1 gill cream
2 tablespoonfuls mayonnaise
6 tablespoonfuls tomato ketchup
$\frac{1}{2}$ teaspoonful Worcester sauce

Method
Trim the mushroom stalks and reserve for soup. Halve the larger mushrooms and cover all with boiling water for one minute. Drain well and cool. Lightly whip the cream and gradually stir in the mayonnaise, ketchup and Worcester sauce, followed by the garlic and mushrooms. Season well and serve on a bed of shredded lettuce, garnished with finely chopped chives.

Prawn Talmouse

$\frac{1}{2}$ oz. butter
$\frac{1}{2}$ oz. flour
5 fluid oz. milk
2 tablespoonfuls fresh cream
4 oz. chopped shelled prawns
1 egg yolk
1 oz. grated cheese (preferably
Lancashire)
Salt and pepper
Cayenne pepper
8 oz. puff pastry
Beaten egg
6 whole prawns and parsley to
garnish

Method
Melt the butter, stir in the flour and blend in the milk. Stir over a medium heat until thick. Stir in the cream, prawns, egg yolk, cheese and seasonings. Stir over a low heat until thick—leave to cool. Roll out the pastry and

Top picture Pink Clouds'   *Scallops Aix en Provence*

cut six 7" equilateral triangles. Divide the cold mixture into six and spoon into the centre of each pastry triangle. Bring up the corners of pastry to meet in a point forming a pyramid, sealing the sides to within 1" from the top. Brush with beaten egg. Bake the Talmouses for approximately 20 minutes at 450°F. (Mark 8). Serve either hot or cold garnished with parsley and a prawn on the top of each Talmouse. *Serves 6 persons.*

Pâté de Poisson Traktir

Take 2 lb. of filleted fish, preferably Brill or Turbot, but fresh Cod can be used. 1 lb. of this fish will be used to make a 'farcie blanche' (white stuffing) viz. mince the fish in the mincing machine, or either crush it with a mortar. To this will be added ½ lb. of Panade (i.e. a thick roux sauce made with butter, flour and stock), to which you will add either cream or condensed milk, mixed altogether which makes the stuffing. The other 1 lb. of fish will be put in a Marinade made of white wine, whisky, thyme, bay leaf, pepper and salt. Then you will make a duxelles of chopped mushrooms and chopped cooked Sorrel, to which you will add reduction of shallots, white wine, a little minced savory and chervil, pepper and salt, and one-third of the white stuffing, so you will have an equal quantity of white stuffing and black stuffing. Prepare a mould which you will line with pancakes, and use the white farcie to make the bottom layer. Then you will put a layer of the fillets of fish which have been cooking in the Marinade. All these farcie layers to be put into the mould through a piping bag. You will then put a layer composed of one stripe of white stuffing and one stripe of black stuffing then a layer of the fish, then a layer composed of one stripe of white stuffing and one stripe of black stuffing, and so on until the mould is finished. You then put the mould into a bain-marie in a slow oven for half an hour. When you take it out, press the mould to drain off any water, leave the mould to cool and take out the following day.

Guard of Honour

This requires 2 joints of best chops. Ask the butcher to chine the joints, then remove surplus fat and skin tissue from around the ends of the rib bones, so that the bones protrude about 1" Place the two joints on end in the roasting pan and close together so that the bone tips cross each. other like swords in a guard of honour. Roast in a moderate oven, 350°F. (Mark 4), for about $1\frac{1}{4}$ hours. To serve, take them just as they are from the roasting pan, stand them on the serving dish and put a few sprigs of watercress along the top where the bones join.

Jacket Potatoes

6 large potatoes
Salt
Oil or butter

Method
Scrub the potatoes well. Rub the skin liberally with oil or butter and salt. Wrap in Alcan foil, place on the lowest shelf and bake in a moderate oven for about $1\frac{1}{2}$ hours.

Top picture Guard of Honour

Jacket Potatoes, Syllabub, Stuffed
Tomatoes Pork Tahaiti

DINNER PARTIES

Syllabub

2 wine glassfuls of sherry or
    sweet white wine
4 oz. castor sugar
$\frac{3}{4}$ pt double cream
1 large lemon

Method

Pare the lemon finely making sure that there is no pith left on the rind. Squeeze the juice and strain it. Pour it into a bowl with the wine and steep the pared rind in the mixture overnight. Next day remove the rind. Put the juice and wine mixture into a large bowl and stir in the sugar. Make sure that all the sugar is completely dissolved. Now gradually add the cream whipping it all the while. Whip until the cream stands in peaks. Turn into small wine glasses or glass custard cups. Chill. Decorate with the finely chopped rind.

Stuffed Tomatoes

6 firm tomatoes
$\frac{1}{2}$ level teaspoonful lemon juice
$\frac{1}{2}$ cucumber
$\frac{1}{4}$ teaspoonful of Tabasco
1 level tablespoonful salad cream
8 oz. cooked mixed vegetables
Salt

Method

Cut a circle 1″ in diameter out of the top of each tomato remove pulp and turn upside down to drain on kitchen paper. Mix vegetables, salad cream and lemon juice. Chop cucumber and add to mixture. Add salt to taste and Tabasco. Pile mixture into tomato shells, and garnish with parsley.

Pork Tahaiti

3 lb. neck-end pork, boned

1 lb. onions
8 oz. breadcrumbs
1 egg
1 bouillon cube
A sprig of sage
$1\frac{1}{2}$ lb. cooking apples
4 oz. pork sausage meat
Pinch of Thyme
1 tablespoonful chopped parsley
$\frac{1}{2}$ pint water

Method

Score boned joints of pork finely. Make stuffing by mixing breadcrumbs, sausage meat, parsley, thyme and seasoning. Bind with beaten egg. Stuff joints and tie firmly. Melt lard and fry gently chopped onions and apples without browning. Cover bottom of baking tin with this mixture. Dissolve the bouillon cube in hot water and pour over apple and onion mixture. Place joint on top, lightly season, add sprig of sage. Cook in moderate oven, 375°F (Mark 4), for $2\frac{1}{2}$-3 hours. Slice meat and serve the apples and onions as sauce.

Fillets of Sole and Mushrooms

cooked in Champagne and garnished with Prawns and Creamed Potato

4 fillets of sole
6 oz. button mushrooms
1 pint prawns
$\frac{1}{2}$ bottle of white wine
2 eggs
$\frac{1}{8}$ pint of cream
3 oz. butter
1 oz. flour
1 bay leaf
1 sliced onion
1 lb. duchesse potatoes
Parsley

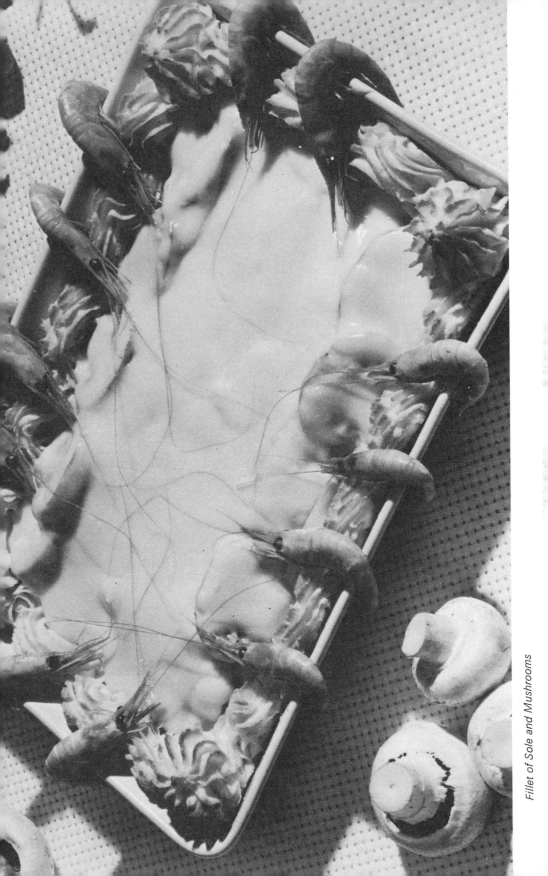

Fillet of Sole and Mushrooms

DINNER PARTIES

Method

Pipe potatoes round the edge of oven-proof serving dish. Place in oven 375°F. (Mark 5) until golden. Put fish into oven-proof dish. Pour over white wine, add bay leaf, parsley, onion, salt and pepper, cover and cook in oven until fish is tender. Make a roux with 1 oz. butter and flour, add stock of fish, check seasoning and bring to the boil. Slice the mushrooms and peel half the prawns. Turn these in hot butter for 2 minutes, arrange fish in a prepared serving dish and place the mushrooms and prawns round the edge. Add cream and beaten egg to the sauce, heat gently and then pour over the fish. Garnish with unpeeled prawns.

Curried Beef in a Rice Ring

Seasoned flour
2 oz. butter or lard
2 lb. beef (cubed)
Curry Sauce
$1\frac{1}{2}$ oz. butter or lard
1 small onion (chopped)
1 cooking apple (peeled and chopped)
2-4 tablespoonfuls curry powder
1 pint beef stock
$\frac{1}{2}$ level teaspoonful salt
$\frac{1}{2}$ bay leaf
1 tablespoonful mango chutney
Juice of $\frac{1}{2}$ lemon
1 level tablespoonful cornflour blended with 2 tablespoonfuls cold water

Method

Toss beef cubes in seasoned flour and brown in hot butter. Meanwhile, prepare curry sauce. Melt butter in a heavy pan, add onions and apples and fry gently for 5 minutes. Add curry powder and gradually stir in water or stock. Bring to Boil, stirring well, then add salt, bay leaf, chutney, lemon juice, raisins and beef. Cover pan with lid and simmer gently for about 1 hour. Discard the bay leaf, and stir in blended cornflour. Bring to the boil. stirring well until thickened.

Rice Ring

1 lb. 8 oz. cooked rice (8 oz. uncooked)
1 tablespoonful diced pimento
1 tablespoonful peas

Method

Combine hot rice with peas and pimento and pack into a $2\frac{1}{2}$ pint ring mould. Cover and place the ring mould in a pan of hot water until serving time. Invert on a warm plate. Serve curry in the rice ring.
Serves 6 persons.

Supreme Sauce

3 pints water
$1\frac{3}{4}$ pints white wine
$\frac{1}{4}$ pint low fat chicken base
2 oz. arrowroot

Method

Blend together water and chicken base and bring to the boil. Blend wine and arrowroot. Add to boiling mixture. Stir until mixture thickens and comes to the boil. Serve over hot cooked rice.
Yield: Approximately $4\frac{1}{2}$ pints.

Marinaded Roast Lamb

1 large leg lamb (weight approximately $4\frac{1}{2}$ lb.)
Marinade:
4 tablespoonfuls olive oil
Grated rind and juice of 1 orange

154

Top picture   *Curried Beef in Rice Ring*   *Supreme Sauce*

1 teaspoonful honey
Salt and pepper
3 good tablespoonfuls Cinzano
    French
To Garnish:
    Slice of orange
To Accompany:
    Creamed potatoes
    Garden peas

Method

Wash and remove skin from lamb. Make marinade: mix all ingredients together and allow lamb to soak in liquid for a couple of hours or preferably overnight. Place lamb in oiled roasting tin and cook with marinade adding more olive oil if necessary and cook at 325°F. (Mark 4), allowing 25 minutes to the lb. and 25 minutes over. Baste frequently with marinade. Test to see if cooked. Only a slight amount of juice should be emitted when skewered. Serve accompanied with creamed potato nests filled with garden peas. Garnish with rings of orange.
Serves 6-8 persons.

Duckling Nambucca

Stuffing
$\frac{1}{2}$ large loaf white bread
$\frac{1}{4}$ pint milk
6 oz. stoned prunes, soaked
    overnight in water
3 oz. skinned almonds
2 oz. Australian stoned raisins
2 eggs
1 apple, cored and peeled
5 lb. duck
3 oz. honey
3 oz. white wine
1 teaspoonful ground ginger
3 oz. pineapple juice
2 oz. brandy

6 pineapple slices
$\frac{1}{2}$ dozen glacé cherries

Method

For the stuffing: Soak white bread in milk for 10 minutes, add stoned prunes, almonds, stoned raisins, eggs and sliced apple. Mix thoroughly. Wash the duck and fill with the stuffing, and season with salt on the outside. Place duck jn a roasting tin. Mix honey, white wine, ginger, pineapple juice and brandy in a small bowl. Add to duck and roast in the oven at 350°F. (Mark 4) for approximately $2\frac{1}{2}$ hours, basting every half hour. Add pineapple slices five minutes before serving. Place duck on a hot serving dish and garnish with pineapple rings and cherries on top of the duck. Pour sauce over and flambe with brandy.
Serves 4 persons.

Veal Escalopes with Yogurt Sauce and Paprika

Veal escalopes—allow one for each
    serving
Butter for frying
Seasoning—paprika
Plain yogurt—amount according to
    number of escalopes being
    cooked. Allow approximately
    $\frac{1}{8}$ pint to each serving

Method

Fry the escalopes in butter until cooked and lightly brown each side. Sprinkle with salt. With the pan over very low heat, pour yogurt over each escalope and sprinkle liberally with paprika. Heat very gently for a few minutes and serve immediately. Duchesse potatoes, peas and grilled mushrooms are suggested as accompanying vegetables.

Duckling Nambucca

DINNER PARTIES

Somerset Chicken

2 chicken portions
3 oz. butter
6 oz. mushrooms
$\frac{1}{2}$ oz. flour
$\frac{1}{2}$ pint dry cider
$\frac{1}{2}$ gill cream
1 bay leaf
Tomato—to garnish

Method

Put the chicken into a good sized pan in which 1 oz. of butter has already been heated. Cook until the chicken skin is a golden brown, then pour in the cider; add the bay, salt and pepper. Cover with a well-fitting lid and simmer gently for about 25 minutes, or until the chicken is tender. Put the chicken onto a serving dish and keep hot. Boil the cider rapidly for a minute. Cut the mushrooms into large dice and turn these in a little hot butter, add the flour and then stir in the cider. Bring the sauce to the boil, add the mushrooms and cream, check seasoning, then pour over the chicken. Edge the dish with sliced tomato.
Serves 2 persons.

Luxury Chicken Casserole

1 chicken
4 onions
$\frac{1}{2}$ lb. mushrooms
$\frac{1}{2}$ lb. streaky bacon
$\frac{1}{2}$ bottle white wine
2 oz. flour
2 oz. butter

Method

Place the chicken, onions, mushrooms and rolled bacon rashers in a casserole. Season and pour in the wine. Cover with a well-fitting lid. Bake in the oven 400°F. (Mark 6) for at least $1\frac{1}{2}$ hours or until the meat is tender. Heat the butter in a pan, add the flour and strain the wine from the casserole. Heat until the sauce thickens. Check seasoning. Lift the chicken onto a serving dish surrounded by the vegetables. Either pour the sauce over the chicken or serve it in a sauce-boat.

Easter Bonnets

4 pork chops
1 oz. butter
4 spoons apple purée (this amount will vary with the size of mushrooms to be filled)
4 large cup mushrooms
4 rashers bacon

Method

Grill the pork chops until tender and place on a serving-dish. Heat the butter in the grill pan, dip the mushrooms in hot butter and grill for 2 minutes each side. Roll the bacon rashers and place on a skewer; grill. Heat the apple purée, then put a spoonful of apple into the mushroom cups, place the bacon rolls in the centre of each; add a touch of parsley. Place the "Easter Bonnets" on top of the chops and serve.

Noisettes de Mouton aux Champignon

4 vol-au-vent cases
6 oz. mushrooms
1 small onion
Watercress
4 noisettes of lamb
$\frac{1}{4}$ pint white sauce
2 oz. butter
Maitre d'hotel butter

158

DINNER PARTIES

Method

Fry the noisettes in hot butter until tender. Slice the onion finely and fry in butter, adding the mushrooms to the pan after a few minutes. Season and cook for a further 3 minutes. Pour in the sauce, heat thoroughly and check seasoning. Fill the hot vol-au-vent cases and top with the noisettes. Garnish with watercress and dot with maitre d'hotel butter.

Roast Duck with Sauce Champignons

1 duckling
2 tablespoonfuls brandy
6 oz. mushrooms
3 tablespoonfuls apple pulp (of which most of the fluid has been boiled away)
$\frac{3}{4}$ pint rich brown stock or consommé
2 tablespoonfuls Italian Vermouth
2 bay leaves

Method

Stuff the carcass with the apple pulp and sew up firmly. Prick the skin of the duckling all over and put into an ovenproof dish with a lid. Put into the oven 425°F. (Mark 7) for 20 minutes. Drain the fat from the dish, pour the brandy over the bird and light. Pour the stock round the bird, add the bay leaves and roast, with the lid on the dish, in the oven 375°F. (Mark 5) until the bird is tender. This will take about 40 minutes, but will vary according to the size and age of the bird. Drain all the liquor into a saucepan; slice the mushrooms and add to the pan, season well and boil quite rapidly until the mushrooms are tender and the sauce

reduced by one-third. Pour in the Vermouth, check seasoning and serve with the roast bird.
Serves 2-3 persons.

Terrine de Canard

1 duck
$\frac{1}{4}$ lb. chicken livers
$\frac{1}{2}$ lb. veal
$\frac{1}{4}$ lb. lean salt pork
6 oz. mushrooms
1 clove garlic
3 tablespoonfuls brandy
2 tablespoonfuls lemon juice
3 tablespoonfuls orange juice
1 teaspoonful orange and lemon zest
1 onion
1 teaspoonful sage
1 beaten egg
12 thin strips bacon fat
2 bay leaves

Method

Skin the duck and remove all the meat from the carcass. Slice the breasts thinly and finely chop the remaining meat. Mince the livers with the veal, pork and mushrooms. Crush the garlic and finely chop the onion. Mix all these ingredients with the chopped duck and blend in the fruit juices and zest. Add the sage and brandy and leave to stand overnight. Add the beaten egg and plenty of seasoning. Pour half the mixture into a greased terrine dish, lined with the bacon fat. Arrange the fillets of duck in the dish and cover with the remaining mixture. Top with strips of fat, and bay leaves, and cover the terrine and bake in oven 350°F. (Mark 4) standing the terrine in a pan of water. Bake for about $1\frac{1}{2}$ hours. Press with weights during cooling.

Turkey in Mushroom and Sherry Sauce

DINNER PARTIES

Turkey in Mushroom and Sherry Sauce

Slices of cold turkey
1 can condensed mushroom soup
Small can evaporated milk
1 glassful dry sherry
1 bouillon cube dissolved in
$\frac{1}{4}$ pint of hot water
1 teaspoonful Oregano
Salt and pepper
Garnish
1 oz. butter
4 oz. mushrooms (with stalks)
4 oz. salted almonds

Method
Combine together soup, milk, sherry, oxo stock, salt, pepper and oregano and heat almost to boiling point. Pour over slices of cold turkey and cook at 350°F. (Mark 4) for approximately 30 minutes. Meanwhile fry mushrooms and salted almonds gently in butter until golden brown. Serve turkey on a bed of noodles with sliced green beans and garnished with the mushrooms and almonds.

Chicken Diable

3 lb. roasting chicken, oven-ready
weight
Seasoned flour
1 oz. butter
1 tablespoonful oil
1 green pepper, seeded and thinly
sliced
4 oz. mushrooms, sliced
4 tablespoonfuls dry white wine
2 level tablespoonfuls Sauce Diable
$\frac{1}{2}$ pint chicken stock
$\frac{1}{2}$ level tablespoonful cornflour
5 fluid oz. carton single cream
Salt and black pepper

Method
Cut chicken into 8 pieces, dip in seasoned flour. Melt butter in a pan with oil and sauté chicken until coloured, about 5 minutes each side. Remove to an ovenproof casserole. Sauté green pepper and mushrooms for a few minutes, stir in wine, Sauce Diable and stock. Bring to the boil and pour over chicken. Cover and cook at 375°F. (Mark 4) for about 1 hour. Stir cornflour blended with a little water into the juices. Add cream, season and return to oven for 5 minutes.

Quiche Lorraine

4 oz. short crust pastry
$\frac{1}{2}$ oz. butter
1 medium onion—chopped
3 oz. lean bacon—chopped
2 eggs
3 oz. grated cheese—Lancashire
for choice
$\frac{1}{4}$ pint milk
3 tablespoonfuls double dairy
cream
Salt and pepper

Method
Line an 8" flan ring with pastry. Melt butter, add onion and fry gently until soft. Add chopped bacon. Fry until bacon is cooked. Beat eggs, add grated cheese, milk and cream. Season with salt and pepper. Stir in bacon and onion. Pour mixture into flan case. Bake in centre of hot oven 400°F. (Mark 6) for 25 minutes. Reduce heat to 375°F. (Mark 5) and cook for a further 10 minutes. Serve hot as the main course with salad or hot vegetables. Serve cold to take on a picnic; serve as part of a cold buffet.

DINNER PARTIES

Roast Duck

Served with Nutted Rice in Fluted Orange Cups.
Roast 1 or 2 ducks, according to size.

Nutted Rice in Fluted Orange Cups

1 pint Chicken Broth
8 oz. uncooked rice
2 dessertspoonfuls Butter or Margarine
4 oz. chopped Pecans or Walnuts
2 level dessertspoonfuls minced Parsley
Pulp and juice of 2 oranges, finely chopped or minced
Salt to taste

Method
In a saucepan, combine Chicken Broth, Orange Juice and Pulp and Rice. Bring to the boil. Stir. Cover and cook over low heat for 14 minutes. Remove from heat. Stir in butter, Pecans and Parsley. Season to taste. Flute orange cups and spoon the rice into the shell.
Serves 6 persons.

Mock Fillet Mignon

9 lb. minced steak
12 eggs
4 cloves garlic, crushed
3 tablespoonfuls salt
3 lb. sliced bacon
4 lb. cooked rice
2 lb. onions, minced
3 oz. powdered mushroom
$1\frac{1}{2}$ teaspoonfuls pepper

Method
Combine above ingredients, except bacon; mix well. Form into steaks $\frac{3}{4}''$ thick. Wrap each with a slice of bacon. Secure with a toothpick. Place on ungreased baking sheet. Bake at 405° for 15 minutes. Serve with mushroom sauce made from canned soup or 12 oz. dehydrated packaged mushroom soup mix.

Creole Jambalaya

$\frac{3}{4}$ lb. cooked ham
$\frac{3}{4}$ lb. jumbo prawns, shelled
$\frac{1}{2}$ lb. chorizo sausage
4 tablespoonfuls olive oil
2 tablespoonfuls butter
2 tablespoonfuls lard
1 spanish onion, finely chopped
$\frac{3}{4}$ lb. risotto rice
1 stalk celery, chopped
1 green pepper, finely chopped
6 tomatoes, peeled, seeded and chopped
1 small tin tomato concentrate
1 bay leaf, crumbled
$\frac{1}{2}$ level teaspoonful oregano
$\frac{1}{8}$ level teaspoonful thyme
$\frac{1}{8}$ level teaspoonful ground cloves
2 cloves garlic
Salt, freshly ground black pepper and cayenne
2 pints well-flavoured chicken stock
1 small glassful dry white wine
4 tablespoonfuls finely chopped parsley (optional)
Pitted black olives (optional)

Method
Cut ham into 1″ squares; shell and clean prawns and cut into smaller pieces if they are a little large; slice *chorizo* sausage (if not available, substitute pork or garlic sausage). Heat olive oil in a thick-bottomed frying pan and sauté ham chunks, prawns and sausage until they are golden brown. Reserve. Melt butter

Top picture Mock Fillet Mignon   Various methods of presenting Potatoes

and lard in the bottom of a large flame-proof casserole and sauté finely chopped Spanish onion until transparent. Stir in Italian rice (the kind you use to make a risotto) and cook over a low heat, stirring gently until the rice is golden. Add ham, prawn and sausage mixture to rice and stir in chopped celery, pepper, tomatoes and tomato concentrate, bay leaf, oregano, thyme, cloves, garlic and salt, freshly ground black pepper and cayenne, to taste. Bring chicken stock to the boil and pour over *jambalaya* mixture. Cover casserole and simmer over a low flame for 25-30 minutes—or until the rice is tender, but still separate— adding a little more liquid from time to time if necessary. Just before serving, stir in dry white wine, correct seasoning and keep warm in the lowest of ovens— or on a candle warmer—until ready to serve. A little finely chopped parsley or a handful of pitted black olives may be added if desired.
Serves 6 persons.

Crown Roast of Lamb with Mushroom Stuffing and Garnish

> 2 best end of neck joints of 6-7 cutlets each
> Stuffing
> Vegetables as desired
> Cutlet frills
> ½ lb. mushrooms

Method
Ask the butcher to cut out the back or chinebone, and then chop off 1-2 inches from both sets of rib bones so that they are all uniform length. Cut through the fat in a straight line about 1-1½ inches from the top of the rib bones, then trim each rib down to that line by cutting away all the fat and meat, leaving the bones bare. Cut away also any surplus fat from around the meat at the other end. Bend the two joints into the shape of a round crown with the meat inside and the bones outside. With a trussing needle or large darning needle and string, thread the flesh between the two end bones in two places at either side and pull the ends together firmly. Sprinkle the meat all over with salt. Stand the crown in a baking tin and fill the centre with stuffing, roughing up the top. Baste with melted dripping and roast at 350°F. (Mark 4) for 2 hours, basting occasionally. Wipe the mushrooms, trim the stalks level with the caps and sauté them in 1 oz. butter and 2 tablespoonfuls water per ½ lb., with the pan covered, for 2-3 minutes each side. Place the crown on a hot dish and put a cutlet frill on the end of each bone. Serve surrounded with the sautéed mushrooms and potato nests filled with peas, or plain piped Duchesse potatoes or new potatoes.

Stuffing

> 2 oz. mushrooms
> 1 small can paté de fois
> 1 small clove garlic (optional)
> 2 oz. breadcrumbs
> ½ teaspoonful chopped mint
> Salt and pepper

Method
Wipe the mushrooms and chop finely. Chop the garlic very finely and crush with the blade of a knife. Mix everything together and season well with salt and pepper.

Roast Duck served with Nutted Rice in
Fluted Orange Cups

DINNER PARTIES

Escalope of Veal with Mushroom and Artichoke Garnish

4 escalopes of veal
2 eggs
Breadcrumbs
Fat for frying
4 artichokes
½ lb. mushrooms
¼ pint double cream
1 teaspoonful cornflour
2 oz. butter

Method
Beat 1 egg and coat the veal in egg and breadcrumbs. Chop the mushrooms and put through a grinder until a fine purée is achieved. Cook the artichoke bottoms in hot water with butter and cornflour, then stir in the cream. Season and cook until the mixture is a thick cream. Fry the veal until just tender. Place the artichokes on top of the veal and fill with the mushroom purée. Add a touch of parsley before serving.

Swiss Veal Fillets

4 veal fillets
½ lb. open mushrooms
¼ pint cooking sherry
2 onions
4 oz. butter
6 oz. Gruyere cheese
¼ lb. white grapes

Method
Beat the veal fillets, season and cook in hot butter until tender. Slice the onions and simmer until tender, but not coloured. Put the veal onto a hot serving dish and cover each with sliced onion. Keep hot. Cook the mushrooms, whole, in plenty of hot butter with salt and pepper. Fry for 2 minutes each side, then place on top of the onions. Pour the sherry into the pan and mix with the juices. Stir over a fierce heat for a few moments, then pour a little over each fillet. Shred the Gruyere cheese and cover each fillet with a generous portion. Put under a hot grill until the cheese melts. Serve garnished with halved white grapes.

Tournedos with Mushroom Flambe

2 tournedos
3 oz. butter
½ gill cream
6 oz. mushrooms
2 tablespoonfuls brandy
Watercress

Method
Heat some butter in a frying pan; season the tournedos and fry quickly on both sides. Arrange on a hot dish. Slice the mushrooms and turn in hot butter with plenty of salt and pepper. Pour over the brandy and set alight. When the flames die down, pour in the cream. Spoon over the tournedos and garnish with bunches of watercress.

Viking Gammon Steaks

Allow approx. 6 oz. of gammon steak per person. Trim off rind, notch fat and brush lightly with melted fat. Grill slowly for 5 to 6 minutes. Turn. Grill other side until cooked through. Garnish with pineapple rings, first drained, dried, sprinkled with sugar and glazed under a really hot grill. Put a maraschino cherry in each ring. Serve with potato chips and watercress.

DINNER PARTIES

Duck with Orange Sauce

1 duck, 5-6 lb. in weight
2 oranges (peel of one to go
* inside the duck, peel of the*
* other one to be cut into julienne*
* strips to go into the sauce with*
* the orange segments)*
1 teaspoonful rosemary
Giblets from the duck
2 oz. onion
1 level teaspoonful salt
Pepper
½ pint water
½ can orange juice
1 oz. margarine
1 oz. flour
1 teaspoonful sugar
Sediment from the roasted duck

Method
Heat the oven to 375°F. (Mark 5). Prepare the duck for roasting, and place the thinly pared rind of one orange and the rosemary inside the duck. Place on trivet, in a baking tin, and place in the prepared oven. Wash the giblets, and put into a saucepan with the onion, salt, pepper, water and orange juice. Simmer for two hours. Pare the rind thinly from the second orange and cut the rind into thin strips about 1½" long. Cut all the pith from both oranges and cut the oranges into segments; put aside on a plate. Melt the butter in a saucepan, add the flour and cook for 2 minutes, strain the stock from the giblets, and gradually pour onto the butter and flour, stirring all the time. Bring to the boil and cook for 3 minutes. Add the julienne strips, cook gently for 2 minutes, then add the sugar and orange segments to the sauce. Arrange the duck on a hot serving dish, and keep hot. Drain the fat from the roasting tin and stir the sediment from the roasting tin into the sauce. Pour some of the sauce over the duck, and serve the rest in a sauce boat.

Kidneys a la berrichonne (rognons a la berrichonne)

Take veal or lamb kidneys from which the fat has been removed and cut into fine slices. Fry in a pan on a very quick fire with a mixture of half oil, half butter. Add a few small rashers of bacon and mushrooms. (The stalks of flap mushrooms will do excellently). When well browned take out the kidneys, bacon and mushrooms; keep hot. Throw a pinch of chopped shallots into the pan; allow to stand for an instant; add a teaspoonful of flour and a large glass of red wine. Let the sauce thicken slightly; season with salt and pepper to taste; finish with a pat of fresh butter and mix this sauce with the kidneys, mushrooms and bacon. Serve with croutons of toast.

Bacon with Leeks and Tomato Sauce

Choose middle cut rashers. Keep them whole and grill them until cooked and well browned. Cook leeks until tender. Make tomato sauce using ½ pt. white sauce flavoured with leek stock, small (5 oz.) tin tomato purée and ½ teaspoonful curry powder. Season to taste. Arrange bacon rashers and leeks alternately on dish. Pour tomato sauce over.

DINNER PARTIES

Luxury Mince Pie

—with the magic of ginger.
Make a rich short-crust pastry and line
a deep flan ring with it. Then fill with
mincemeat to which has been added
the grated rind of an orange and lemon.
2 tablespoonfuls chopped stem ginger
and a glassful of ginger wine. Cover
with a short crust and brush over with
water and a little castor sugar. Bake in
a hot oven (400-425°F. or Mark 6/7).

Maple Rice Pudding

2 lb. 12 oz. uncooked rice
4¾ pints water
2 tablespoonfuls salt
18 eggs
7 pints warm milk
1½ lb. sugar
¾ lb. melted butter
2 lb. raisins
2 tablespoonfuls vanilla
2 tablespoonfuls maple flavouring
¾ teaspoonful salt
10 oz. chopped nuts
1 lb. sugar

Method
Combine rice, water, and salt in a large
pan. Bring to the boil, lower heat,
cover and simmer about 18 minutes or
until rice is tender and liquid absorbed.
Divide rice in half and turn into two
long steam table pans, buttered.
Sprinkle 1 lb. raisins into each pan.
Beat egg yolk slightly; add milk,
1½ lb. sugar, butter and vanilla. Pour
over rice mixture; mix well. Cover and
bake at 350°F about 45 minutes
stirring occasionally. Beat egg white
until foamy. Add 1 lb. sugar gradually
and continue beating until whites
stand in stiff peaks. Fold in maple
flavouring and salt. Spread over cooked
pudding. Sprinkle with nuts. Bake at
350°F for 10 minutes or until golden
brown. Serve warm or cold.
Serves 50 persons.

Chocolate Orange Soufflé

3 eggs
½ gill water
2 oz. castor sugar
½ oz. gelatine
1 dessertspoonful cocoa
1½ gills evaporated milk or
   fresh cream
2 tablespoonfuls orange curacao
For decoration
   Tin mandarin oranges
   Glacé cherry
   Fresh whipped cream

Method
Cut a strip of paper long enough to go
round the soufflé dish, overlapping
slightly, and sufficiently deep to reach
from the bottom to approximately 2″
above the top of the dish. Place round
the outside so that it fits exactly. Pin
firmly into position, or tie with string.
Put sieved cocoa, egg yolks, and
sugar into a bowl and heat over a pan
of hot water whisking all the time, until
thick and creamy. Add the curacao.
Whip the cream or evaporated milk
and add this to the thickened mixture.
Dissolve the gelatine in 1 tablespoonful hot water. Stir into the other
ingredients. Allow to cool and then
fold in the· stiffly beaten egg whites.
Pour into the prepared dish and stand
in a cold place until firm. Just before
serving remove the paper from the side
of the soufflé and decorate with flaked
almonds, mandarin oranges and fresh
whipped cream.

169

DINNER PARTIES

Spicy Rice Peaches

8 large canned peach halves
6 oz. cooked rice
2 tablespoonfuls brown sugar
$\frac{1}{8}$ teaspoonful cinnamon
2 tablespoonfuls slivered almonds
1 tablespoonful butter or margarine

Method
Drain peach halves. Place rounded side down on baking sheet. Combine rice with brown sugar and cinnamon. Spoon into peach halves. Insert slivered almonds into rice. Dot with butter. Grill about 5 minutes.
Serves 4 persons.

Almond Mallow Trifles

4 almond macaroons
4 tablespoonfuls fresh orange juice, sherry or brandy
Approximately 8 apricot halves
$\frac{1}{4}$ pint double cream
2 oz. Marshmallows, each cut into 4
1 oz. blanched almonds, lightly toasted then coarsely chopped (optional)

Method
Break up macaroons and mix with fruit juice or sherry. Leave for 30 minutes—or till macaroons have absorbed most of the liquid — then divide equally between 4 individual dishes. Arrange apricot halves on top. Whip cream till thick, add Marshmallows then spoon on top of apricots. Chill. Sprinkle with nuts before serving.
Serves 4 persons.

Four Fruit Flan

Colourful—and a good way of using up left-over fruits.

A baked 7-8" sandwich cake (1 layer only)
3-4 tablespoonfuls apricot jam or redcurrant jelly, melted
8 Marshmallows, halved
4 different fruits (sliced bananas, halved grapes, stoned cherries, small strawberries, raspberries, tinned mandarins, tinned pineapple, tinned peach slices, etc.)

Method
Spread top of sandwich cake with melted jam or jelly and divide into 4 equal sections with halved Marshmallows. Cover each section with a different fruit then spoon over melted jam or jelly to glaze. Accompany with cream.
Note: Even better if the cake is first sprinkled with a little sherry.
Serves 4-6 persons.

Mallow Jelly Trifle

Stale sponge cake
4 oz. Marshmallows, halved
1 raspberry, strawberry or blackcurrant jello,
$\frac{1}{2}$-$\frac{3}{4}$ pint stewed fruit (not too sweet)
1 pint custard, freshly made

Method
Break up cake then put, with the Marshmallows, into a large serving dish. Make up jello as directed on the packet and when cool and just beginning to thicken, pour over cake and Marshmallows. Leave to set then cover with a layer of stewed fruit. Top with freshly made custard and cool. Just before serving, decorate with pink and white Marshmallows and angelica.

Spicey Rice Peaches

DINNER PARTIES

Lemon and Pineapple Soufflé

Lemon jello mix
1 medium-sized tin pineapple
3 eggs
2 oz. castor sugar
¼ pint whipped cream or
    evaporated milk

To decorate
Angelica
Glacé cherries
Little extra whipped cream

Method

Strain juice from the tin of pineapple. Add enough water to the pineapple juice to make ¾ pint liquid. Heat this and dissolve the lemon jello in the hot liquid. Allow this to cool. Meanwhile chop most of the pineapple finely and add to the lemon jello. Beat egg yolk and sugar and fold this mixture into the cold lemon jello together with the whipped cream. Lastly, when the mixture is just beginning to stiffen, fold in the stiffly beaten egg whites. Pour into a prepared soufflé dish. When quite firm decorate with tiny flower shapes of cherry and pineapple and leaves of angelica. Pipe a little cream round edge of the soufflé.

Paradise Pears

¼ pint red wine
¼ pint cold water
4 medium-sized pears (not too
    soft)
4 oz. lump sugar
1 heaped teaspoonful powdered
    arrowroot
3 or 4 drops cochineal

Method

Mix wine and water in a saucepan with a heavy base. Add sugar and cochineal. Dissolve over gentle heat. Then boil until syrupy. Do not stir but watch pan from time to time. Peel each pear carefully, leaving stalk but removing eye. Stand pears, stalk upwards, in the pan of syrup. Take a circle of paper and place it over the pears. Make four holes in paper for stalks to poke through. Boil for about 7 minutes. Baste pears once or twice. Pears should be tender but not too soft. Carefully remove pears. Put them on to a nice dish (stainless steel, silver or white for effect). If syrup is too thin boil it again until it thickens. Mix arrowroot with a little cold water. Stir into mixture. Boil, stirring, for about 7 minutes. When thickened and really clear, allow to cool. Pour over and around pears and serve.

Strawberry Mousse

12 oz. strawberries, washed and
    hulled (reserve a few for
    decoration)
3 oz. castor sugar
1 envelope gelatine
4 oz. Marshmallows
¼ pint orange juice, fresh or tinned
4 tablespoonfuls single cream
2 egg whites

Method

Crush fruit and combine with sugar. Over a very low heat, melt gelatine and Marshmallows in the orange juice. Add to crushed fruit then leave in a cool place till thick but not set. Stir in cream. Whisk egg whites till stiff then fold into strawberry mixture. Turn into a fancy 2-pint mould—first rinsed with cold water—and leave till firm and set. Turn out on to a dish.

Paradise Pears

Rice Pear Melba

Rice Pear Melba

4 oz. uncooked rice
½ pt. water
½ teaspoonful salt
¾ pt. milk
2 cinnamon sticks
2 oz. sugar
½ pt. double cream, whipped
16 pear halves, drained
¼ pt. red currant jelly, melted
2 tablespoonfuls Kirsch (optional)
2 oz. Cashew nuts (chopped)

Method
Combine rice, water, and salt. Heat to boiling. Cover and cook 5 minutes. Add milk, cinnamon sticks, and sugar. Cook over low heat, stirring occasionally until thickened, about 30 minutes. Remove from heat; discard cinnamon sticks. Cool. Fold in whipped cream. Chill. Fasten pear halves together with a little of the rice mixture, the remainder spoon into dessert dishes and top with pear halves, cut side down. Mix melted jelly with Kirsch. Spoon over fruit and sprinkle with nuts.
Serves 8 persons.

Trifle

8 sponge cakes
Apricot and raspberry jam
6 oz. macaroon biscuits
4 oz. ratafias
2 oz. shredded almonds
Sherry as required
¾ pint thick custard
½ pint cream

Method
Halve sponge cakes lengthwise. Put halves together with apricot jam. Cut in three cross-wise. Spread cut sides with raspberry jam. Pile in glass trifle dish. Crumble the macaroons and sprinkle over the cake. Arrange the ratafias round the edge. Sprinkle evenly with the almonds then with sherry, using only ¼ pint of sherry then adding up to ½ pint if required. It must all be absorbed. Stand for 30 minutes. Leave custard till tepid, then pour over. Chill. Whip cream. Sweeten with castor sugar and flavour with vanilla essence. Pile rockily on top. Decorate with posies of glacé cherries and angelica.

Make the most of the strawberry season, but instead of just strawberries and cream try:

Chocolate Flan Whip

2 eggs
2 oz. castor sugar
2 oz. self-raising flour
1 dessertspoonful cocoa
½ packet plain gelatine
¼ pint boiling water
¼ pint evaporated milk or cream
Glacé cherries
Almonds

Method
Whisk the eggs and sugar until thick and fluffy. Fold in the sieved flour and cocoa. Pour into a well greased 8" flan tin. Bake in oven 375°F. (Mark 5) for about 15-20 minutes. Cool on a wire tray. Dissolve the gelatine in the boiling water. Allow to cool and thicken slightly. Add the evaporated milk or cream and whisk until the mixture is light and fluffy. Pour in to the flan case. Put in to a cool place until firm. Decorate with glacé cherries and split almonds.

DINNER PARTIES

Banana Chartreuse

Lemon jello mix
$\frac{1}{4}$ pint whipped cream
1 pint milk
Packet banana-flavoured
   blancmange powder
2 oz. sugar
4 or 5 sliced bananas
To decorate
   Angelica
   Glacé cherries
   Whipped cream

Method
Dissolve the lemon jello in hot water. Pour a little into a mould and allow to set. Arrange the sliced bananas and tiny pieces of angelica and cherry on this jello. Carefully spoon over a little more jello and allow to set. Leave the remainder of the jello in a basin to set. Make the banana-flavoured blancmange as directed on the packet using the milk and sugar. When cool, fold in the whipped cream and the remaining sliced bananas. Pour over the jello. Turn out and decorate with whisked lemon jello, leaves of angelica and cherries.

Florence Creams

$1\frac{1}{4}$ oz. custard powder or
   cornflour or a packet of vanilla-
   flavoured blancmange powder
1 pint milk
1 oz. sugar
2 or 3 egg yolks or 2 whole eggs
For the caramel
   3 oz. granulated or castor sugar
   3 tablespoonfuls water
To decorate
   Little cream
   Shredded browned almonds

Method
First make the caramel. Put the sugar and water into a saucepan and stir until the sugar has melted. Boil steadily, without stirring, until sugar is golden-brown. Cool, then add $\frac{3}{4}$ pint milk to the caramel and heat gently until the milk has absorbed the caramel flavour. Blend custard powder with the remainder of the milk and sugar, and pour warm caramel liquid over this, then return to the pan and cook until thick and smooth. Add beaten eggs and cook *without* boiling for several minutes. Pour into glasses and allow to set. Top with lightly whipped cream and browned almonds. To brown almonds first remove skins (blanch) by putting the almonds into a saucepan of boiling water for a minute. Dry nuts, cut into thin shreds and brown under the grill or in the oven.

Pineapple Cardinal

Drain canned pineapple rings, allow two per person. Place a slice of jam Swiss roll or other sponge cake in the base of individual glasses. Spoon over a little pineapple juice and kirsch. Top each with two twisted pineapple rings, glaze with Sauce Melba. Serve with Chantilly cream (optional). Or from the refrigerator take a block of vanilla or walnut ice cream, cut into thick slices, spoon over Banana Dessert Sauce, top with toasted almonds and crushed brittle. For a split, slice a whole banana lengthwise, fill with ice cream and Banana Dessert Sauce. When a more hearty pudding is called for offer hot canned chocolate or ginger pudding with Apricot Dessert Sauce.

176

DINNER PARTIES

Apricot Cream Flan

7 or 8 in. pastry.flan case—baked
  until crisp and golden-brown
Medium-sized tin apricots
½ packet vanilla blancmange
  powder
2 oz. sugar
¼ pint milk
½ gill whipped cream
For the glaze
¼ pint apricot syrup
1 teaspoonful cornflour
To decorate
Halved apricots
Little cream if wished
Angelica and almonds

Method

Open tin of apricots and drain fruit. Mash half the apricots or put them through a sieve. Blend blancmange powder with a little cold milk. Bring rest of milk to the boil, pour over blancmange, return to pan and thicken, adding sugar. Cool, then fold in cream and apricot purée. Pour into flan case. Top with halved apricots and angelica or almonds. To make the glaze blend the cornflour and fruit syrup until smooth. Put into pan and boil until thick and clear. Cool, then coat the top of the fruit with this. Decorate with cream if wished.

Orange Ice Cream Baskets

4 large oranges
1 small block vanilla ice cream
Glacé cherries and angelica to
  decorate

Method

Cut a large slice from the stalk end of orange to form a cup shape. Scoop out half of the orange flesh by cutting around outer rim between flesh and pith and removing this section of orange. Fill remaining cavity of orange with a large scoop of ice cream and decorate with a glacé cherry and leaves of angelica.

Note: An excellent idea of using oranges for parties !

Caroni Rum Truffles

4 oz. best plain chocolate
2 oz. unsalted butter
1 tablespoonful Navy Rum
1 tablespoonful fresh cream
Icing sugar
Chocolate vermicelli

Method

Chop the chocolate, and melt it with the butter in the top of a double saucepan. When smooth, remove from the heat and stir in cream and rum. Stand in a cool place until set. Beat up well and stir in sufficient icing sugar to produce a soft paste (2-3 oz.) Set aside again to firm, then roll into balls between the hands and coat with chocolate vermicelli. Allow to harden in a cool place.

Baked Bananas

6 small bananas
2 tablespoonfuls apple or quince
  jelly
2 tablespoonfuls claret
Castor sugar as required

Method

Peel, and halve bananas lengthwise. Place side by side in a shallow buttered fireproof dish. Spread each with jelly, then sprinkle with claret. Dredge lightly with castor sugar. Bake in a moderate oven, 350°F., for 20 minutes. Serve with cream.

CHILDREN'S PARTIES

Yogurt Drop Scones

$\frac{1}{4}$ pint yogurt
1 egg
2 level tablespoonfuls plain flour,
   sifted with a pinch of salt
A little lard for frying

Method
Beat the egg. Put the yogurt into a bowl, add the egg and beat well. Add the sifted flour and salt, and fold into the mixture. Heat a little lard in a frying pan and when a haze rises from it, drop dessertspoonfuls of the mixture into it. Cook until golden brown on underside, then, using a palette knife, turn to cook the other side in the same way. Drain on kitchen paper when cooked and keep hot, until all are cooked. Serve immediately with butter, jam or honey for tea, or as a sweet, with lemon juice, sugar or syrup.
Makes approximately 12 scones.

Chocolate Mallow Pie

1 x 9" pie case or flan case—
   baked blind
1 pint milk
2 oz. plain chocolate
3 oz. flour
$\frac{1}{2}$ level teaspoonful salt
$\frac{1}{4}$ pint milk
4 oz. marshmallows (about 16)
3 eggs
2 tablespoonfuls butter or margarine
1 teaspoonful vanilla essence
6 tablespoonfuls castor sugar

Method
Heat the pint of milk with the chocolate and marshmallows in a double pan until melted. Into a basin sieve the flour and salt. Mix to a smooth paste with the $\frac{1}{4}$ pint of cold water, gradually stirring in the chocolate mixture. Return to the cleaned pan and heat until the mixture thickens. Continue to cook over boiling water for 5-7 minutes, stirring occasionally. Stir 3 tablespoonfuls of the mixture into the slightly beaten egg yolks. Return to the mixture in the double pan. Cook for a further 3-5 minutes, stirring all the time. Remove from heat. Stir in the butter and vanilla essence. Cover and cool. When cooled sufficiently pour into the flan case and chill in the refrigerator or a cool place. Prepare the meringue by beating the egg whites and salt until very stiff. Fold in the castor sugar using a metal spoon. Pile the meringue onto the filling, being sure to seal it to the crust. Bake at 350°F. (Mark 4) for 10-15 minutes or until the meringue is delicately brown. Cool. Streak meringue with melted chocolate.

Cream Swiss Roll

3 eggs
4 oz. castor sugar
3 oz. flour
$\frac{1}{2}$ tablespoonful hot water
1 gill whipped cream
$\frac{1}{2}$ tablespoonful warm jam

Method
Grease a swiss roll tin and line with greased paper. Warm and sieve the flour. Beat eggs and sugar until thick and creamy. Fold in flour. Add sufficient tepid water to make a pouring consistency. Turn into a prepared tin and spread out to corners. Bake in a hot oven 7-10 minutes. 450-475°F. (Mark 7-8). Turn onto a sugared paper. Roll with paper and leave to cool. Unroll, spread with warm jam and whipped cream. Then roll up.

Chocolate Mallow Pie

CHILDREN'S PARTIES

Honey Christmas Cookie Trees

Every child likes to have 'one of my own' and with these Honey Christmas Cookie Trees every child can have his own little tree. The trees are made from a simple honey biscuit mixture sandwiched together with a delicious fruity filling. The height of the trees can vary according to the size and numbers of cutters used.

Cookie mixture
- *1 lb. self-raising flour*
- *½ level teaspoonful cinnamon*
- *¼ level teaspoonful ginger*
- *1 level teaspoonful grated lemon rind*
- *6 oz. butter or margarine*
- *7 level tablespoonfuls honey (clear)*

Filling
- *1 packet whipped topping mix*
- *1 teaspoonful vanilla essence*
- *7 oz. chopped seedless raisins*
- *2 oz. chopped nuts*
- *2 oz. chopped green glacé cherries*
- *2 oz chopped red glacé cherries*

Method
To make cookies, sieve dry ingredients together, add lemon rind and rub in butter until mixture resembles fine breadcrumbs. Melt the honey over a very gentle heat and pour into the mixture. Work in by hand until a dough is formed. Knead lightly on a floured board and roll out thinly. Using graduated plain cutters 2½", 2", 1¾", 1½" and 1¼", cut eight circles of each size, or more if there is dough over. Bake on greased baking sheets in a cool oven 300°F. (Mark 2) for 20-25 minutes. Cool on a wire tray. Prepare filling by whipping topping as directed on pack. Add remaining ingredients. Spread over cookies and stack in graduated sizes to make five-layer 'trees'.
Makes 8-9 trees

Fruit Cocktail and Mallow Whip

- *1 lb. can fruit cocktail*
- *¼ lb. marshmallows*
- *1 small can of milk*
- *1 dessertspoonful castor sugar*
- *Juice of half a lemon*

Method
Cut the mallows into eighths. This will be easy if the knife blade is dipped into icing sugar first. Drain most of the juice from the fruit and then add the fruit to the mallows. Mix together then place in the refrigerator for about one hour. Whip the milk until thick and creamy. Add the lemon juice and sugar and continue to beat for a few minutes more. Combine the milk with the fruit and mallows. Place in individual dishes and serve.
Serves 5-6 persons.

Cream Slices

- *1 packet frozen puff pastry*
- *Raspberry jam*
- *¼ pint double dairy cream*

Method
Roll out pastry to fit baking sheet 10" x 12". Using back of knife, cut into 15 squares. Brush with water and sprinkle with castor sugar. Place in centre of oven at 450-475°F. (Mark 7-8), and bake for about 10 minutes. Split and fill with jam and whipped cream. Makes 15 cakes.

Honey Christmas Cookie Trees

CHILDREN'S PARTIES

Creamed Strawberry Shortbreads

5 oz. flour
1 dessertspoonful cocoa
Pinch of salt
2 oz. castor sugar
4 oz. butter
Fresh cream or butter cream
Strawberries

Method
Sieve the flour, cocoa and salt into a bowl. Stir in the sugar. Add the butter and mix until a smooth paste is obtained. Roll out and cut into rounds. Bake in oven 350°F. (Mark 4) for 20-30 minutes. Sprinkle with sugar while still hot then allow to cool. To decorate just before serving pile or pipe on the fresh whipped cream and decorate with strawberries.

Party Chicks

Sponge
4 oz. margarine
4 oz. castor sugar
2 eggs—slightly whisked
4 oz. self-raising flour—sieved
Decoration
Apricot preserves, sieved and boiled
Desiccated coconut—coarse
Skinned halved almonds
Saffron yellow colouring
Currants

Method
Grease and line a 12″ x 8″ x ½″ Swiss Roll tin with greaseproof paper to a depth of 1″. Cream margarine and sugar till light and fluffy. Add egg in tablespoonfuls to avoid curdling and beat in well after each addition. Fold in (do not beat) flour and mix in

thoroughly. Transfer the mixture to the prepared tin, smooth and level the mixture in the tin and bake in a moderately hot oven 350°F. (Mark 4) for about 25-30 minutes. Cool on a wire tray. When cold, cut into rounds with a 2½″ pastry cutter. Use a 1″ pastry cutter for the head. Fix body to stand with preserves. Brush stand, body and head with preserves and toss in coconut. Join head to body with preserves. Position almonds and currants to represent beaks and eyes.
To Colour Almonds
Halve lengthwise and soak for 15 minutes in saffron colouring. Rinse in cold water and dry ready for use.

Butterscotch Sauce

(for Sundaes and Ice Cream Topping)
4 oz. Golden Syrup
4 oz. soft brown sugar
1 oz. butter
2 tablespoonfuls boiling water
4 tablespoonfuls evaporated milk or thin cream
½ teaspoonful vanilla essence

Method
Put syrup, sugar and butter in a heavy saucepan and stir gently over a low heat until sugar is dissolved. Boil steadily for three minutes. Remove from heat and add boiling water carefully. Cool slightly, then add milk and vanilla essence. Serve hot or cold, adding a little more milk if the sauce is thicker than desired.
To assemble Butterscotch Sundae
Fill a tall glass with alternate spoonfuls of a favourite ice cream, sauce, and fruit such as sliced banana. Top off with whipped cream. Decorate with toasted nuts, or grated chocolate, and a cherry.

Top picture Creamed Strawberry Shortbreads

Party Chicks

Raisin Mocha Meringue Pie

Meringue:
  2 egg whites
  Pinch cream of tartar
  4 oz. castor sugar
  ½ teaspoonful vanilla essence
Filling
  8 oz. seedless raisins
  8 fluid oz. water
  2 rounded teaspoonfuls instant coffee
  6 oz. semi-sweet chocolate
  ½ pint double cream

Method

To make meringue case, whisk egg whites and cream of tartar together until stiff. Gradually add sugar and continue whisking. Blend in vanilla essence. Butter a deep 8-inch pie plate and spread meringue over bottom and up sides. Bake in a slow oven (gas No. 2–275°F.) for 1 hour. Turn off heat, open door and leave in oven for another half an hour. Cool thoroughly. To make filling, put raisins, water and coffee into a small pan, bring to boil and simmer for 5 minutes. Cover and let stand until cold. Melt chocolate in a basin over warm water. Whip cream. Fold chocolate into cream and add raisins. Turn into meringue case. Chill.

Strawberry Gateau

  4 oz. margarine
  4 oz. castor sugar
  1 level dessertspoonful honey
  2 eggs
  5 oz. self raising flour
  ½ level teaspoonful baking powder
  3 tablespoonfuls milk

Decoration
  ¼ pint double cream
  Strawberries

Method

Slice up margarine and put into a warm mixing bowl, with honey, eggs and all other ingredients. Beat well for ½-1 minute. Put into a well-greased 7-inch ring tin. Bake in a moderately hot oven (gas No. 5–375°F.) for 25-30 minutes. Cool. Whip cream and sweeten if liked. Coat cake all over. Fill centre with strawberries and decorate round edge.
Serves 4-6 persons.
Note: The centre may be filled with ice-cream if liked, and decorated with strawberries.

Pineapple Upside-Down Cake

  1 packet pineapple flavour jello
  *12 oz. can pineapple rings
    (do not use fresh pineapple)*
  2 oz. glacé cherries
  1 layer 8" sandwich cake
  4 tablespoonfuls sweet sherry
  For decoration
  2 oz. finely chopped almonds

Method

Place jello in basin. Add ½ pint boiling water, stir until dissolved. Drain syrup from can of pineapple. (Fresh pineapple should not be used). Dry rings, place with cherries in base of an 8" cake tin. Spoon over four tablespoonfuls of jello. Place cake on top, moisten with sherry and a little pineapple juice. When remaining jello is beginning to thicken, pour over cake. Leave to set. Turn out onto plate. Decorate sides with chopped almonds.
Serves 6 persons.

Top picture Raisin Mocha Meringue Pie   *Strawberry Gateau*

CHILDREN'S PARTIES

Melbourne Walnut and Pineapple Log

1 swiss roll
Pineapple jam
Chopped walnuts
1 can pineapple rings
¼ pint double cream
Glacé cherries
Angelica
Swiss Roll
3 eggs
3 oz. sugar
2 oz. plain flour
Caster sugar
3 teaspoonfuls finely chopped
*   walnuts*

Method

Swiss Roll: Whisk the eggs and sugar until thick and creamy. Fold in sieved flour and chopped nuts. Pour into a flat 12" baking tin lined with greased greaseproof paper. Bake in the oven at 450°F. (Mark 8) for 7 minutes. Turn out onto sugared paper and spread with warm pineapple jam. Trim edges and roll. Leave to cool on wire rack. Spread outside of the roll with whipped cream, then roll in chopped walnuts. Cut into slices. Re-assemble the swiss roll with slices of pineapple between slices of sponge. Decorate with whipped cream, cherries and angelica. *Serves 6 persons.*

Old-fashioned Toffee

2 oz. Golden Syrup
1 lb. cube sugar
¼ pint water
2 teaspoonfuls vinegar or lemon
*   juice*
½ level teaspoonful cream of tartar
3 oz. butter

Method

Put syrup, sugar, water and vinegar into a large, heavy saucepan and dissolve together carefully over low heat, stirring as necessary. Add cream of tartar dissolved in a little water, bring to the boil and cook briskly, without stirring, to 285-290°F. At this temperature a drop tested in cold water will snap easily. Remove from heat and add butter in small pieces without stirring, then reboil to previous temperature (285°F.). Pour into an oiled tin and break up when cold.

Coconut Ice

Use about four times weight of sugar to coconut. Dissolve sugar in a little cold water and boil the syrup until it reaches 240°F. or until it will form a soft ball when dropped into cold water. Remove from the fire and add the coconut. Stir until thick, pour into a greased tin and cut into bars when cold. A knob of butter added after boiling will improve the flavour.

Coconut Ice (Fudge type)

1 lb. sugar
½ pint water
1 large tin condensed milk
½ lb. coconut

Method

Place the sugar and water in a saucepan and bring to the boil. Add the condensed milk and cook at 235-240°F. or until it will form a soft ball when dropped in cold water. Remove from heat and add the coconut. Stir until beginning to thicken. Pour the mixture into an oiled or wetted tin. When cold cut in bars.

187

CHILDREN'S PARTIES

Toffee Apples

12 medium-sized dessert apples,
 preferably with rosy red skins
6 oz. Golden Syrup
12 oz. soft brown sugar
1 oz. butter
¼ pint water
1 teaspoonful lemon juice or
 vinegar

Method

Wash and dry apples thoroughly. Remove stalks and force a wooden skewer into the stalk end of each. Put all the other ingredients into a heavy saucepan and heat gently until the sugar is fully dissolved, stirring as necessary. Bring to the boil and cook briskly, without stirring, until a drop tested in cold water will snap cleanly (290°F.). Dip apples into the toffee, twisting to coat completely, and then immediately into a bowl of cold water. Leave to set on a greased tray. Eat soon afterwards as toffee tends to become sticky on exposure to atmosphere.

Crispy Fruit Balls

4 oz. marshmallows
2 oz. butter
2 oz. glacé cherries, chopped
2 oz. sultanas
1 oz. walnuts, chopped
1 teaspoonful grated orange rind
2 oz. (two 10-oz. measuring cups)
 Rice Krispies

Method

Melt marshmallows and butter together. Remove from heat and stir in remaining ingredients. Cool slightly. With well-greased hands, form the mixture into 1" balls. Leave in a cool place until set. Makes approximately two dozen.

Orange and Banana Ring

¼ lb. sugar
¼ pint water
6 bananas
Juice of 2 oranges
1 teaspoonful lemon juice
Sponge flan case
½ pint double dairy cream
 (whipped)
Crystallised orange slices

Method

Dissolve the sugar in the water. Bring to the boil, then add the bananas and cut into slices. Simmer for 10 minutes. Add the orange and lemon juice. Leave to cool. Place the sponge flan case on a serving dish. Fill the centre with the cold mixture and pile stiffly whipped cream on top. Decorate with crystallised orange slices.

Velvet Cream

Cold custard made with ½ pint milk
 (same consistency as cream)
¼ pint double dairy cream
¼ oz. gelatine
2 tablespoonfuls water
Glacé cherries
Angelica

Method

Blend the custard with most of the double dairy cream (leaving the remainder for decoration). Dissolve the gelatine in 2 tablespoonfuls warm water and strain it into the cream mixture. Stir lightly until the mixture begins to set, then pour into a wetted mould. When set, turn out and decorate with glacé cherries, angelica and remaining double dairy cream (whipped).

Toffee Apples

CHILDREN'S PARTIES

Chocolate Banana Sundae

1 banana
Flaked or chopped almonds
Ice cream
Ice cream wafers
Chocolate Sauce
  3 oz. brown sugar
  1½ oz. cocoa
  ¼ pint milk
  Vanilla essence

Method
To make the Chocolate sauce
Put all the ingredients into a saucepan. Stir until the sugar has completely dissolved, then boil for 2 minutes or until thick enough to coat the back of a spoon. Allow to cool. Now put the ice cream into individual sundae dishes. Quickly cut each banana into eight pieces and dip in lemon juice to prevent discolouration. Arrange around the edge of the ice cream. Pour chocolate sauce over the ice cream and sprinkle with chopped nuts. Top each with an ice cream wafer. Serve at once.
Serves 1 person.

Pineapple and Banana Ice Cream Topping

2 bananas
1 tin crushed pineapple
Juice of half a lemon
1 block dairy ice cream

Method
Mix the pineapple, lemon juice and sliced bananas together taking care to see that all the banana slices get covered by the pineapple to prevent browning. Divide the ice cream onto individual plates and top with the fruit mix. Serve at once.
Serves 5-6 persons.

Orange Meringue Cups

Perfect for a children's party, being hot on the outside, cold inside, and wonderfully pretty indeed.
  2 egg whites (large eggs)
  4 large oranges
  4 oz. castor sugar
  1 ice-cream brick

Method
Cut 'lids' off oranges, scoop out pulp and remove pith. Chop pulp, divide it into 4 and return to orange cups. Put in a cold place for ½ hour. Beat whites until very stiff (so they stay in the basin when turned upside-down). Beat in 2 dessertspoons of the sugar; when stiff fold in the rest. Put meringue in a forcing bag. Place a portion of ice cream on top of orange pulp, then pipe a generous whirl of meringue on top, completely covering the ice cream. Put the orange cups in a very hot oven, for about 1 minute, to allow meringue to lightly brown. Serve immediately.

Moroccan Jelly Cups

4 oranges
1 packet orange jello
Angelica
Whipped cream to decorate

Method
Cut top from oranges approximately ⅓ of the way down. Scoop out flesh leaving pith intact. Make up packet jello as directed making up quantity with orange pulp. Pour jello into orange cups. Leave to set in refrigerator. When set, pipe whipped cream round edge of cup and decorate with angelica leaves or angelica handles.

Chocolate Banana Sundae

Top picture   Custard Slices

Party Layer Loaf

CHILDREN'S PARTIES

Custard Slices

$\frac{1}{2}$ lb. Puff Pastry
Water-Icing
Custard Filling
$\frac{3}{4}$ oz. Custard Powder
2 oz. sugar
$\frac{1}{2}$ pint milk

Method

Roll out pastry $\frac{1}{8}$" thick and cut into strips, 4" wide. Bake for about 15 minutes at 475°F. (Mark 9). Prepare the custard in the normal manner but return to the saucepan and bring to the boil. Allow to cool. When the pastry is cold spread custard on one strip and cover with another strip. Coat with a little water-icing, flavoured with vanilla essence. When the icing has set cut into pieces about $1\frac{1}{2}$" wide.

Orange Chiffon Pie

1 packet orange flavour jello
8 oz. shortcrust pastry
2 eggs
3 oz. castor sugar
For decoration
$\frac{1}{4}$ pint double cream
1 orange

Method

Line a 7-8" shallow pie dish with pastry. Bake at 450°F. (Mark 7) until golden brown. Boil $\frac{1}{4}$ pint of water in a saucepan and remove from heat; put jelly in pan and stir until dissolved. Leave until beginning to thicken. Meanwhile whisk eggs and sugar until thick in basin over pan of simmering water. Remove from heat, whisk until cold. Fold in jello. When beginning to set, spoon into pastry shell. When set, decorate with whipped cream and orange segments. As an alternative to pastry, a sponge flan case can be used. Serves 6 persons.

Party Layer Loaf

1 lb. cottage cheese or
    2 large cartons
2 tablespoonfuls whipped cream
    (optional)
1 tablespoonful mayonnaise
Seasoning to taste
1 sandwich loaf
Varied sandwich fillings
Fruit and salad garnish such as
    peach halves or pineapple slices
Clusters of grapes, radishes,
    cucumber, tomato, olives, cress
    or lettuce.

Method

Beat or sieve the cottage cheese and blend with the cream and mayonnaise. Season to taste and chill. (If the weather is very hot add 1 level dessertspoonful gelatine dissolved in 1 tablespoonful boiling water). Slice the crust off the loaf (reserving crusts for fruit scallops or oven-crisped crumbs) and cut the length of the loaf in 3 or 4 slices. Sandwich with savoury colourful fillings, buttering only if the filling needs the blandness and moisture of the butter. Place on serving platter and spread the cottage cheese mixture over top and sides. Garnish with fruit and salad vegetables.

Suggested fillings:

Minced gammon dressed with mustard, a little chopped gherkin and mayonnaise. . . flaked tuna fish and capers bound with mayonnaise. . . chopped hard-boiled eggs, a little chopped anchovy and mayonnaise. . . minced beef moistened with tomato purée, seasoned with mustard.

CHILDREN'S PARTIES

Fruit Ice

$\frac{1}{4}$ lb. sugar
$\frac{3}{8}$ pint (15 tablespoonfuls) water
1 egg
2 cans strained pears
Juice of 1 lemon
$\frac{1}{8}$ pint double cream

Method
Boil the water and sugar for 10 minutes. Separate the egg yolk from the white and add the yolk to the strained pears. Add the hot sugar syrup, stirring continuously. Stir in the lemon juice and place in a shallow container in the freezing compartment of a refrigerator. When set to a creamy consistency fold in the stiffly beaten egg white and the lightly whipped cream. Return to the freezer until stiff.
This basic recipe can be used in several ways:
Set the fruit ice in a ring mould, turn out and fill the centre with fruit. Set the fruit ice in a deep container, spoon into sundae glasses and serve with pears, chocolate sauce and chopped nuts. Set the fruit ice in a deep container, spoon out into an orange skin basket, and intersperse the fruit ice with the orange segments.

Puff Brittle

6 oz. Golden Syrup
8 oz. granulated sugar
$\frac{1}{2}$ teaspoonful vinegar
4 tablespoonfuls water
1 oz. butter
1 level teaspoonful bicarbonate of soda
2 oz. puffed breakfast cereal

Method
Put syrup, sugar, vinegar and water into a heavy saucepan and heat gently until sugar is quite dissolved, stirring as necessary. Bring to the boil and cook, without stirring, to 290°F. At this temperature a drop tested in cold water will snap cleanly. Remove from heat and add butter in small pieces. Stir in bicarbonate of soda, and cereal. Mix together quickly and pour into a greased tin. Break up when cold.

Seafoam Candy

3 oz. Golden Syrup
8 oz. granulated sugar
6 tablespoonfuls water
1 egg white
$\frac{1}{2}$ teaspoonful vanilla essence
2 oz. glacé cherries
$\frac{1}{2}$ oz. angelica

Method
Put syrup, sugar and water into a heavy saucepan and heat gently until sugar is quite dissolved, stirring as necessary. Bring to the boil and cook, without stirring, to 250°F. At this temperature a little tested in cold water will form a firm ball. Meanwhile cut cherries into quarters and chop angelica roughly. Pour the syrup mixture in a thin continuous stream over the stiffly whisked egg white, beating continuously with a wire whisk or electric beater. Add the essence and continue beating until mixture whitens and will hold a trail when dropped from the beater (about 7 minutes). Stir in cherries and angelica and spread in a greased tin. Cut in squares when cold. If mixture becomes too stiff to spread, beat in a few drops of hot water and use a wet knife for spreading.

Fruit Ice

Top picture Honey Boats

The Toadstool Ring

CHILDREN'S PARTIES

Honey Boats

Join the celebrations and bake some Gypsy Moth Cakes. Children will love them.

6 oz. shortcrust pastry
2 oz. butter or margarine
1 oz. castor sugar
1 tablespoonful clear honey
1 egg
3 oz. self-raising flour
2 tablespoonfuls milk
1 level tablespoonful lemon
   preserve
Coffee or chocolate glacé icing
To decorate
   White paper sails

Method

Roll pastry thinly, and use it to line eight 4½-inch boat-shaped patty tins. Trim and chill for at least 30 minutes. Cream butter and sugar until light and fluffy, add honey and beat in egg, adding a teaspoonful of flour. Fold in remaining flour and milk. Spread ½ level teaspoonful of lemon preserve in base of each 'boat', and divide the creamed filling between them. Smooth surfaces, and bake in a moderately hot oven (gas No. 5–375°F.) for 20 minutes. Cool. Coat sponge part of 'boats' with coffee or chocolate icing. Leave to set. Decorate with 'sails' made from triangles or white paper speared with cocktail sticks.
8 honey boats.

Toadstool Ring

Children love a hallowe'en party. There's fancy dress, ducking for apples, witches hats and plenty of excitement. The food for tea can easily take on a hallowe'en atmosphere, too. This Toadstool Ring looks unusual and attractive, yet the only cooking which has to be done is to make the little meringue toadstools—the cake itself is basically made of biscuit crumbs

The Toadstool Ring

6 oz. sweet biscuits
3 oz. digestive biscuits
3 oz. plain biscuits
4½ oz. biscuits
1½ oz. castor sugar
4½ level tablespoonfuls Clear
   Honey
1½ oz. cocoa
6 oz. seedless raisins
Toadstools
1 egg white
2 oz. castor sugar
Green tinted coconut
Icing
3 oz. butter or margarine
6 oz. icing sugar
1 dessertspoonful cocoa

Method

Crumble biscuits and roll into fine crumbs. Cream butter and sugar. Add honey and cocoa and beat well. Work in crumbs and raisins. Press into an ungreased 8" sandwich tin, and leave overnight pressed well down. To make toadstools, make 8 small tops and stalks from the meringue (using a ¼" plain vegetable pipe). Bake in a cool oven 275°F. (Mark 1) for 1-1¼ hours. Make up chocolate butter icing and ice top of cake, leaving some icing for toadstools. To assemble, remove a little of the toadstool top with a small, sharp knife, put on a little of the remaining butter icing and press in stems firmly but gently. Arrange round edge of cake. Sprinkle toadstools with a little cocoa.

CHILDREN'S PARTIES

Ginger Danish Pastries

12 oz. plain flour
Pinch of salt
$\frac{1}{2}$ oz. yeast
$1\frac{3}{4}$ oz. caster sugar
1-1$\frac{1}{2}$ gills tepid milk
7 oz. butter
Filling—(A)
2 oz. ground almonds
5 globes Stem Ginger, chopped
2 tablespoonfuls ginger syrup
Filling—(B)
2 oz. ground almonds
5 globes Stem Ginger, chopped

Method
Cream the yeast with one teaspoonful of sugar. Pour one gill of the milk at blood heat onto the yeast. Sift the flour and salt into a bowl, add the remaining sugar. Make a well in the centre and pour in the yeast mixture. Work into the flour adding the remaining milk if necessary, to form a light but dry dough. Knead until smooth. Roll into an oblong $\frac{1}{2}$" in thickness and place knobs of butter, the size of walnuts, over two thirds of the surface. Fold and roll as for rough puff pastry and repeat once. Wrap in greaseproof paper and place in a refrigerator or cool place for 15 minutes or until firm. Repeat the rolling and folding until all the butter is worked in. Chill for one hour or overnight. When firm, roll out into a square $\frac{1}{4}$" thick. Cut in half. Spread one half with the ground almond filling. Roll up into a sausage shape and cut into six pieces. Cut each slice twice two-thirds of the way down and fan out. Cut the other half into squares.

Fill half the squares with chopped ginger and nuts and fold the corners to the centre. Make the rest of the pastry and filling into your favourite shapes. Place, covered in a warm place to prove for 10-15 minutes. When the pastries have increased their size by half, glaze with egg white, beaten. Place in a preheated oven at 450°F. or Mark 8 for 15-20 minutes until golden brown.
Makes approximately 15 pastries.

Chocolate Hazelnut Gateau

8 oz. castor sugar
1 rounded dessertspoonful cocoa
4 egg whites
2 oz. hazelnuts
$\frac{1}{2}$ pint double cream

Method
Mark 7" circles on 3 pieces of grease-proof paper on 3 baking sheets then brush with oil. Sieve the sugar and cocoa together. Whisk the egg whites until stiff. Whisk in half of the sugar and cocoa. Gradually fold in the remaining sugar. Using a $\frac{1}{2}$" nozzle pipe or spread the meringue on the marked rounds. Cook in a slow oven 200°F. (Mark $\frac{1}{2}$) for approximately 2-3 hours or until meringues dry throughout. Carefully remove from paper and turn onto a cooling tray. Chop the hazelnuts keeping back a few for decoration. Whip the cream until stiff. Sandwich layers of meringue together when quite cold, with cream and chopped nuts. Spread cream on the top and decorate with whole nuts and grated chocolate.

Top picture   Chocolate Hazelnut Gateau   *Ginger Danish Pastries*

CHILDREN'S PARTIES

Australian Catherine Wheel Cake

6 oz. butter
6 oz. castor sugar
3 eggs
8 oz. self-raising flour
1 oz. ground rice
Pinch salt
4 oz. sultanas
4 oz. glacé cherries, halved
1-2 tablespoonfuls milk
1 heaped teaspoonful mixed spice
Cochineal

Icing

Pink glacé icing
½ lb. butter icing (½ chocolate, ½ plain)
1 dozen candles approximately

Method

Prepare an 8″ round cake tin. Cream butter and sugar until light and fluffy. Whisk eggs and beat in a little at a time. Sift flour, salt and ground rice and sprinkle a tablespoonful over the cherries and sultanas. Fold in dry ingredients and fruit alternately adding the milk at the end. Divide mixture into three portions. Portion 1—Add mixed spice. Portion 2—Tint with cochineal. Portion 3—Leave plain. Place in layers into prepared tin and bake in the oven, at 350°F. (Mark 4) for 1-1¼ hours. When cool, completely cover cake with a glacé icing which has been tinted with cochineal. Prepare butter icing and divide in half. Colour and flavour one half with chocolate or dissolved cocoa. Pipe from base to centre of cake alternate circles of chocolate and plain butter icing to give wheel effect. When firm insert candles around side of cake and light to give sparkling effect of the firework— catherine wheel.

Fruit and Cream Tartlets

Pastry:
6 oz. plain flour
Pinch of salt
1½ oz. butter
1½ oz. lard
Filling:
1 x 8 oz. tin fruit
¼ pint double dairy cream
4 oz. icing sugar

Method

Prepare shortcrust pastry and bake tartlet cases. Cool on a wire tray. Prepare the filling: Drain the fruit (reserving some of the juice for icing) and cut it into small pieces. Whip the cream stiffly and add most of the fruit (reserving some for decoration). Fill the tartlet cases with the cream-and-fruit mixture. Level the tops with a knife. Make a little glacé icing by gradually adding some of the fruit juice to the icing sugar. This should be fairly stiff. Cover the top of each tartlet and decorate with the remaining fruit.

Marshmallow Crispies

4 oz. butter or margarine
4 oz. marshmallows
4 oz. toffee
Small packet Rice Krispies.

Method

Melt butter, marshmallows and toffee in a large saucepan over a low heat, stirring occasionally. When melted add the Rice Krispies and mix well together. Turn out into greased tin and when cool cut into fingers.

Australian Catherine Wheel Cake

CHILDREN'S PARTIES

Chocolate Soufflé

¼ *pint milk*
1½ *oz. chocolate*
1 *oz. butter*
1 *oz. plain flour*
1 *tablespoonful castor sugar*
3 *large eggs*
Vanilla essence to taste

Method
Warm the milk and dissolve the chocolate in it. Melt the butter in a saucepan and add the flour. Pour in the chocolate milk, add sugar and stir until mixture thickens. Beat well until the mixture leaves the sides of the pan and is quite smooth. Remove the pan from the heat, and add the egg yolks one at a time, beating the mixture well. Add vanilla essence. Whisk the egg whites to a stiff froth and fold lightly into the mixture. Pour at once into a prepared soufflé dish and bake for approximately 30 minutes at 400°F. (Mark 6). Remove the paper band and serve immediately.

Caramel Soufflé (cold)

1½ *oz. brown sugar*
Water
¼ *pint hot milk*
6 *egg yolks*
2 *oz. castor sugar*
¼-½ *oz. gelatine (short weight)*
1½ *oz. crushed ratafia biscuits*
½ *pint double dairy cream*
4 *egg whites*
Whipped cream

Method
Put the brown sugar and one teaspoonful of water into a saucepan and cook to caramel colour. Add the hot milk to the caramel, re-dissolve, and pour on to the beaten yolks and castor sugar. Cook gently until thick. Dissolve the gelatine in four tablespoonfuls of water over a gentle heat, add it to the custard and cool. Half-whip cream and stir this in together with the crushed ratafia biscuits. Whip the egg whites very stiffly and fold them into the mixture. Pour the mixture into a prepared souffle ·case and allow to set. Before serving decorate with whipped cream.

Maroc Biscuit Cake

12 *oz. Whole Wheat biscuits (or broken biscuits)*
4 *tablespoonfuls olive oil*
2 *tablespoonfuls golden syrup*
2 *oz. chopped walnuts*
Rind and juice of 1 orange
Decoration
Walnuts
Oranges
8 *oz. icing sugar*
Orange colouring—optional

Method
Crush biscuits with rolling pin between sheets of greaseproof paper or in a large greaseproof bag. Chop walnuts reserving four for decoration. Gently heat oil and syrup in saucepan until fully dissolved. Add rind and juice of orange. Add to crushed biscuits, add walnuts and mix well. Press mixture well down into a lightly oiled 7" flan ring on a serving plate and refrigerate for approximately 3 hours. Remove flan ring and cover with orange icing :– sieve icing sugar and mix with orange juice until smooth but not runny. Colour if necessary. Decorate with reserved walnuts and orange segments. Refrigerate for a short while just before serving as a cake or sweet.

Chocolate Drops

4 oz. butter
2 oz. castor sugar
3 oz. plain chocolate
2 dessertspoonfuls milk
4 oz. marshmallows
3 oz. (three 10-oz. measuring cups)
Rice Krispies

Method

Combine all ingredients except Rice Krispies in a saucepan and heat slowly, stirring, until mixture is smooth and well-blended. Cool slightly. Stir in Krispies then spoon into small paper cases and leave in a cool place until set. Makes approximately four dozen.

Igloo Cake

Cake
8 oz. self-raising flour
Pinch salt
8 oz. butter or margarine
8 oz. castor sugar
Finely grated rind of 1 large lemon
4 eggs
Butter Cream
4 oz. icing sugar, sifted
2 oz. butter, softened
1 tablespoonful lemon juice
Decoration
About 50 white marshmallows
(approximately 8 oz. halved)
1 individual swiss roll

Method

Sift together flour and salt. Cream fat, sugar and lemon rind until light and fluffy, then beat in eggs, one at a time, adding a tablespoonful of flour with each. Lightly fold in remaining flour with a metal spoon. Turn mixture into a well-greased, 2½-pint pudding basin. Bake in the centre of a moderate oven, 355°F. (Mark 4) for 1½ hours or until well risen and firm. Turn out and cool on a wire tray. Cream sugar and butter together till light and fluffy, then gradually beat in lemon juice. Spread the cake with butter-cream then cover with halved marshmallows. To make the tunnel—stand in individual swiss roll at base of Igloo and cover with butter-cream and halved marsh-mallows.

Strawberry Mousse

1 lb. (or one 16 oz. tin)
strawberries
2 oz. castor sugar
1 egg white
½ pint double dairy cream

Method

Sprinkle fresh strawberries with sugar and leave for 1 hour, then rub through sieve. Whip the egg white and the real dairy cream separately, then fold together. Add the sieved fruit gradually. Put into a serving dish and chill well before serving.

Butterscotch Sauce

2 oz. soft brown sugar
2 oz. butter
1 small can evaporated milk

Method

Melt the sugar and butter together over a low heat, then cook slowly, stirring constantly until the mixture turns a golden colour (about 5 minutes). Add the milk and continue to stir until all the sugar mix is dissolved into the milk. The sauce will thicken as it cools.

Excellent served with ice-cream.

Orange Souffle

2 oranges
½ pint milk
¾ oz. castor sugar
1½ oz. butter
2 oz. plain flour
3 egg yolks
4 egg whites
Icing sugar

Method

Grate orange rind into the milk and boil with ½ oz. castor sugar. Strain and keep hot. Melt the butter in a large saucepan, stir in the flour and add the milk. Whisk the mixture until it is smooth, then allow it to cool slightly. Beat in the egg yolks one at a time. Whisk the egg whites until stiff, then fold into the mixture. Place in a prepared soufflé dish and sprinkle the inside of the greased dish and band with castor sugar. Bake at 400°F. (Mark 6) for approximately 40 minutes until well risen. Lightly dredge with icing sugar and serve immediately.

Fruit Cake

½ lb. plain flour
Pinch of salt
3 level teaspoonfuls baking powder
1½ level teaspoonfuls ground
    mixed spice
2 oz. ground almonds
4 fluid oz. olive oil
5 oz. demerara sugar
2 large eggs
Grated rind of 1 orange
Approximately 3 tablespoonfuls
    Cinzano Red
4 oz. raisins (stoned)
4 oz. sultanas
4 oz. currants
2 oz. mixed chopped peel
2 oz. glacé cherries (quartered)
7" round cake tin

Method

Wash and dry fruit and leave to soak in the Cinzano Red preferably overnight. Sieve flour, salt, baking powder and mixed spice. Add ground almonds and sugar. Add the soaked fruit and grated orange rind. Lightly beat eggs in the measured oil and add to the flour and fruit mixture. Mix until of a soft dropping consistency. Mixture should fall gently from wooden spoon when lightly shaken. Place mixture in an oiled and greaseproof lined cake tin and bake, centre shelf, at 325°F. (Mark 3) for approximately 1¾-2 hours, until cake is well browned and cooked through—test with a skewer. Allow to cool slightly before removing from tin. *Note:* This mixture can be used for baking a Celebration, Christmas or Dundee cake (covered with halved or whole blanched almonds prior to cooking). A little additional Cinzano Red can be skewered into the cake when cooled.

Honeycomb Lime Mould

1 packet lime flavour jello
2 eggs
¼ pint milk
2 oz. castor sugar

Method

Boil ¼ pint of water in a saucepan and remove from heat; put jello in pan and stir until dissolved. Place 2-3 tablespoonfuls jello in 2 pint mould. Allow to set. Separate whites from yolks. Whisk egg yolks, add milk, place in double saucepan. Cook, stirring continuously until mixture thickens. Add

Orange Soufflé

sugar and jello leave until beginning to set. Fold in stiffly beaten egg whites. Pour into mould. Turn onto plate when set.

Serves 4 persons.

Strawberry Macaroon Trifle

2 packets strawberry flavour jello
12 almond macaroons or
8 oz. ratafia biscuits
4 tablespoonfuls sweet sherry
For decoration
¼ pint double cream
Fresh, canned or frozen strawberries
1 oz. almonds, blanched, split and
roasted (optional)
Serves 8 persons.

Method

Place jellies in basin. Add 1 pint boiling water, stir until dissolved. Add ½ pint cold water. Leave until beginning to set. Place macaroons in trifle bowl, moisten with sherry, cover with nearly all the thickened jello. Leave to set. Chop remaining jello with wet knife, and use with whipped cream, strawberries and almonds for decoration. Swiss roll, sponge cakes or fingers may be used in place of macaroons.

Jelly Jewels

1 packet of your favourite jello
2 level tablespoonfuls desiccated
coconut
For decoration
Angelica leaves

Method

Place jello in basin. Add ½ pint boiling water, stir until dissolved. Add ¼ pint cold water. Pour ⅓ of the jello into another basin, leave to set. When remaining jello is beginning to thicken stir in coconut. Divide mixture between four sundae glasses. Leave to set. Top glasses, with plain jello roughly chopped with wet knife. Decorate with angelica leaves.

Serves 4 persons.

Golden Mousse

4 eggs
2 tablespoonfuls orange marmalade
(not jelly type)
2 tablespoonfuls undiluted
orange squash
¼ pint double dairy cream
Glacé cherries

Method

Separate the eggs. Beat the yolks with the marmalade, then add the squash. Put into a saucepan and cook over very gentle heat, whisking the mixture until it thickens. Put aside to cool. Whisk the egg whites and fold into the mixture. Finally add the cream, stiffly whipped, reserving a little for decoration. Pour the mixture into a serving dish and chill thoroughly. Before serving, decorate with the remaining whipped cream and glacé cherries.

Cherry Pudding

2½ oz. brown breadcrumbs
Grated rind of ½ lemon
1½ oz. castor sugar
½ lb. cherries (stoned)
½ pint double dairy cream
2 eggs

Method

Put the breadcrumbs, lemon rinds and sugar into a basin. Add the cherries. Warm ¼ pint cream slightly and pour over the breadcrumbs mixture. Separate the eggs and add the yolks to the

CHILDREN'S PARTIES

mixture. Fold in stiffly whipped egg whites. Transfer to a greased pudding basin, cover and steam slowly for about an hour. Turn out and serve with the remaining cream.

Meringues

4 egg whites
4 oz. castor sugar
4 oz. granulated sugar
Glacé cherries
¼ pint double dairy cream

Method
Place the egg whites in a basin and whisk until very stiff. Fold in the sugar. Place greaseproof paper onto a baking sheet and either pipe in shapes or place onto the tin in tablespoonfuls. Sprinkle with castor sugar. Put immediately into oven and bake for 3½-3 hours at 250°F. (Mark ¼). The meringues are 'dry' when they can be lifted off the paper. Sandwich together with whipped cream and decorate with glacé cherries. Makes 12 meringues.

Chocolate Eclairs

7½ oz. water
Pinch of salt
4 small eggs
½ pint double dairy cream
2 oz. butter
4 oz. plain flour
Chocolate icing

Method
Add salt and fat to water and bring to boil. Add flour, stirring over heat until mixture leaves sides of the pan. Leave to cool, then beat in the eggs gradually. Pipe mixture with a forcing bag and ½" plain tube onto a greased tray. Bake about 25 minutes at 475°F. (Mark 8).

Split whilst hot, leave to cool and fill with whipped cream and coat with chocolate icing. Makes 18 eclairs.

Sponge Cake

This one merits the order of the bath !

4 oz. butter
4 oz. sugar
2 eggs
4 oz. self-raising flour
1½ tablespoonfuls ginger wine
1 oz. stem ginger (chopped)

Method
Cream the butter and sugar together until light and creamy, then add the beaten eggs a little at a time. Lightly fold in the flour and chopped ginger. Add the ginger wine to form a soft dropping consistency. Put into two greased 7" sandwich tins and bake in a moderate oven 375°F. (Mark 5) for about 20 minutes. Cool and sandwich together with butter icing. Sprinkle the top with icing sugar or ice with glacé icing.

Butter Icing

4 oz. icing sugar
2 oz. butter
1 dessertspoonful ginger wine

Method
Sieve icing sugar and cream together with butter and ginger wine. Beat until smooth.

Glacé Icing

4 oz. icing sugar
1½ tablespoonfuls ginger wine.
(approximately)

Method
Sieve the icing sugar and mix to a smooth consistency with the ginger wine.

Potatoes in their Jackets

WINE & CHEESE PARTIES

English Cheese & Wine Parties for the Sophisticated Twenties

When you are in your twenties parties are most fun. Friends will always help with preparation, you may be a host or hostess for the first time, your friends will want to bring friends and you will meet many interesting people. If you haven't been to a party for a long time, find an excuse and give one.

Keep food as easy to manage as possible. There's no need to spend a lot of money as the basic requirements for a really wonderful spread can be quite inexpensive—bread, biscuits, butter and English cheese, with just one or two odds and ends to give colour. Hot homemade soup served at the very end of your party will be greatly appreciated, particularly on chilly nights.

Cheese Board

Buy a selection of loaves, biscuits and crispbread and a variety of fruit and vegetables for garnish. These should include grapes (green and black), tomatoes, celery, chicory spears and olives. You will also need plenty of butter.

Dice some of the cheese early in the day and keep it fresh in polythene bags. Later on the cheese can be displayed on a variety of dishes and boards accompanied by the bread, biscuits and garnishes.

Here are a few suggestions:

Cheddar with French bread and green grapes
Cheshire with slices of tomatoes
Stilton with Granary bread and curls of butter
Leicester with French bread and black grapes
Double Gloucester with horse-shoe rolls and black olives
Derby with cream crackers and chicory spears
Caerphilly with wholemeal biscuits and celery snippets

Bottles or flagons with bottle openers and glasses can be put out early in the day together with brightly coloured napkins. And don't forget plenty of ash trays.

If some of the cheese has been diced in advance it will take less than an hour to arrange the cheese attractively on the dishes and boards.

Once a party has really got going there comes a time when the hostess can slip away without being missed. That is the time to prepare a fondue.

English Cheeses

No matter how you buy it—cut from a whole cheese or a rindless block, or in a vacuum pack—English cheese tastes better. As full of tradition as the country-side it comes from. The nine traditional varieties each with its own individual characteristics have nine distinctive flavours.

English cheeses were traditionally made in country farmhouses. Different soil, grass, climate and maturity resulted in subtle differences in the flavours of each of the cheeses. Before the old crafts were forgotten, the famous regional cheeses were successfully

WINE & CHEESE PARTIES

reproduced in modern creameries. English cheeses today have all the flavour produced by the craftsmen and in addition a high standard of hygienic production.

Cheddar

A rich nutty-tasting cheese with a close creamy texture. Cheddar is specially good with fruit but is really an "all purpose" cheese. Try it with ham or crisp bacon.

Cheshire

The oldest English cheese of all. There are red, white and blue versions of Cheshire, all with a good solid flavour. Try mellow red or white Cheshire for an extra special "elevenses"

Wensleydale

A mild cheese with a delicious honeyed aftertaste. The subtle flavour and flaky texture make Wensleydale much beloved by Northerners with apple pie— and no wonder—it's very good.

Leicester

Mild and mellow with a rich russet colour, Leicester has a slightly flaky texture and looks particularly well on a cheeseboard. It is especially delicious as a dessert.

Derby

A close-textured cheese with a pale honey colour. Mild when young, Derby develops a definite tang as it matures. Sage Derby—flavoured with chopped sage leaves—has long been a Christmas favourite.

Caerphilly

Creamy and white with a mild delicate flavour, Caerphilly is a favourite with Welsh people. Especially good for tea with celery and thin slices of bread and butter.

Stilton

The King of Cheeses! Blue Stilton has a close texture and its blue veins give it a special tangy flavour. White Stilton is a mild crumbly white cheese which is delicious in salads.

Double Gloucester

A smooth mature cheese which makes excellent sandwiches. Harvest gold in colour, Double Gloucester combines well with a pint of beer or, strangely enough, fresh fruit salad and cream.

Lancashire

A crumbly, white cheese with a creamy mild taste which grows stronger with maturity. Splendid with biscuits, Lancashire is also ideal for topping soups or toasting.

French Cheeses

Gruyère

Three traditionally produced varieties of cheese from the Jura, Vosges and the French Alps are:
Beaufort
Emmental Francais
Comté

WINE & CHEESE PARTIES

Cantal

One of the oldest known cheeses, and one of the most appreciated in France. The best are made on the slopes of the Auvergne mountains, between 3,600 and 4,500 ft. A semi-hard cheese, fairly strong in flavour. It matures after 2½ months; average weight ½-¾ cwt.

Bleu des Causses

A rich blue-veined cheese made from rich cow's milk of the Bordeaux district in Gascony. Weighing around 5 lbs. each and gold-foil wrapped. Matured in the local caves in which it develops its characteristic blue mould. Of creamy texture, full flavoured.

Coeur de Bray Bondon de Neufchatel

Also sold under the name of BONDON, it is a small cylindrical whitish cheese, which is made in the region of Bray and in the north-eastern part of the Seine-Maritime department. It has a high proportion of fats (45-50%) and weighs 4 lbs.

Triple Cremé

Soft or thinly rinded cheese, containing 75% fat, made into a variety of shapes mild and natural, or flavoured with aromatic plants.

Fromages de Chévre

These little cheeses, weighing between 3 and 8 oz. Made from rich goat's milk. Found in a variety of shapes. Thin white or blue mould covered rinds, the curd is close and white, and of mild flavour.

Brie

Made in the province of Brie and adjoining districts. On the same soft texture as Camembert and made from rich cow's milk. Averaging 4-5 lbs. and 15″ in diameter, but, for your convenience, is cut into smaller wedge shaped portions of ½ lb. or ¼ lb. and boxed.

Pont L'Eveque

A square cheese in a wood-chip box, named after the small town in Calvados. Somewhat close curd, thin rinded and full flavoured on becoming fully matured.

Carre de L'Est

A soft cheese from the Champagne and adjacent district of N.E. France. Made from pasteurized rich cow's milk, and packed in square boxes. Like Camembert, it softens on ripening. When ripe, of a buttery texture and mild flavour.

Carre Demi-Sel

Made in Normandy from rich cow's milk. Of white, soft texture, rindless, and whilst slightly salted, mild in flavour. Square in shape and foil wrapped. Immediate consumption is desirable in order that the true delicacy of flavour may be enjoyed to the full.

Petit-Suisse

Made in Normandy, a small very rich cream cheese, freshly made and un-salted. Of white creamy consistency. Cylindrical in shape. Immediate consumption (as for Demi-Sel) essential. Delicious sprinkled with fine sugar and eaten with digestive biscuits.

211

French Cheeses

Coulommiers

Originated in the department of Seine-et-Marne, it is made from rich cow's milk and is round, flat, and packed in wood-chip boxes. Weighing around 1 lb., it is larger than a Camembert, but smaller than a Brie, ripening in a similar fashion.

Camembert

The well-known soft cheese of Normandy, made from rich cow's milk. It originated from the village of Camembert around 1791. Camembert softens on ripening.

Livarot

This cheese comes from Normandy and has been made for centuries. It has a strong flavour and can be recognized by its girdle of dark chestnut-green threads. These threads are hollow reeds which keep the cheese in shape while it is softening. A lovely light terra-cotta in colour, it is one of the most praised regional cheeses of France.

Grape Cheese

With the rinds covered with the black grape skins and seeds from the local wine pressings, and weighing around 4 lbs. each, it is made in the Haute-Savoie district. The texture is white and buttery, flavour mild.

Bleu de Bresse

A small blue-veined cheese, made from rich cow's milk in Servas (Ain). Average weight $\frac{1}{2}$ lb., foil wrapped, soft buttery texture, thin rinded, mild flavour.

Saint-Nectaire

Cheese from the Auvergne district, semi-hard, at its best when very soft and almost runny. The rind is purplish-brown and therefore easily recognized. Made locally at the spa town from which it takes its name, this cheese is best when the milk comes from the high mountain pastures between 3,600 ft. and 4,500 ft. The output of this cheese is one of the largest. Weight: 3-3$\frac{3}{4}$ lbs.

Reblochon

This cheese is known to have first been made centuries ago and is still very well known on account of its soft, buttery consistency. The best is produced in the Alps above 3,000 ft. With its mild, nutty flavour it is one of the most popular cheeses. It weighs 1 lb. To-day, a smaller cheese is also made in dairies and weighs $\frac{1}{2}$ lb., but this is not the traditional size.

Saint-Paulin

Made chiefly in the N.E. of France, from rich cow's milk. A slightly pressed cheese, averaging 4lb., thin rinded, close buttery consistency, mild flavour.

Roquefort

The blue-veined cheese made entirely of rich ewe's milk, it is the oldest blue-veined cheese of France, its production dating back nearly 2,000 years. Made in the Aveyron department, S.W. France, where it is matured in the famous local caves of Roquefort. Weighing around 4 lbs. each; and foil wrapped. Creamy but crumbly in texture, its flavour is delicious, but somewhat pungent.

WINE & CHEESE PARTIES

Munster

Originating from Alsace, it has a very strong flavour. The rich paste, made wholly of cow's milk, has a high proportion of fat (45-50%). Coming in various sizes—from ½ lb. to 2 lbs.

Maroilles

Known to have been made as long ago as the thirteenth century this traditional cheese of the Thiérache, Champagne and Flanders regions is still praised by great epicures today. It stimulates the palate so that the full-bodied Bourgogne wines can be better appreciated. Square in shape it comes in four sizes: Quarter size—½ lb., MIGNON—about 1 lb.; SORBAIS—about 1 lb. 6 oz.; whole 2 lbs.

German Cheeses

Tilsiter

A typical German product, available since 120 years in old unequalled quality. Tilsiter is piquant, anyhow unique and original.

Emmentaler

King of cheeses! Made in the Allgaeu Alps (Bavaria) of delicious milk from brown highland cattle. Mild flavour, of a nutty taste.

Raeucherkaese

Smoked cheese, mild and creamy.

Raeucherkaese M. Schinken

Smoked cheese with cottage smoked Ham. Delicious!

Bianco

Made of full flavoured, aromatic Alpine milk and cream. Bianco is creamy and mildly piquant.

Blue Cheese

A top quality Bavarian dairy product. Fresh milk from healthy cows, high fat content, full flavoured.

Limburger

Spicy and full flavoured, is the connoisseur's delight. Low fat content.

Romadur

Mild, spicy and piquant. Delicious and creamy.

Camembert Champignon

The Champignon Camembert with its typically aromatic savour is relisted by gourmets for its prime quality that will never change!

Camembert Edelweiss

Regular Camembert mould, white to cream colour, aromatic.

Brie

Soft ripened cheese of an excellent mild flavour.

Wine-Cheese (Weinkaese)

A strongly flavoured cheese. Creamy.

Camembert and Brie in tins

Vacuum packed. Preservation warranted for a minimum of six months at proper storage. No rind—edible to the last crumb.

WINE & CHEESE PARTIES

Chives-Cheese (Schnittlauchkaese)

Choice qualities of cheeses of different origin mixed with butter, cream and chives.

Cream Cheese (Sahne-Kaese)

Mixed with butter and cream, very mild flavour.

Caraway Cheese

A cheese-spread with caraway, with natural spices.

Mereta

A delicious processed cheese with horse-radish and dill.

Pfefferoni

A tangy processed cheese with freshly ground black Brazilian pepper and fine spices.

Picado

A delicious cheese-spread, with cucumber, paprika, tomato and fine spices.

Meisterpastete

A delicious processed cheese in the style of the chef containing 10% of meat-pie, ham, cucumber and spices.

Bierwuerfel
Butter Cheese (Butterhappen)
Beer Cheese (Bierhappen)
Wine Cheese (Weinhappen)

Choice quality of cheeses mixed with butter, cream and spices.

A Danish Cheese Board

At parties several kinds of cheese are needed to make sure there is something for everyone's taste. Danish cheeses provide plenty of choice, ranging from the piquant, blue-veined Danish Blue and creamy Mycella to the milder varieties like Samsoe and the very interesting Havarti and Esrom. There are also cream cheeses and delicately flavoured processed cheeses soft enough to spread or make into dips. Cheese lends itself perfectly to a colourful display decorated with various fruits and salads. Cut some slices ready to serve and let guests help themselves to as much or as little as they want from the larger pieces. Biscuits, bread and plenty of fresh Danish butter will be needed. As a change, or when only light refreshments are called for, hand round an assortment of cubed cheeses with fruit, nuts or pickles or make the midget Danwiches called slicelets. The Danish word for these slicelets is 'snitter'. They are made by using half the usual size bread cut across diagonally.

Danish Blue

Has a well developed piquant flavour and creamy consistency. It is made from pasteurised and homogenised milk with the addition of a beneficial mould to produce the blue veins from which it is named. The cheese is pierced with stainless steel prongs to introduce air and allow the characteristic blue veining to develop. Danes have made Danish Blue cheese for over fifty years.

WINE & CHEESE PARTIES

Mycella

This is another veined cheese with the golden yellow colour of rich cream and green, not blue, veins. It is a fine, richly-flavoured, table cheese. The process of making it is similar to that for Danish Blue.

Havarti

This cheese gets its name from a farm on Zealand where it was first made, not far from Denmark's capital—Copenhagen. It is light yellow with numerous holes, big and small. It has a clean, aromatic flavour. In olden days the taste was said to be in the holes. Wherever it is, it's delicious.

Samsoe

Named after the island of Samsoe. This is the staple cheese of Denmark, often eaten even at breakfast time. It is a fine textured, pale yellow cheese with a few large shiny holes. The taste is mild with the flavour of nut kernels.

Esrom

This cheese is soft, and wonderfully mellow. Esrom has numerous small holes which give it an uneven surface when cut. It is practically rindless and can be eaten and enjoyed to the last crumb.

WINE & CHEESE PARTIES

Marrow with Cheese Sauce

1 medium-sized marrow
Sauce
1 oz. butter
1 oz. flour
½ pint milk
4 oz. grated cheese.
Salt and pepper

Method

Cut the marrow into 1½ in. thick rings. Peel and remove the central seeds and pith. Cook in boiling salted water until just tender. Make up the sauce by melting the butter and stirring in the flour. Cook together for 1-2 mins., then gradually add the milk. Bring to the boil and simmer for several mins. Add most of the cheese and season with salt and pepper. When the marrow is cooked, drain thoroughly and arrange the rings on a heated serving dish. Pour over the sauce and sprinkle with the remaining cheese. Brown under a hot grill for 2-3 mins. *Serves 4.*
Other vegetables, such as cauliflower, carrots, leeks and celery, are delicious served in this way, either as a dish on their own or as an accompaniment to grilled meat, sausages, etc. Prepare the vegetables in the usual way and cook in boiling salted water until tender then finish as above.

Cheese Aigrettes

2 oz. butter
¼ pint milk and water mixed
2½ oz. plain flour
2 eggs, beaten
2 oz. grated cheese
Salt and pepper
Oil for frying

Method

Place the butter and liquid in a saucepan and bring to the boil. Remove from the heat and add the flour. Beat until smooth, then cool slightly. Gradually beat in the eggs and add the cheese, salt and pepper. Leave until quite cold. Heat a deep-fat pan of oil and drop in teaspoonfuls of the cheese mixture. Fry, turning once until puffed and golden. Drain on kitchen paper. Serve hot or cold.

Cheese on sticks

For a cocktail party serve cheese on sticks. Cut cheese into ½ in. cubes, using a knife dipped in hot water. Arrange on cocktail sticks with mandarin orange segments, stuffed olives, maraschino cherries, pineapple cubes or black grapes.

Tomato Baskets

8 firm tomatoes
3 oz. cheese
¼ cucumber
Salt and pepper
Watercress

Cut the tomatoes into basket shapes, using a sharp knife. With a small teaspoon scoop out and discard all the centre. Invert the baskets on a piece of kitchen paper and leave to drain. Cut some of the cheese into small sticks and the rest into tiny dice. Cut the cucumber into the same-size dice. Mix the cheese and cucumber dice and season well. Use to fill the tomato baskets, arranging the cheese sticks. Serve garnished with watercress.

Serves 4 persons.

218

WINE & CHEESE PARTIES

Cheese and Apricot Pilaff

6 oz. patna rice
1 tablespoonful chopped chives
8 oz. Cheddar cheese, cut into
$\frac{1}{4}$" cubes
3 oz. melted butter
Salt, pepper and cayenne pepper
Tinned halves apricots
Watercress

Method
Cook rice in fast boiling salted water
for 12-15 minutes. Drain and rinse with
cold water. Place rice in a basin with
chives, cheese and butter. Season to
taste and mix lightly together. Put
mixture into a greased loose-bottomed
7" cake tin. Smooth and leave for half-
and-hour. Turn out on to a plate,
decorate with apricots and sprigs of
watercress.
Serves 4-6 persons.

Cheese and Tuna Medley

1 x 7 oz. tin tuna fish
4 oz. potato crisps
Small packet frozen peas
2 oz. mushrooms, sliced
1 medium chopped onion
6 oz. grated Cheddar cheese
Salt and pepper
3 eggs
Scant $\frac{1}{2}$ pint milk

Method
Flake tuna fish into a mixing bowl,
crush potato crisps and mix in. Add
peas, mushrooms, onion, 4 oz. cheese,
seasoning and mix well together. Beat
eggs lightly and add milk. Pour into fish
mixture. Put into a buttered ovenproof
dish and sprinkle on remaining cheese.
Bake in a moderate oven at 350°F.
(Mark 4), for 30-40 minutes. Serve hot.
Serves 4 persons.

Hot Cheese Stuffed Eggs

4 hard-boiled eggs, shelled
3 oz. butter
5 oz. grated Cheddar cheese
1 clove garlic crushed with a little
salt (optional)
Pinch salt and cayenne pepper
1 tablespoonful cream or top of
milk
1 oz. flour
$\frac{1}{2}$ pint milk
Salt and cayenne pepper
8 cooked mushroom caps

Method
Cut the eggs in half lengthwise,
remove yolks and mash with a fork.
Add 2 oz. softened butter, 2 oz. cheese,
garlic, seasoning and cream or top of
milk, and mix well together. Divide the
mixture equally among the halved egg
whites, piling up smoothly, and place
in a buttered fireproof dish. Make
cheese sauce with remaining butter,
flour, milk, 2 oz. cheese and seasoning,
pour over eggs. Sprinkle with a little
grated cheese, and brown quickly
under a hot grill. Garnish with mushroom caps, and serve hot.

Gang Sandwiches

2 slices bread
1 slice Cheddar cheese
1 slice ham
Chutney

Method
Toast bread on one side only. Place
cheese on untoasted side of one
piece and place under a hot grill until
cheese melts. Place ham on untoasted
side of other piece of toast, spread with
chutney and sandwich the two together. Serve hot or cold.

WINE & CHEESE PARTIES

Lancashire Fondue

6 oz. Lancashire cheese
1 small glassful white wine
¾ oz. English butter
Pinch of black pepper and salt

Method
Cut the cheese into very small thin slices. Put the cheese, butter, wine and seasoning into a fireproof dish over a very low heat and leave, stirring occasionally, until the cheese and butter have melted and are well blended. Do not allow to boil, or the cheese will be stringy instead of creamy. Serve the dish on a table heater. The fondue must be kept very hot and it should be eaten as soon as it is cooked.

Blue Boy

3 slices Danish Blue cheese or
  Mycella cheese
Small piece lettuce
2 halves black grapes
Buttered bread

Method
Press the piece of lettuce into the butter at one end of the bread. Slice the cheese neatly and arrange the slices in slightly overlapping layers. Decorate the top of the cheese with two buttons' of de-seeded black grapes.

Hello Havarti

2 slices Havarti cheese
Lettuce leaf
Tomato quarter
Cress
Buttered bread

Method
Arrange the two slices of Havarti in layers taking care to cover the buttered bread. Decorate with lettuce, tomato quarter and cress.

Welsh Rarebits

8 oz. grated cheese
1 tablespoonful Worcester sauce
Salt and pepper
½ level teaspoonful dry mustard
Milk or beer
Hot buttered toast
Tomato slices

Mix the cheese, Worcester sauce, salt, pepper and mustard with enough milk or beer to make a stiff paste. Spread on the toast and place under a hot grill until melted and browned. Garnish with a tomato twist. Makes enough for 4 large or 8 small rarebits. For a change try some of the following variations:

Top the toast with a slice of ham or boiled bacon before spreading with the cheese mixture.

Garnish the Welsh Rarebit with heated canned baked beans.

Top the Rarebit with sliced tomatoes before grilling.

Cover the cooked Rarebit with a slice of hot bacon and a poached egg.

Cheese Straws

4 oz. cheese pastry (4 oz. flour, etc.) as in recipe on page 222

Method
Knead the pastry until smooth and roll out thinly. Trim into strips about 4 in. wide and cut into narrow straws. Roll out the trimmings and cut into rings using a 3 in. and a 2 in. plain cutter. Place on a baking tray and bake at 425°F. (Mark 7) for 6-8 mins. Cool on a wire rack. Serve with the straws threaded through the rings.

WINE & CHEESE PARTIES

Shrimp-Cheese Vol-au-Vents

12 oz. frozen puff pastry, thawed
Beaten egg to glaze
Filling
$\frac{1}{2}$ oz. butter
$\frac{1}{2}$ oz. flour
$\frac{1}{4}$ pint milk
2 oz. grated cheese
Salt and pepper
5 oz. can shrimps or prawns,
    drained
Parsley sprigs for garnish

Method
Roll out the pastry to $\frac{1}{2}$ in. thickness and cut into 6-8 circles, using a $2\frac{1}{2}$ in. cutter. Place upside down on a wetted baking tray and brush with beaten egg to glaze. Mark the centre of each pastry circle with a $1\frac{1}{2}$ in. cutter and with a sharp knife cut through half the depth of the pastry. Bake at 450°F. (Mark 8) for 15-20 mins., lowering the oven temperature if the pastry becomes too brown. When the vol-au-vents are cooked remove the centre piece of pastry and any soft inside. Make up the filling by melting the butter and stirring in the flour. Cook together for 1-2 mins., then gradually add the milk. Bring to the boil and simmer for several mins. Add the cheese, salt, pepper and most of the shrimps. Heat gently, then divide between the vol-au-vent cases. Decorate with the remaining shrimps and a little parsley. Serve hot or cold.
Makes about 8.
Note: Puff-pastry trimmings should not be kneaded together but carefully folded. Vol-au-vents made from the second rollings are not very satisfactory so we suggest you use the trimmings to make the Cheese Palmiers.

Cheese and Date Pastries

4 oz. bought puff pastry
Approximately 18 chopped dates
$4\frac{1}{2}$ oz. grated Cheddar cheese
Nutmeg to taste

Method
Divide pastry in 12 pieces and roll each out into a small circle. Mix dates, 4 oz. cheese and nutmeg together in a basin and put a spoonful of the filling into each pastry round. Damp edges and bring them together in the centre, pinching well. Turn over and roll out gently into an oval, so that the dates just show through. Make cuts across lightly. Brush with water, sprinkle with remaining cheese. Bake in a hot oven at 425°F. (Mark 7), for 10-15 minutes.

Cheese and Sardine Tricorns

4 oz. cheese pastry (4 oz. flour, etc.) as in recipe on page 222
$4\frac{3}{4}$ oz. can sardines in oil
Salt and pepper
1 teaspoonful lemon juice
Beaten egg for glazing

Method
Roll out the pastry thinly and cut into circles, using a 3 in. round cutter. Drain off most of the oil from the sardines. Turn out and mash well with the salt, pepper and lemon juice. Divide this mixture among the pastry circles. Damp the edges of the pastry and fold into tricorns. Brush with beaten egg and bake at 400°F. (Mark 6) for 12-15 mins. Serve hot or cold, garnished with parsley sprigs.
Makes about 8.

WINE & CHEESE PARTIES

Curry Cheese Eggs

4 eggs
1 oz. butter
2 oz. grated cheese
1 level teaspoonful curry powder
Salt and pepper
Milk if necessary
Pimento
Lettuce

Method
Hard-boil the eggs, then cool in running cold water. Shell and cut each egg in half lengthwise. Scoop out the yolks. Cream the butter until soft and mix in the cheese, egg yolks and curry powder. Season with salt and pepper and add a little milk if necessary to give a piping consistency. Place in a piping bag fitted with a star vegetable pipe. Refill the egg whites and garnish each with a piece of pimento. Serve with lettuce.
Serves 4 persons.

Cheese Palmiers

Puff-pastry trimmings (see recipe for Shrimp-Cheese Vol-au-vents)
Beaten egg to glaze
2-3 oz. grated cheese
Salt and cayenne pepper
Paprika

Method
Layer the trimmings and roll out thinly into an oblong. Brush with beaten egg and sprinkle with the cheese. Sprinkle with salt and cayenne pepper. Fold the long sides to the middle, brush with beaten egg and then fold in half again. Brush again with egg and cut across into thin slices with a sharp knife. Lay the slices downwards on a baking tray, allowing room for spread-ing. Bake at 450°F. (Mark 8) for 10 mins. Cool, then sprinkle with paprika.

Cheese Pastry

4 oz. plain flour
Salt and pepper
2 oz. butter
3 oz. grated cheese
1 egg yolk
A little water

Method
Sift the flour with the salt and pepper. Rub in the butter and mix in the cheese. Add the egg yolk and enough water to make a stiff dough. Use as required.

Fiery Dip

Beat 1 level teaspoonful curry powder into 1 teacupful of thick mayonnaise.

Rosy Dip

Beat 1 tablespoonful of the juice from a jar of pickled beetroot into a teacup-ful of thick mayonnaise. Colour with cochineal.

As you can see, this is an easy way to prepare for a party and when your guests have left you'll find that there isn't very much washing up to do, so if you are very tired you will be able to leave it until the morning.

Order a light-bodied red wine or rosé and a dry white wine.

There are some excellent wines available at prices varying from 10s. to 15s. a bottle. Your wine merchant will usually agree to take back unopened bottles and extra glasses can often be hired from him.

222

PARTY DRINKS

To make your party a success, there must be a touch of *novelty*. That's what we hope you'll find in these pages . . . . things easy to make and serve, but so 'different' they'll give your party that all-important element of surprise.

Most important of all items on any party menu are the drinks. So, in this section, you'll find new, delicious and amusing ways to serve both soft drinks . . . and alcohol . . . and ways to make punches that you've never tried before.

A bottled carbonated beverage is something you can't make or 'brew' at home. Its quality of flavour and lively effervescence requires a strictly-accurate blending of ingredients—plus the skilled technique of bottling under pressure. Years of careful research and advancement have brought the early versions of 'soda' to the high standards of purity and goodness we enjoy in soft drinks today.

Whether *your* 'crowd' are teenagers, grown-ups, or youngsters, bottled carbonated beverages, with their sparkle and zest, will add party pleasure, so don't forget them when planning your party.

EMERALD FROST

12 small bottles lemon soda or
    3 quart-size bottles club soda
$\frac{1}{2}$ *cup mint jelly*
$\frac{1}{2}$ *cup water*
3 tablespoonfuls lime juice
8 slices of lime

Empty 4 small bottles (or 1 quart bottle) into freezing tray and freeze. Chill remaining bottles. Heat mint jelly and water in small saucepan to make a syrup. Cool: add lime juice. *To serve:* shave, or crack carbonated beverage ice and place in tall glasses. Pour two tablespoonfuls of the syrup over ice in each glass. Garnish glasses with lime slices. Serve together with the chilled bottles of carbonated beverage; let each guest fill his own glass.
Serves 8 persons.

FROZEN MINT FIZZ

2 egg whites, beaten stiff
$\frac{1}{3}$ *cup mint jelly*
3 tablespoonfuls lemon juice
1$\frac{1}{2}$ cups (12 oz.) carbonated
    beverage*, chilled

Turn refrigerator control to freezing as far in advance as convenient. Beat mint jelly and lemon juice into beaten egg whites. Slowly pour and fold in very cold carbonated beverage. Transfer to two freezing trays. When frozen to a snow soft consistency, remove to a chilled bowl and beat until smooth and blended. Return to refrigerator tray and freeze. Serve in individual sherbet glasses—plain, or topped with fresh frozen strawberries.
Serves 6 persons.
* Use ginger ale, club soda or lemon-lime beverage.

Outback Peach Punch

PARTY DRINKS

Outback Peach Punch

1 large can peaches
Miniature bottle brandy
1 bottle medium sparkling wine
1 bottle of lemonade
Slices of fresh orange to decorate
  if liked
Sprig of mint

Leave wine and lemonade to chill in refrigerator for 4 hours or more. Tip the peaches and their juice into a large jug or very large bowl. Pour in brandy. Leave to stand overnight. Just before serving—stir in wine and lemonade. Float slices of fresh orange on top if liked and add a sprig of mint. Serve iced.
Serves 8 persons.

Beat the Breath Test

Impromptu parties are popular these days . . . at the last minute friends decide to drop in . . . as a gracious hostess, always be prepared.
Bottled soft drinks, now, are the *expected* thing — besides alcoholic drinks — so, order them as regularly as you do your groceries — they'll never go to waste !
Chill them well (the cold holds the effervescence) and serve them right in the bottle. Or have fun, and mystify your guests, by mixing one of these :

JOCKEY FLIP

1 quart-size bottle cherry soda
1 small bottle orange soda
1 small bottle lemon soda

Chill bottles of carbonated beverages thoroughly in refrigerator. Pour slowly into pitcher (do not stir) and serve at once.
Serves 6 persons.

CREOLE COOLER

1 quart-sized bottle raspberry soda
1 bottle kola-type beverage
1 small bottle ginger ale

Chill bottles of carbonated beverages thoroughly in refrigerator. Pour slowly into pitcher (do not stir) and serve at at once.
Serves 6 persons.

Soft drinks can be made into a superlatively good sherbet-type dessert . . . easy to prepare, and quick to freeze when the bottles are *very* cold before you start.

ORANGE BLISS

5 small bottles orange soda
2 small bottles lemon soda
1 small bottle cream soda
3 egg whites
2 cups fresh, or frozen strawberries
2 tablespoonfuls lemon juice

Chill bottles of carbonated beverages in refrigerator. Beat egg whites until they form small peaks, add strawberries and beat lightly. Slowly add one bottle orange soda, lemon juice and mix. Quickly place in the freezing tray of refrigerator, with controls set at freezing. When the mixture begins to freeze, remove from freezing tray and beat with egg beater until foamy. Return to the freezing tray and freeze until ready to serve. *To serve:* remove the strawberry ice from freezing tray and place in bottom of punch bowl. Slowly add remaining bottles of chilled carbonated beverages.
Serves 10-12 persons.

PARTY DRINKS

PINK SPICE

6 small bottles ginger ale
½ cup currant jelly
½ cup water
10 cloves
4 teaspoonfuls lemon juice
4 lemon slices

Empty 2 bottles into freezing tray and freeze. Chill remaining 4 bottles. Heat currant jelly, water and cloves in small saucepan, combine to make a syrup. Cool: remove cloves and add lemon juice. To serve: shave, or crack carbonated beverage ice and place in tall glasses. Pour ¼ cup syrup over ice in each glass. Garnish glasses with lemon slices. Serve together with chilled bottles of carbonated beverage. *Serves 4 persons.*

CHERUB CLOUD

2 quart-size bottle cherry soda
2 bottles kola-type beverage
1 quart-size bottle cream soda
1 pint vanilla ice cream

Chill carbonated beverages thoroughly. Just before serving, pour beverages into punch bowl. Add ice cream dividing the pint into four large table-spoonfuls. *Makes 32 punch size cups.*

BLOSSOM PUNCH

1 quart-size bottle raspberry soda
12 small bottles lemon soda
1 lime for slicing
Small fresh flowers
2 bottles (8 oz. size) maraschino cherries
⅔ cup lime juice

Chill bottled carbonated beverages thoroughly. Cut lime into 5 or 6 slices. Pull the stem of a small flower through the centre of each so that the blossom rests on the slice, trim stem short. Chop maraschino cherries fine; add together with the syrup to lime juice in punch bowl. Add the chilled raspberry and lemon carbonated beverages. Float lime-flower slices on top. *Serves 15-20 persons.*

BLUEBERRY SHRUB

8 (12-oz.) bottles, orange carbonated beverages
1¼ cupful lemon juice
½ cupful grape jelly or jam
½ cupful cultivated blueberries

Place four bottles of beverage in refrigerator to chill. Dissolve grape jelly in lemon juice; add remaining four bottles of beverage into two freezing trays. Sprinkle ¼ cup of blueberries in each tray. Freeze solid. *To serve:* fill punch bowl with shaved or cracked iced beverages. Pour over this the remaining chilled beverages.

PUNCH WITH COLA

1 (12-oz.) bottle cola, chilled
¼ cupful cream
¼ cupful powdered sugar
¾ cupful milk

Mix ingredients with egg-beater or fork. Pour into tall glasses. Serve with a dash of nutmeg on top of each glass. *Serves 4 persons.*

CRANBERRY GLOW

1 can frozen lemonade concentrate
1 cupful cranberry juice cocktail
1 quart sparkling soda
Lemon slices, small candles

Combine ingredients. Pour into suitable punch bowl filled with finely crushed ice. Float lemon slices and light candles.

226

PARTY DRINKS

A SPECIAL TIP

Instead of using water to reconstitute frozen fruit concentrate or ades for punches, try carbonated water or soft drinks of matching or appropriate flavours. Carbonated beverage flavours are constant, while ordinary tap water may vary in taste from area to area.

Frost Rims. For elegant service, dip edge of glass into slightly beaten egg white, then into granulated sugar, white or tinted.

SPARKLING TEA PUNCH

3 quarts ginger ale
1¼ cupfuls granulated sugar
1 cupful hot water
1 cupful lemon juice
3 cupfuls orange juice
1 cupful pineapple juice
3 cupfuls double-strength tea
1 (12-oz.) bottle raspberry soda
  mint leaves

Freeze one quart ginger ale for beverage cubes. Boil sugar and water five minutes. Combine with fruit juices and tea. Chill. Just before serving, add thoroughly chilled carbonated beverages. Float sparkling cubes and mint leaves.
Serves 40 punch-size cups.

ISLAND PUNCH

1 cupful canned crushed pineapple
  with juice
4 quarts ginger ale
2 quarts orange soda

Freeze one quart ginger ale for beverage cubes. Chill pineapple and remaining beverages. Combine just before serving. Garnish with orange slices and mint leaves.
Serves 40 punch-size cups.

As a novel punch bowl, use a hollowed-out watermelon. Fill with Sweetheart Punch, a three-way blend of cherry, orange and lemon-lime soft drinks. Garnish with lemon slices, stemmed cherries, mint leaves, and floating carbonated cubes.

CHERUB CLOUD PUNCH

4½ quarts cola, chilled
2 cupfuls sugar
1 pint heavy cream
½ tablespoonful cinnamon

Pour 1½ pints of cola into ice cube trays and freeze until mushy. Whip cream until frothy, mix with sugar. Scrape out frozen cola into punch bowl, add cream, then pour in remaining bottles of cola. Stir lightly, sprinkle with cinnamon.
Serves 36 punch-size cups.

CHERRY GINGER JUBILEE

3 quarts cherry soda, well chilled
3 quarts chilled ginger ale
1 can fruit cocktail (No. 2)
¼ cup lemon juice
2 bananas, sliced
2 tangerines, sectioned

Chill fruit cocktail in refrigerator. When ready to serve, empty into punchbowl. Pour in lemon juice; stir. Slowly add the chilled carbonated beverages. Float banana slices and tangerine segments. Makes 1½ gallons of punch. Serves approximately 16, allowing three punch-sized cups per person.
Note: Heart-shaped meringue floats and cut-out paper cupids make any punch a Sweetheart.

PARTY DRINKS

CHRISTMAS CHEER

3 large bottles ginger ale
3 large or 8 small bottles
lemon-lime soda
1 firm orange
12 maraschino cherries
12 green coloured cherries

Chill unopened bottles in refrigerator. Pour some of the ginger ale and lemon-lime in separate ice cube trays. Place a green or red cherry or chunky slice of orange in each cube compartment, freeze as quickly as possible. When ready to serve, put cubes in punch bowl and pour in chilled carbonated beverages. Place bowl on bed of Christmas greens; tuck gold or silver ornaments in the greens. Makes about 30 glasses of punch.

COLA-COOLER

$4\frac{1}{2}$ quarts cola, chilled
$\frac{3}{4}$ cup water
16 cloves
8 slices of orange, cut in half
$\frac{1}{2}$ cup orange marmalade
4 tablespoonfuls raisins
1 cup grapefruit juice

Place marmalade, water, raisins and cloves in saucepan; stir over low flame for five minutes, or until syrupy. Cool; add grapefruit juice. Remove cloves. Pour mixture into punch bowl, slowly add cola. Float orange halves as garnish.
Serves 40 punch-size cups.

CRANBERRY HOLIDAY PUNCH

2 quarts ginger ale
1 quart orange soda
8 oz. lemon-lime soda
2 cups cranberry juice cocktail

Freeze one quart ginger ale for beverage cubes. When ready to serve pour cranberry juice and carbonated beverages into punch bowl. Float beverage cubes. Garnish with orange slices and mint leaves.
Serves 24 punch-size cups.

TEXAS FLIP

1 quart grape soda
1 quart ginger ale
$1\frac{1}{2}$ quarts cola

Combine some of the cola and grape beverages in ice cube tray and freeze. Place other bottles in refrigerator and chill. When ready to serve, empty carbonated cubes into punch bowl and add chilled beverages.
Makes 32 punch-size cups.

ORANGE COOLER

$\frac{3}{4}$ pint milk
$\frac{1}{4}$ pint orange squash
Whipped double dairy cream
Crystallised orange slices

Whisk the milk and orange squash together. Pour into glasses and top with whipped cream and garnish with crystallised orange slices.

HONEY-AND-ALMOND SHAKE

1 tablespoonful clear honey
1 oz. ground almonds
1 pint milk
1 egg white
Whipped double dairy cream
Chopped almonds
Little green colouring (optional)

Whisk the honey and ground almonds into the milk. Add colouring. Whisk egg white stiffly and fold into the mixture. Pour into glasses and top with whipped cream and chopped almonds.

PARTY DRINKS

COLA PEACH CUBES

1 cupful mashed ripe peaches
2 tablespoonfuls lemon juice
¼ cupful sugar
Chilled cola

Mix lemon juice, sugar and peaches and put into ice cube tray. Fill tray with cola up to half inch from the top. Set refrigerator controls to coldest and freeze.

PINK FROST CUBES

½ cupful currant jelly
2 tablespoonfuls lemon juice
¼ cupful water
Chilled ginger ale or lemon-lime

Put jelly and lemon juice and water into saucepan. Heat, stirring until jelly completely melts. Pour into freezing tray and cool. When cold fill tray with chilled carbonated beverage to about ½ inch from top. Turn control low and freeze.

Hospitality is a new dimension in our lives. Homemakers busy with scores of outside interests no longer spend days preparing for a party. Here a brandy-snifter punchbowl with complementing glasses, a colourful sparkling punch and gay Christmas decorations set the stage for a gala holiday.

For a big crowd, twin pitchers double as punch bowls. The sparkling tea punch uses a double-strength tea, fruit juice and ginger ale combination. The Island Punch blends orange soda, pineapple juice and ginger ale. Sparkling beverage cubes float in each punch.

SWEETHEART PUNCH

2 quarts cherry soda
1 quart orange soda
1 quart lemon-lime soda

Freeze one quart cherry soda for beverage cubes. Chill remaining soft drinks. When ready to serve, shave or crack beverage cubes. Place in punch bowl, add other soft drinks slowly. Garnish with orange or lemon slices. *Makes 24 punch-size glasses.*

ROSE BOWL FLOAT

2 quarts raspberry soda
2 small bottles orange soda
1 quart cream soda or ginger ale
1 pint vanilla ice cream

Chill carbonated beverages thoroughly. Just before serving pour beverages into punch bowl. Add ice cream, dividing the pint into four 'floats'. *Makes 32 punch-size cups.*

ROMAN FIZZ

2 quarts grape soda
2 small bottles lemon-lime soda
1 quart ginger ale
1 pint vanilla ice cream

Chill thoroughly. Just before serving, pour into punch bowl; add ice cream in large spoonfuls.
Serves 10 to 16 persons, allowing 2 to 3 punch-size glasses for each.

Ice cubes made with carbonated beverages are ideal for punches, or for serving soft drinks right from the bottle. Sparkling cubes freeze fast, keep your drink lively, and never dilute the beverage. Cubes may either match or complement the flavour of the beverage you serve.

230

PARTY DRINKS

Short Punches

FRUIT

Mix $\frac{1}{4}$ pint apricot, peach, pear, or pineapple syrup with 2 tablespoonfuls lemon juice. Chill. Add $\frac{1}{2}$ pint Sparkling Lemon. Pour into 4 small glasses. Add to each a chopped maraschino cherry.

HONEY

Place 1 tablespoonful honey in a basin. Strain in 2 tablespoonfuls Lemon Squash and 1 tablespoonful Orange Squash. Add 4 tablespoonfuls maraschino syrup taken from a bottle of cherries. Chill. Place a tablespoonful of this mixture in the bottom of 8 small tumblers. Fill up with chilled Soda Water or Cream Soda. Garnish each with a slice of maraschino cherry and poise half a cherry on the edge of each glass.

MOCK SHANDYGAFF

2½ teaspoonfuls tea
1 pint boiling water
¾ lb. sugar
Juice of 5 lemons
3 pints Ginger Beer

Infuse tea in boiling water for 3 minutes, then strain. Add sugar. Stir until dissolved. Strain in lemon juice. Chill. When required, place a block of ice hollowed out in centre, in a glass punch bowl. Pour the flavoured tea over, then add Ginger Beer. Garnish with thin slices of lemon, orange or tangerine, and green or red cherries. Arrange a bunch of borage or mint in hollow in ice. When cherries are in season, arrange a cluster of cherries in centre, otherwise, a small bunch of green grapes.

RASPBERRY CUP

1 pint raspberries
Sugar to taste
2 tablespoonfuls Lemon Squash
2 tablespoonfuls non-alcoholic Orange Wine
3 bottles (splits) Sparkling Lemon
Water as required

Crush berries in a saucepan. Heat slowly till all the juice is extracted, then drip through a jelly bag. Sweeten juice to taste. When chilled, add Lemon Squash, Orange Wine, and Sparkling Lemon. Dilute with enough cold water to give you 2½ quarts. Serve with a sprig of mint and 1 or 2 berries floating in glasses.
Serves 10 glasses.

FRUIT FIZZES

Combine equal quantities of chilled Fruit Squash and Ginger Ale or Ginger Beer. Pour into glasses, quarter filled with cracked ice.

ICE FANCY

A tumbler half full with juice, top the glass with lemonade and a portion of vanilla ice with whipped cream. To be served well cooled.

ORANGE BLOSSOM

Mix one-half glass of buttermilk or yoghourt, with orange juice and two tablespoonfuls of sugar, add cola and a slice of orange as decoration. Cool.

SANDYMAN

Fill a glass half full with buttermilk or yoghourt, mix well with two tablespoonfuls of buckthorn and an egg yolk, top the glass with cola. Well cooled.

Mulled Wine

PARTY DRINKS

WIDDICOMBE FAIR

¼ bottle dry cider
1 bottle Pepsi-Cola
Apple
Ice

Method
Pour cider over ice in a half-pint tankard and fill up with Pepsi-Cola.
Float a good slice of apple on top.
For twelve people allow six each of the following varieties:
Hans Andersen's Favourite
Oliver Twist
Danwich International
Picnic Fancy
Copenhagen Salad
The Continental
For twenty-five people, increase the number to nine of each, and add a further nine each of the following:
Chef's Special
Master Mariner
Kirsten's Fruit Salad

PINEAPPLE AND BANANA WHISK

2 ripe bananas
¼ pint pineapple juice
1 pint milk

Mash the bananas until they are smooth. Add pineapple juice and milk. Whisk until frothy and serve immediately.

"Do-It-Yourself" Ice Cream Sodas

To make a soda properly, the bottled beverage should be pre-chilled to retain its full carbonation. Uncap the bottle and pour slowly in the glass just before serving.

Solo Serving

1 tablespoonful sweetened flavouring
1 to 2 scoops ice cream
Bottled soft drink, chilled

Put sweetened flavouring (frozen fruit, crushed, canned or fresh berries, etc.) in bottom of tall glass. Add 1 to 2 scoops of ice cream. Fill up glass with chilled freshly-uncapped carbonated beverage. Sodas pictured follow a patriotic motif—red, white, and blue.
Red Sodas: start with red fruits (strawberries, cherry preserves, or chopped maraschino cherries); add pink ice cream; cherry or raspberry soft drink, and garnish of whole strawberries or maraschino cherry.
White Sodas: crushed pineapple, pineapple preserves, canned or frozen fruit cocktail; vanilla ice cream; ginger ale, lemon-lime soda or cream soda; garnish, pineapple slice with maraschino cherry or sprig of mint.
Blue Sodas: blackberry jam, grape conserve, elderberry jam or frozen raspberries; black cherry or black raspberry ice cream; kola, black cherry, raspberry or grape soft drink; garnish, whole blueberries, blackberries or black cherries.

Cold Milk Drinks

Milk drinks are always enjoyable and they are so easy to prepare. Do not spoil the creaminess of the drinks by adding lumps of ice. If you prefer your drinks really cold, use milk straight from a refrigerator or make those which include dairy ice cream.

ICED COFFEE

2 oz. sugar

233

PARTY DRINKS

¼ *pint hot strong coffee*
¾ *pint milk*
Brickette or small carton dairy
   ice cream
Grated chocolate

Dissolve the sugar in the coffee. Add the milk and chill well. Pour into glasses and top with dairy ice cream and sprinkle with grated chocolate.

BLACKCURRANT WHIP

4 tablespoonfuls sieved
   blackcurrant jam
or
¼ *pint fresh blackcurrant purée*
1 pint milk
Sugar to taste
Brickette or small carton dairy
   ice cream

Whisk the blackcurrant jam or purée into the milk, add sugar and chill well. Pour into glasses and top with dairy ice cream.

CHOCOLATE MINT JULEP

2 oz. bar milk chocolate
1 pint hot milk
1 oz. castor sugar
¾ *teaspoonful peppermint essence*
Whipped double dairy cream
A few chopped nuts
Fresh mint leaves

Dissolve the chocolate in the hot milk. Add the sugar and essence and chill well. Pour into glasses and top with whipped cream and sprinkle with nuts. Decorate with mint leaves.

COUNTRY MILK SHAKE

1 pint milk
1 tablespoonful rosehip syrup
Brickette or small carton dairy
   ice cream

Coloured sugar strands

Whisk the milk and syrup together. Pour into glasses and top with dairy ice cream. Sprinkle with coloured sugar strands.

Hot Milk Drinks

Stir, sprinkle, whisk or whip—these recipes make delicious drinks. Everyone knows how comforting a glass of hot milk can be. But have you ever thought of the enormous variety of drinks you can make with hot milk? Here's a selection to start you experimenting. All these recipes make 3 drinks.

HONEY AND LEMON CUP

1 pint milk
2 tablespoonfuls clear honey
1 dessertspoonful lemon juice

Heat the milk with the honey, remove from heat, add the lemon juice and serve immediately.

BANANA AND COCONUT DRINK

1 pint milk
1 tablespoonful desiccated coconut
2 bananas
1 dessertspoonful icing sugar
3 teaspoonfuls double dairy cream
A little nutmeg and toasted
   coconut to decorate

Heat the milk with 1 tablespoonful desiccated coconut and allow to stand over very gentle heat for 15 minutes. Mash the bananas with the icing sugar. Strain the milk on to this mixture and whisk thoroughly. Reheat before serving. Float* (see p. 236) a teaspoonful of double dairy cream on the top of each drink and sprinkle with desiccated coconut, which has been toasted in the oven.

Summer Cups

PARTY DRINKS

ALMOND WHISK
1 egg white
1 oz. ground almonds
1 oz. castor sugar
1 pint milk
Whisk the egg white. Fold in the ground almonds and sugar. Heat the milk. Remove from the heat and fold in the egg-white mixture. Serve immediately.

COFFEE MARSHMALLOW FOAM
¼ pint strong coffee
¾ pint milk
1 oz. sugar
8 marshmallows
Grated chocolate to decorate
Heat the coffee and milk together. Add the sugar and stir in the marshmallows. Sprinkle each drink with grated chocolate before serving.

FRUIT PUNCH
1 small (8 oz.) tin fruit cocktail
¾ pint milk
A good pinch mixed spice
Add ¼ pint juice from the tin to the milk. Drain the fruit and rub through a sieve. Heat the milk. Pour into the sieved fruit and whisk. Add mixed spice and reheat before serving.

TREACLE MILK
1 pint milk
2 tablespoonfuls black treacle
3 teaspoonfuls double dairy cream
A little cinnamon
Heat the milk and dissolve the treacle in it. When sufficiently hot, pour into cups and float* double dairy cream on top. Sprinkle with cinnamon.
*Cream will float if it is poured over the back of a cold spoon.

CHOCOLATE NOG
2 egg whites
2 dessertspoonfuls brown sugar
1 dessertspoonful chocolate powder
1 pint milk
1 tablespoonful brandy (optional)
Whisk the egg whites, add the sugar and chocolate powder. Heat the milk and fold in the egg-white mixture. Add brandy, if used, and serve immediately.

EGG FLIP
1 egg
1 teaspoonful sugar
1 dessertspoonful sherry
½ pint milk
Beat together the egg, sugar and sherry. Warm the milk and add it to the mixture. Heat slowly but do not allow to boil.

Some like it Strong
When you want to serve alcoholic drinks, here are a few recipes for cocktails and cups made with soft drinks and hard liquor or wine : there is no need to use expensive imported wines. Empire wines are quite suitable for the purpose.

GIMLET
¼ lime juice cordial
¾ dry gin
Shake well. Strain into a sherry glass. Fill up with chilled soda water.
Serves 1 person.

INDIAN COCKTAIL
½ dry gin
⅔ Indian Tonic Water
2 dashes orange bitters
Shake well with ice. Strain into a cocktail glass. Garnish with a stuffed olive.

PARTY DRINKS

PINK WINK

Lump of ice
2 oz. Cinzano Bianco
3 dashes Grenadine
1 dash Angostura
Fill up with soda water.

PLAZA

⅓ dry gin
⅓ Cinzano Bianco
⅓ Cinzano Extra Dry
Shake well and strain. Add 1 slice of
pineapple.

BRONX COCKTAIL

⅓ Cinzano Extra Dry
⅓ Cinzano Bianco (or Red)
⅓ gin
Dash of orange juice
Shake well with ice

MARTINI COCKTAIL

⅓ Cinzano Extra Dry
⅔ dry gin or vodka
Shake or stir and strain. Serve with an
olive.

RED INDIAN

¼ dry gin
¼ Cinzano Extra Dry
¼ Cinzano Red
¼ sherry (medium)
1 dash Crème de Noyeau
1 dash orange bitters
Stir and strain. Add a cherry.

COLONIAL

½ teaspoonful sugar
1 dash Angostura
Fill up with Cinzano Red. Stir and
strain. Add sprig of mint.

TROPICAL DAWN

Into each tumbler put crushed ice, a

measure (1-2 oz.) of cherry brandy
or grenadine and top up with Tropical
Lemon. To make this a more potent
sundowner you can also add a
measure of brandy, vodka or gin.

HIGH JINKS

⅔ dry gin
⅓ grapefruit squash
3 dashes non-alcoholic raisin wine
Shake well with ice. Strain into a cocktail glass. Garnish with a snippet of
lemon rind.
Serves 1 person.

KING'S NAVY

⅔ glass Jamaica rum
⅓ glass lime juice cordial
Castor sugar to taste
Shake well with ice. Strain into a cock-
tail glass.
Serves 1 person.

RASPBERRY COCKTAIL

1 teacup fresh raspberries
2 glasses gin
1 liqueur glass raspberry flavoured
    cordial
2 glassfuls dry white wine
Shake well with ice. Strain into 6
cocktail glasses. Garnish each with a
raspberry.
Serves 6 persons.

GLAMOUR GIRL

1 tablespoonful pineapple juice
1 teaspoonful blackcurrant
    flavoured cordial
The white of 1 egg
¼ Italian Vermouth
⅔ dry gin
Shake well with ice. Strain into a
medium-sized glass, not a cocktail
glass.

238

PARTY DRINKS

THREE COOL ACES

1 bottle Red Burgundy
3 tablespoonfuls of Brandy
3 tablespoonfuls Tawny Port
2 slices each of orange and
*   lemon peel*
1 pint lemon squash
Block of ice

Pour Red Burgundy over block of ice adding Brandy and Tawny Port and leave for half an hour in refrigerator or cool place. Add already chilled lemon squash and orange and lemon peel. Stir well and serve chilled.
Serves 25 glasses.

SHILLINGFORD SPECIAL

A very old and popular mull of the 18th Century.
1 quart Claret
Orange Curaçao
Brandy
Orange slices
Sugar
Cloves
Nutmeg

Pour Claret into saucepan, put with it sliced orange, twelve lumps of sugar and six cloves. Bring these nearly to the boil. Boil one pint of water and add to the mixture. Add one wine glassful of Curaçao and—if you want to give your guests something to remember—add one wine glassful of Brandy. Pour into glasses and grate nutmeg on top.

BAISH'S BOMBSHELL

1 bottle Burgundy
1 tablespoonful sugar
Cinnamon
Cloves
Lemon juice
½ measure Brandy

Curaçao
Heat half a bottle of water in large saucepan, adding sugar, pinch cinnamon, a few cloves and a dash of lemon juice. When water is nearly boiling add wine. Add Brandy and 1 quarter of a sherry glassful Curaçao. Bottle mixture and keep warm.

MIDDLETON'S MULL

1 bottle Burgundy
2 lemons
1 cup granulated sugar
4 cloves
2 cupfuls of water
4 sticks of cinnamon (or ground
*   cinnamon equivalent)*

Boil water with sugar, cinnamon and cloves for five minutes. Add lemon thinly sliced and allow to stand for ten minutes. Add wine and heat slowly but do not allow to boil. Put it in a pitcher or jug and serve very hot. A silver spoon in each glass will prevent it from cracking.

VELDT VELVET

1 bottle South African Burgundy
2 lemons
1 cup granulated sugar
4 cloves
2 cups water
4 sticks cinnamon (or ground
*   cinnamon equivalent)*

Boil water with sugar, cinnamon and cloves for five minutes. Add lemon thinly sliced and allow to stand for 10 minutes. Add wine and heat slowly. Do not allow to boil. Put into a pitcher or jug and serve very hot.

PARTY DRINKS

PALL MALL

 $\frac{1}{3}$ dry gin
 $\frac{1}{3}$ Cinzano Bianco
 $\frac{1}{3}$ Cinzano Extra Dry
 1 teaspoonful white Crème de
    Menthe
 2 dashes orange bitters

Stir and strain.

VERMOUTH COBBLER

 Fill glass with cracked ice
 3 oz. Cinzano Red
 1 teaspoonful sugar
 4 dashes Curaçao

Stir and decorate with fruit. Add sprig of mint (optional). Serve with straws.

ORANGE NECTAR CUP
(for slimmers)

 2 bottles sparkling orange
 2 bottles tonic water
 3 tablespoonfuls dry Vermouth
 1 orange
 1 lemon
 Small can drained crushed
    pineapple

Peel orange and lemon rind thinly. Add to pineapple with mint. Allow to stand for one hour. Remove rind and mint. Add sparkling orange, tonic water, dry Vermouth and the juices of the orange and lemon. Serve very well chilled. Delicious on its own or with gin.

PARTY DRINKS

ALGERIAN MULL
1 quart Algerian Red Wine
Sliced orange
1 wine glassful Curaçao
1 wine glassful Brandy
12 lumps sugar
6 cloves
Grated nutmeg

Pour wine into saucepan. Put with it sliced orange, sugar and cloves. Bring mixture nearly to boil. Add the Curaçao and—if your guests are hard-headed and you want to give them something to remember—the Brandy. Pour into glasses. Grate nutmeg on top.

BOATHOOK (rum base)
1 jigger rum
Juice of half a small grapefruit
Dash of Angostura Bitters
1 bottle Pepsi-Cola
Sprig of mint
Ice

Pour the rum and grapefruit juice over the ice in a tall glass, add the dash of Bitters and top up with Pepsi-Cola. Garnish with mint.

JUNIPER JOY
(Dubonnet and gin base)
1 jigger gin
*Pink ice
1 baby bottle tonic water
1 jigger Dubonnet Red
Juice of ½ lemon
Slice of lemon

Pour the gin over pink ice (*made by adding Angostura Bitters to water when making ice cubes). Add the lemon juice and tonic water and fill up with Dubonnet Red. Garnish with a slice of lemon.

DUBONNET CHRISTMAS PUNCH
1 large bottle Dubonnet
1 bottle Red Wine
1 pint freshly infused fragrant
   China tea
Juice ½ orange
Juice ½ lemon
Twist orange peel
Twist lemon peel
3 cloves
1 coffee spoon cinnamon
Good grating nutmeg
Brown sugar to taste

Strain the tea into a saucepan and add the lemon and orange juices and peels, spices and sugar. Simmer for 15 minutes and strain into another saucepan. Add the Dubonnet and Red Wine, heat quickly. Do *not* in any circumstances boil. Decorate punch bowl or jugs with slices of lemon and orange if liked. If the drink is required milder, increase the quantity of China tea and if stronger, a little brandy may be added at the discretion of the hostess. This quantity makes 24-30 reasonable glasses.

RIESLING CUP
3 bottles Riesling
2 miniature Grand Marnier
6 bottles bitter orange
1 packet frozen strawberries
Ice

Slice the strawberries and place in a large bowl. Pour over the Grand Marnier and marinade 1 hour. Add the

PARTY DRINKS

wine and bitter orange, mix well and add a large piece of ice.

FRUIT CUP (non alcoholic)

1 bottle dry ginger ale
1 bottle bitter orange
1 bottle bitter lemon

Mix ingredients and garnish with pieces of fruit.

RED DEVIL

You don't need a parachute to fall for this one. Take ½ measure of ginger wine, ½ measure of blackcurrant cordial. Add boiling water to taste—and keep glowing.

SUMMER CUP

Thirst Aid. Place a few lumps of ice into a cool jug. Pour ¼ bottle of ginger wine into it and add an equal quantity of fresh or tinned fruit juice or squash. Top up with sparkling water.

LONG LIME

Worth a Calypso to itself. ½ measure of ginger wine, ½ measure lime juice ; add ice and top up with 2 measures of soda water or tonic and you'll be singing.

PINK PEACH

1 bottle Rosé wine
1 bottle Sauternes
1 miniature Peach liqueur
¼ pint soda water
1 fresh sliced peach or tinned equivalent

Pour Rosé wine over block of ice adding fruit. Stir in Sauternes, Peach liqueur and sugar to taste. Leave for half an hour in refrigerator or cool place. Add soda water immediately before serving.
Serves 19 glasses.

Hot Spiced Punch

1 bottle inexpensive red wine
2 sherry glassfuls of sherry
1 port glassful of port
3 tablespoonfuls brandy
1 level teaspoonful ground cinnamon
1 dozen cloves
¼-½ pint water
Sugar to taste

Method

Pour all the ingredients into a saucepan with the exception of the brandy, sugar and water. Bring to near boiling point, then add hot water, sugar and brandy and serve piping hot.
Serves 12 persons.

WINE CUP

3 tablespoonfuls non-alcoholic orange flavoured wine
Rind of 1 orange
Rind of ½ lemon
2 oz. castor sugar
2 teacups rich white wine
1 quart soda water

Add non-alcoholic orange flavoured wine to rinds and sugar. Cover. Stand for 2 hours. Add wine. Strain. Chill on ice. When required, add chilled soda water. Garnish with slices of orange or tangerine and lemon, sprigs of mint, and a dozen cherries, or strawberries.
Serves 12 persons.
Sparklers:
Pour 2 tablespoonfuls of non-alcoholic ginger wine into a small tumbler. Fill up with chilled ginger ale. Yield: ½ pint. Pour 1 tablespoonful each of non-alcoholic raisin wine and Italian vermouth or sweet sherry into a small tumbler. Fill up with chilled ginger ale.

PARTY DRINKS

HAT TRICK

1 bottle Red Burgundy
6 tablespoonfuls of Tawny Port
4 tablespoonfuls of Benedictine
Thinly sliced orange and lemon
  pieces
1 pint Kola
Soft brown sugar to taste
Block of ice

Place in bowl, block of ice and fruit. Add Red Burgundy, Tawny Port and Benedictine. Leave for half an hour in cool place or refrigerator. Add sugar and stir well and just before serving add Kola.
Serves 25 glasses.

PRIDE OF OPORTO

2 bottles Tawny Port
1 siphon soda water
¼ bottle Orange Curacao
2 lemons
Block of ice

Chill siphon of soda water and 2 bottles of Tawny Port in refrigerator for one hour. Squeeze 1 lemon and put juice in bowl. Slice 1 lemon very thinly and put into bowl with juice. Place block of ice in bowl and pour over 2 bottles Tawny Port. Leave for fifteen minutes after stirring well. To serve fill glasses ⅔ full and fill up rest with chilled soda water and decorate with slice of lemon.
Serves 32 glasses.

BORDEAUX BOWL

1 bottle Claret
½ sherry glassful Orange Curaçao
1 tablespoonful sugar
Grated nutmeg

Heat mixture but do not boil. Add 1 sherry glassful Port instead of Curaçao if preferred.

A BISHOP

1 quart Port
Cloves
2 oz. lump sugar
2 lemons
Mixed spices
1 pint water

Stick a lemon with cloves and roast it. Put a quart of Port into a saucepan and bring to the boil. Boil one pint of water, adding a good pinch spices. Add boiled water and spices and roasted lemon to hot wine. Then rub the 2 oz. of lump sugar on the rind of another lemon, put it into a bowl adding half the juice of the lemon and pour in the wine. Serve as hot as possible.

PORT WINE NEGUS

1 glassful of Port Wine
1 lemon
Sugar to taste
1 long glass
Boiling water

Put wine in long glass, add sugar and the rind and juice of the lemon. Fill up with boiling water and strain.

SOUTHERN CROSS PUNCH

1 bottle Australian Tawny Port
  type wine
2 tablespoonfuls sugar
½ teaspoonful mixed spice
Juice and rind of 1 lemon
1 cupful water
½ cupful grapefruit juice
A few raisins

Heat wine with sugar, spice and grapefruit juice, lemon juice and lemon rind. Do not boil. Boil slowly a handful of raisins in cup of water. Add to wine mixture. Do not strain. Serve with raisins still in Punch Bowl.

PARTY DRINKS

HOCK SPARKLER

3 bottles Hock
1 bottle Sparkling Hock
3 tablespoonfuls Brandy
9 tablespoonfuls Orange Curaçao
1 lb. melon cubes or other fresh
    fruit in season
Sugar to taste
Block of ice

Pour over ice block the still Hock, Brandy, Orange Curacao, stir well and add cut fruit. Leave for half an hour in either refrigerator or cool place. Add Sparkling Hock and serve immediately.
Serves 36 glasses.

FROZEN SUNSHINE

3 bottles dry white wine
¼ bottle Cognac brandy
9 tablespoonfuls Benedictine
½ lb. cut pineapple, either fresh or
    tinned
1 pint lemonade
Sugar to taste
Block of ice

Soak pineapple in Brandy for fifteen minutes. Add three bottles of well chilled white wine, lemonade and Benedictine. Leave for half an hour in refrigerator or cool place and then add sugar to taste.
Serves 36 glasses.

CRYSTAL ROSE

1 bottle Rosé wine
3 tablespoonfuls of Green
    Chartreuse
Pieces of ice
Juice of ½ lemon
Handful of peeled and de-pipped
    grapes

Pour Rosé wine over ice adding Green Chartreuse and juice of ½ lemon.

Leave for half an hour in either refrigerator or cool place. Serve garnished with very thinly sliced lemon peel and grapes.
Serves 9 glasses.

CLARET AND SAUTERNES FRAPPE

1 bottle Claret
1 bottle Sauternes
6 tablespoonfuls Orange Curaçao
2 tablespoonfuls Brandy
Strawberries to taste (preferably
    fresh)
Juice of one lemon
½ pint soda water
Sugar to taste
Sprigs of mint to decorate
Block of ice

Pour wine, Orange Curaçao and Brandy over block of ice and chill for half an hour in refrigerator or cool place. Add juice of a lemon and sugar and stir well. Garnish with strawberries and mint sprigs. Add soda water just before serving.
Serves 21 glasses.

COOL MOON

3 bottles white Burgundy
¼ bottle Pernod
3 tablespoonfuls Crème de Menthe
Thin strips of cucumber peel
Siphon of soda water
Castor Sugar
Block of ice

Pour over ice block the white Burgundy, Crème de Menthe and Pernod. Leave for half an hour in either refrigerator or cool place. Add sugar to taste and at the last moment siphon of soda water.
Serves 36 glasses.

PARTY DRINKS

TROPICAL GOLD

Into a cocktail shaker put some crushed ice, a tumbler of Tropical Lemon, 2 oz. Curaçao and 2 beaten egg yolks. Shake well, strain and serve in cocktail glasses with a cherry on a stick.

TROPICAL CUP

Pour four 11½-oz. bottles or cans of Tropical Lemon into a large jug and add plenty of ice-cubes and a ½ bottle of light rum (Barbados or Cuban, for instance). Stir it up, add slices of unpeeled cucumber, sprigs of mint or borage and—for the West Indies way —a sprinkling of grated nutmeg. It gives 15 to 20 drinks.

CAMPARI COOLER

The sheer elegance of Campari makes it more and more in demand as an apéritif—usually topped up with soda water. Try it—in the same proportions —with Tropical Lemon instead of soda, and plenty of ice.

VERMOUTH CASSIS

*1 large bottle of dry French
   Vermouth
6 tablespoonfuls of Crème de
   Cassis
1 siphon soda water
Block of ice*

Pour Vermouth and Crème de Cassis over the ice. Leave for half an hour in either refrigerator or cool place. Add already chilled soda water immediately before serving.
Serves 20 glasses.

VERMOUTH SORBET

1 bottle sweet Italian Vermouth

*Juice of lemon
1 siphon soda water
Block of ice*

Pour Vermouth and lemon juice over the ice. Leave for half an hour in either refrigerator or cool place. Add already chilled soda water immediately before serving.
Serves 20 glasses.

SHERRY SHIVER

*1 bottle Sherry
1 pint ginger beer
Block of ice*

Pour Sherry over ice block. Leave for half an hour in either refrigerator or cool place. Add already chilled ginger beer just before serving.
Serves 15 glasses.

SHERRY COBBLER

*1 bottle sweet Sherry
1 pint soda water
2 glasses of Benedictine (or other
   liqueur)
Cocktail cherries
Sugar to taste
Apples, strawberries or other
   fruits in season*

Pour Sherry and liqueur over fruits. Leave for one hour. Add ice, soda water and sugar to taste and serve in glass with cherry on stick.
Serves 16 glasses.

ESKIMO CUP

Cool man—cool! Place a few lumps of ice into a jug. Into it pour ¼ bottle green ginger wine and the same quantity of gin or vodka. Add the juice of a lemon and top up with sparkling water.

PARTY DRINKS

SIR ROGER DE COVERLEY

1 bottle Light Red Wine
1 glassful of Port Wine
½ sherry glassful Orange Curaçao
Small teaspoonful cinnamon
Small teaspoonful mixed spices
Dash nutmeg
6 cloves
Sugar to taste

Tie spices, etc. in muslin bag. Pour wines and Curaçao into pot, insert muslin bag and bring slowly to the boil. Simmer two minutes, stirring continuously. Strain and serve in warmed glasses.

HOPE'S HOTTENTOT

1 bottle full-bodied Red Wine
8 fluid oz. medium dry Sherry
4 fluid oz. Brandy
½ bottle Cassis or Blackcurrant
*   Liqueur*
1 quart water
Lemons
Ginger
Sugar to taste

Grate rind of three lemons into saucepan, add ¼ lb. granulated sugar and pour juice of three lemons on top. Add 1 teaspoonful ground ginger and mix thoroughly. Then add liquid ingredients and bring slowly to the boil, stirring continuously. Sweeten to taste, and then strain and serve hot.

TABASCO VODKA

Heat a 6-oz. bottle of clam juice cocktail with 1 tablespoonful tomato ketchup, pinch of celery salt and dash of Tabasco. Pour measure of vodka in tall glass, fill with piping-hot clam juice.
Serves 2 drinks.

TWELFTH NIGHT

1 apple
1 bottle Algerian Wine
Cloves
Hot Water

Stick an apple full of cloves and float in a bowl filled with one bottle heated Algerian Wine. Add hot water to weaken according to taste.

SPANISH BOLLAN

1 quart Spanish Red Wine
Lemon slices
1 cupful sugar
Grated nutmeg

Heat wine, sugar and nutmeg to boiling point. Remove grated nutmeg. Pour into glasses with slice of lemon in each glass. (Place a silver spoon in glass before pouring in mixture, to prevent glass breaking).

CHRISTMAS CUP

1 bottle Red Wine
1 tablespoonful sugar
Grated nutmeg
½ sherry glassful of Orange Curaçao
1 egg

Take one bottle red wine. Add ½ sherry glassful of Orange Curaçao and one tablespoonful of sugar, plus grated nutmeg. After taking the brew off the fire add a well beaten egg to the mull. To make it even more Christmassy, add glassful of Port instead of Curaçao.

BACCHUS' BOWL

As for Christmas Cup above, but add ½ sherry glassful of Brandy instead of Curacao or Port.

SNAKE BITE

A rattling good one. ⅓ measure of green ginger wine, ⅔ measure of cider or

PARTY DRINKS

Babycham, add ice. Sip it, roll it round your tongue and you'll agree it's 'Great Snakes!' A convenient method for party use is to add ½ bottle green ginger wine to a flagon of cider.

SUSPENSION

Gets the party going. ⅓ green ginger wine. ⅓ scotch whisky, ⅓ orange squash. Mix well with ice and serve very cold with a cherry. If you are making large party quantities you can put all the ingredients in a liquidiser and mix until all the ice is completely dissolved, then serve immediately. *Note:* For the best results with Snake Bite, Suspension and Eskimo Cup cool all the ingredients before mixing and use a cool jug.

GINGER TODDY

Nobody sniffs at this one. Place one wine-glassful of ginger wine into a tumbler and add the juice of half a lemon and one dessertspoonful of honey. Top up with boiling water and drink piping hot. You'll go off to bed all aglow and equally satisfied, whether you're fighting a cold or just hoping you're not getting one.

GINGER PUNCH

This really is a knockout. In a muslin bag place 3 or 4 sticks of cinnamon, 20 cloves, the peel of a lemon and orange. Boil in a saucepan with 2 pints of water for 15 minutes. Strain the liquid into a large saucepan and add 3 bottles of red wine, 1 bottle green ginger wine (and if you're after an extra kick, 1 pint of brandy). Add sugar to taste, ladle into glasses and serve piping hot.

VODKA CACAO

Mix 1 oz. vodka with ¾ oz. white Crème de Cacao, ¾ oz. sweet cream. Shake well with cracked ice. Strain into cocktail glass.

TAIL TWISTER

Mix 1 measure vodka with ½ measure green Crème de Menthe. Fill tall glass with lemonade and orange slice.

VODKA AND STOUT

Pour 1 measure of vodka into the bottom of a tall beer goblet. Add stout to fill glass, pouring slowly to build a fine head of foam.

DUBONNET BLONDE PINEAPPLE BOWL

1 bottle Dubonnet Blonde
5 bottles pineapple juice
A fifth of a bottle of vodka
Ice
Soda to taste
Cucumber rind
Pineapple rings
Cucumber slices to decorate

Place either a block of ice or crushed ice in the bottom of a bowl. Put in slivers of cucumber rind. Add Dubonnet Blonde, pineapple juice, vodka and soda to taste. Mix well—do not shake— and allow to stand for half an hour. Decorate the bowl with pineapple rings and cucumber slices. This is a light but mellow, cool drink.

VODKA AND BITTER LEMON

1 measure vodka; top up with bitter lemon to taste, add ice and garnish with a slice of lemon.

249

ACKNOWLEDGEMENTS

The publishers are pleased to acknowledge the help and assistance provided by the undermentioned firms and organisations all of which have provided information, recipes or illustrations for this book.

Birds Eye Foods

Booths Distilleries Ltd

Brown and Polson Ltd

Campbell's Soups Ltd

Cadburys Chocolate

J. & J. Colman Ltd

John Crabbie & Co Ltd

Robert Carrier

The Danish Centre Ltd

The Dairy Centre

Dubonnet

Haig (The Distillers Co)

Heinz, H. J. Ltd

Horlicks Ltd

International Distillers & Vintners Group

Kraft Superfine

Libby, McNeill and Libby Ltd

Shirly Lord

The U.S. Rice Council

"Maroc" Oranges

Meredith & Drew Ltd

Madame Prunier

The Mushroom Marketing Board

New Zealand Dairy Board

The Norwegian Food Centre

The Outspan Organisation

The Potato Marketing Board

Quaker Oats Ltd

Rowntrees Jellies

C. Shippam & Co

Symington & Co Ltd

S.O.P.E.X.A. Ltd

Tabasco Ltd

Wine and Spirit Association of Gt. Britain

The White Fish Authority

Australian Recipe Service

Simon Dee

Tate and Lyle Ltd.

INDEX

INDEX

INDEX

INDEX

INDEX